Evil Media

Evil Media

Matthew Fuller and Andrew Goffey

The MIT Press
Cambridge, Massachusetts
London, England

MIT Press books may be purchased at special quantity discounts for business or sales promotional use. For information, please email special_sales@mitpress.mit.edu or write to Special Sales Department, The MIT Press, 55 Hayward Street, Cambridge, MA 02142.

This book was set in Stone Sans and Stone Serif by Toppan Best-set Premedia Limited, Hong Kong. Printed and bound in the United States of America.

Library of Congress Cataloging-in-Publication Data

Fuller, Matthew.
Evil media / Matthew Fuller and Andrew Goffey.
    p.   cm.
Includes bibliographical references and index.
ISBN 978-0-262-01785-5 (hardcover : alk. paper)
1. Information society. 2. Social media. 3. Social networks. I. Goffey, Andrew. II. Title.
HM851.F855   2012
006.7′54—dc23
                                                                    2012002755

10   9   8   7   6   5   4   3   2   1

With thanks to our informants

Contents

Structures 83

Technicalities 105

Productivity 125

Excellence 147

Introduction

Evil Media is an attempt to develop an understanding of contemporary media systems, techniques, and practices of mediation in an era of participation, of massive networks in which contests are waged as much between technical systems as between ideas or more ostensibly social forces, and in which such conflicts in turn ramify into new crazes, passions, projects, and plans. Much of what we will discuss are the "gray media" most recognizable from the world of work and administration, affecting the habits of government, business, and culture, yet rarely recognized or explored as media in their own right. By gray media, we mean things such as databases, group-work software, project-planning methods, media forms, and technologies that are operative far from the more visible churn of messages about consumers, empowerment, or the questionable wisdom of the information economy.

As Marshall McLuhan has argued, media are rather more pervasive than is commonly perceived, and the technologies that are encompassed by this broader view of media knot together some surprisingly disparate objects, practices, techniques, and knowledge. Part of the underlying argument of *Evil Media* is that the presence of media in our lives, and the abstract social relations that they bear, are more diffuse and extensive than is usually imagined. Moreover, increasingly more diverse and numerous things, habits, and roles are becoming media or are being activated as mediation.

Although researchers schooled in the concepts and concerns of media studies have for a long time been prepared to question simplistic views of communication and have sought to convey the concrete, material "thickness" of media processes in contemporary social life, they have often overlooked the dull opacity of devices and techniques not commonly viewed *as* media or forms of mediation. In this book mediation, and the gaming of the disparate processes that make it up, becomes a general principle that extends from the basic building blocks of software to management methods, psychic techniques, linguistic factors, and the hidden cunning of the work of manipulation. Media here become less about the movement of signs that refer to other things but active as tangible, biddable things in their own right. A set of words in a report, article, or illicit data dump becomes significant in a different way when placed in a mechanism that allows or even solicits unfettered access, than when that set of words is lodged in a closed directory or laid out as a book; allowing such open access has direct and pragmatic effects on the reception of ideas, to mention just one scale at which they might be operative. That texts, for example, also have automated readers—such as search engines—does not necessarily imply that readers become automatons but suggests that a transit of dynamics flows between one sort of material kind and another. This insight is in some ways fundamentally cybernetic, but it further implies that the fine grain of affordances provided by different kinds of scales, processes, objects, stuff, always complicates things, introducing subtle shifts susceptible of leading others (things, persons) astray. More is going on in processes of mediation than can possibly be handled by a set of rules (the hunger for which, in certain kinds of gray literature—documents of policy and procedure, self-improvement manuals, and so on—seems to know no bounds).

Rather than the dreamy promise of rules for success, then, this book takes the form of a series of stratagems, each of which is either aimed at giving a particular angle into a certain scale of operation or calls attention to a way of working. We're interested in the unintended or secondary effects of media as much as in their ostensibly obvious consequences. At the same time, following Giorgio Agamben, such a stratagematic perspective rejects the presumption that the point of view of the spectator is the privileged vantage from which to understand the operations of media. Conventional media studies, not to mention ethics, are far too concerned with thinking things through from the spectator's perspective. An evil media approach suggests that mediation entails the process of becoming activated, whether one consciously takes on the role of spectator or not. The following five short texts—on the ways in which media might be said to be evil, on the nature of the book, on grayness as a compositional form, on the technics of sophistication, and on the notion of the stratagem—set out the underlying concerns and issues with which the book as a whole operates.

Evil

"Don't be evil." Google's well-known maxim,[1] reworked as something of a publicity device, finds broad resonance in other expressions of practical reason today—from the imperative to think good thoughts, to have positive feelings, and to show compassion and pity for others to the historically well-established tendency to qualify organized productive activity in moral terms. It is an injunction that thus displays, perhaps more clearly than any other, the theological residue of economic thinking and its associated sociotechnical practices, to say nothing of the fundamentalist propensities of contemporary forms of imperialism for which the incontestability of transcendent values offers a clever ruse for alliance building, chest beating, and even technological development.[2] The subject of the Manichaean puppetry of Hollywood, of military-industrial-corporate governance, the tracking down and rooting out of evil, and the orchestration of support for geopolitical strategies of domination aligned with the "good" adopts a rhetoric that is generally as excessive in its intensity as the malice against which it purports to mobilize.[3] The maxim "don't be evil" and its rather more bellicose sibling, the ultimatum to be with us or to be against us, both portend, with cartoon simplicity, the coming of a world in which every byte of information and every tap on a screen, every waking thought and action, are expunged of the deviant and devious propensities of contrary forms of vital energy. Propensities to think and to act in ways that do not conform to social commands are neutralized and pacified by the shaping of behavior through media forms that aspire to friction-free transparency. Any activity that fails the pragmatic test of globalized informatics is thereby proscribed, leaving itself open to condemnation as malicious, viral, terroristic, or more simply to disqualification through cheery indifference.[4]

In this context, to propose the hypothesis of evil *media* is something of a paradox. If a pervasive sense of dark foreboding is at work today—a sense of foreboding that helps to legitimate simplistic injunctions against malice in all its real or imagined forms—then this foreboding is at least in part due to the operations of mediation that help to propagate it. Not just in the obvious way that forms of media feature narratives of the triumph of light over dark, good over evil, right over wrong (the mediation of evil), but in the more obscure and perhaps more enduringly visceral sense that the material construction of media ecologies themselves plays a critical role in disseminating the very feelings of dread, fear, and foreboding that give rise to preemptive judgments in the first place. The all-pervasive extension of digital communication in particular contributes to the removal of a sense of the boundaries or of the territorial fixity that otherwise anchors experience in the relatively known and familiar. Mediation facilitates and amplifies the creation of troubling, ambiguous social processes, fragile networks of susceptible activity, opaque zones of nonknowledge—the evils of media. And while the idealization of globalized networks today continues a prevalent tradition of linking technology with aesthetic sensibilities,[5] this is perhaps done with little consideration of ethics other than through the simplifying problematic of representation, leaving us at a loss to grasp the axiology of media as such. Instead of shock and awe, or the sublime and lofty feeling of destiny that might be produced in a spectator riveted to a screen, what is interesting here are the mixed feelings of terror and wretchedness, delight and joy, produced for and by active cogs in sociotechnical machines.[6]

Researchers have paid much attention to the importance of affect in contemporary capitalism in recent years, to its difference from identifiable emotion, and to the links between affective labor and the economic tendency toward more abstract forms of materiality and infrastructure. Less attention, however, has been paid to the precise ways in which the dimly sensed links between affective configurations and the broader, unstable networks of agents and mediators of which we are a part, with their difficult-to-perceive boundaries and their correlative scope for producing troubling uncertainties, are being assembled.[7] Media, in the very broad sense that can be given to the term via science and technology studies, management theory, or even speculative philosophy,[8] are irreducible elements in the composition and configuration of affect. Delight, terror, geeky enthusiasm, mildly hypnotic euphoria, ugly feelings, and paranoid rage find their conditions in the objects and objective forms that make up their environment. The nagging insecurity when a phone does not ring or rings too often, the panic generated by unusual patterns of traffic of data, the raging fury of a mild-mannered but well-encapsulated executive on the road to a meeting: such subjective dispositions are the outcome of specific sociotechnical configurations, conferring a plus or a minus, a tick or a cross, a yes or a no, or sometimes a more ambiguous sign, on the processes in play.

The transparency of the facilitation of activity that is produced when devices, practices, protocols and procedures, gadgets and applications, mesh and synchronize simultaneously creates vast black-boxed or obscurely grayed-out zones, taken for granted, more or less stabilizing and stabilized artifacts, that permit the abstract social relations characteristic of "frictionless" communication to take root.[9] But how these zones of configured operations work, with what effects, with what latitude for maneuver, with what "play" in their gearing, is an open question, one with the scope for experimentation that contingency allows. Under the conditions of programmable control that digital mediation creates, the sophisticated infrastructures and practices of communication enter into the calculus of decision making of all sorts, not always as an explicit factor but more typically as an environmental variable with a hoped-for or unnoticed stability that allows the objectives of decision making to proceed untroubled.

This book explores the hypothesis of evil media in an "extramoral" sense. Our approach eschews the deadlocked, blackmailing logic of the supposedly irreducible moral oppositions that provide the Western production of "infernal alternatives" (and the compulsive necessities they induce) with a helpful coefficient of guilty feeling: be good, don't be evil, or (if you can't avoid it) at least opt for the calculus of the lesser evil.[10] Far from considering media to be neutral means with regard to the ends they come into relation with, we consider media and mediation as creating a troubling opacity and thickness in the relations of which they are a part, with an *active* capacity of their own to shape or manipulate the things or people with which they come into contact. At a time when "transparency" receives suspiciously excessive praise, we seek to examine specific stratagematic logics of mediation as they are developed in a range of practices, devices, techniques, and technologies. That such things can be component elements in both a slavish devotion *to* and an effortless enslavement *of* work within the confines of production for exchange is well known. Forming the object of countless forms of denunciation, media are frequently absolved and divested of any specific active qualities of their own by means of broad concepts such as that of "instrumental rationality" or visions of preconfigured social agents to whose service such means are harnessed (class domination, liberal elites, vested interests). Viewing media as transparent to human intentions—albeit intentions that are often distorted or misrecognized through ideology—is a conception of mediators as intermediaries, which is built on a moral presupposition the construction of which it is unable to understand or sense its own active contribution to.[11] In this context, the phrase "evil media" makes this troubling but often unacknowledged opacity palpable, situating at the heart of processes whose transparency is typically presumed an opacity that usually only surfaces when things go wrong.[12] It is a matter not so much of unveiling or making this opacity legible but of drawing useful effects from it.

But if we adopt the qualification "evil" in our exploration, we do so as a convulsive response to the more pervasively onto-theological climate of global culture, wherein humanity substitutes itself for God and then acts out goodness in a servile obedience to its own commands—a lacerating operation of subjection, with which any endeavor to explore ethics beyond good and evil has to contend through an inevitably scorched humor. Nietzsche may have seen the zone beyond good and evil as the province of the superman, but the same Nietzsche glimpsed the superfluity of profoundly theological values in the practices of the sophists, providing a helpful pointer to a set of practices that might offer a productive way of escaping the endless moral injunctions and solicitations to be solely good.[13] Challenging the entrenched censoriousness of the

One, the Good, and the True and opening up the path of nonbeing as the path one was supposed not to follow,[14] the sophists' attack on duality, a position both on this side of and beyond good and evil, practically invites the slander, malice, and cunning trickery, the evil imputed to them in turn. Suspect from the point of view of reason that is blind to its own conditions of operation, an amoral stance toward media and mediation that calls into question the *presumed* moral superiority of those who seek "the truth" is one that will find its interest in a consideration of the manipulation of symbols, and in an artful use of forms of communication and mediation.

Already we can sense the chaotic heterogeneity of the uses to which the term "evil" can be put. But such a term is not to be invoked with impunity. One can but admire the humorous understatement of the philosopher Alfred North Whitehead in his remark that the "trick of evil," as he called it, is "to insist on birth at the wrong season."

The focus in this book on particular media systems and mediating processes does not establish for them any direct translation into the spectacular values of good and evil, but neither does it exonerate them as simply being means at the transparent service of ends. What it seeks to do is to use the habitual ways in which values are distributed and experiment with the possibilities this opens up: Why not consider the irreducibly constitutive role of machines, techniques, or technologies in the problematic axiology of power? Why assume that the moral diktats of representation exhaust mediating processes? Recurrent panics about the effects of media technologies on one's ability to empathize or to think pose an interesting problem, but usually they get bogged down in pseudoscientific solutions that tend to miss both the point and the politics. Rather than being transparent to the intentions of use, any object affords specific opportunities in specific circumstances—a certain latitude or room for maneuver, a dynamic or curve of development that allows for particular kinds of inflection or scope for variation. Knowing how to manipulate such objects or processes (while knowing yourself to be manipulated or manipulable in turn),[15] as well as the effects or consequences that the trickery or cunning of such manipulation produces, brings into play questions of timing, of the propitiousness of the opportune moment, as well as an appreciation of the relative instability of the relations into which such objects, processes, techniques, or technologies are a part. But knowledge of such—which perhaps has more the form of a practical wisdom, a virtue,[16] than a science—must still be cultivated and those objects explored. That is what we propose here.

Machiavelli placed a great deal of emphasis on fortune and other qualities of contingency in the counsel he offered. With him, we can observe that one's efforts in this regard can "flourish one day and come to grief the next,"[17] pointing to the importance of a constant vigilance in stratagematic thought.

Book

For a globalizing culture that is more than prepared to give unilateral credence to the virtues of the digital, operations that involve the book as a significant media object are at risk of seeming anachronistic. Specific defenses of the book as a cultural form might appeal to antiquarians, to the profound traditions of library-based humanism, or to the possibility of sustained engagement with discursive objects, among other things; but given that the book is part of an ecology of media forms that is itself subject to rapid shifts and mutations, such defenses endow it with a status and a niche akin to the death-on-hold that is normally reserved for protected species. In any event, such defenses are easily defanged and brushed aside—by the rhetoric of digital democratization—as the all-too-predictable demurs and cavils of a backward-looking cultural elite anxious to retain its privileges and peculiarities, raising in turn the question of the value of the agency of the book in an era of pervasive digital networks.

Clearly, in the rapidly shifting ecology of contemporary media, the historically dominant place of the book is less than assured. Although writing has crossed numerous thresholds in its tangled histories—aesthetic, scientific, political, amorous, organizational—it would be a mistake to consider the more obviously aesthetic qualities of writing as having preeminence. The more obscure and less glorious instances of writing and of books within the systems and networks of gray media—accounts, manuals, instruction books, policy guidelines, strategy documents—are historically as significant a resource and topic for analysis as the literary or scientific text and, although demure, are also equipped with a certain aesthetic. There are many types of writing—those connected to the bureaucratic world of the document, the memo, and the reminder—other than those that directly convey a sense of the sublime, conduct an infinite conversation, or offer the generativity of the open work, and these others also deserve careful attention as media forms and agents in their own right.

Theories of the text have done much to aid in the exploration of the silent, surreptitious role of the mediations of writing and the writerly. But the vast mass of writing, originating historically in the keeping of accounts, the organizing of societies, the tallying and making of measures, has often escaped the attention of such theories, riveted as they are to culture as a repository of values resistant to economic conformity.[18] What, then, of books that, while evidently important component parts of the material of culture, have not crossed a threshold of scientificity, literariness, aesthesis, or spirituality? What of the book as an active—if not necessarily stable—mediator in apparently more mundane processes? The book as what science and technology studies might call a *boundary object*,[19] or the psychic ergonomist an *influencing machine*? If the book were considered within a generalized pragmatics of evil media as the bearer of sets of opportunities and affordances (of which textual play is merely a subset), then it might be considered an object that—to a greater or lesser extent—provides a way of exploring and exploiting potentially antagonistic practices.

A book, on this count, somewhat paradoxically seems able to sustain interactions between, and give the appearance of, consensus to very different groups. To qualify as such in the more technical sense of the boundary object, the book would have to offer a high degree of interpretive flexibility—you read it your way, I'll read it mine— and operate as a way to structure working arrangements in a collective situation; it would have to entail the capacity to generate both standardized and ill-formed uses, such as those that occur when a semiliterate miller produces a cosmology from the Bible, decidedly not adopting the same kind of use as a literate monk at vespers.[20] Here, misprision, freely varied constructive use, and a failure to follow due norms or standards all allow the book itself to gain agency rather than relinquish it to readers, thus becoming the center and organizing principle of multiple acts of interpretation or reference.

From a pragmatic point of view, a boundary object gives material shape to ambiguity, which thereby ceases to be simply an issue of semantics in games of language. On the one hand, the object effects a kind of consensus—typically in institutional settings—but on the other, that consensus does not erase or crush differences. Marking and negotiating the frontiers between different territories, whether conceptual or material, such objects, like the components that produce an "imagined community,"[21] would seem to envelop degrees of variation in their capacity to unify differences, never quite accomplishing the mental standardization of a meeting of minds, but achieving only resonances, coordination, and points and counterpoints of contact between groups (a bit like the consensus that an artful sophist produces).[22] The preconditions for antagonism and conflict between groups should be located in relation to the shifting patterns of interaction accomplished in complex media ecologies. As those ecologies change, so the lines of stability between groups shift and falter: "All was chaos . . . and out of that bulk a mass formed—just as cheese is made out of milk—and worms appeared in it, and these were the angels."[23]

Evil Media proposes a consideration and practice of the book as medium that brings it into productive connection with sociotechnical media of other kinds, under conditions of heterogeneity and difference. In this context, manuals that purport to provide advice, short essays that codify sets of moves in the unfolding play of verbal jousting, guidance on tactics, or sets of instructions have offered it a way to explore and experiment with the kind of agency, beyond the perpetual play of meaning or of textual *différance*, that such a practice of the book might hanker after. To learn the art of "always being right" with Schopenhauer, for example, is to learn the maneuvers that are made, with or without wiles or premeditation, with the ductile material of language. In focusing on habitual ways of doing in the art of arguing and on the slips and cracks in language that can be exploited in the temporal unfolding of discourse, Schopenhauer's tract offers a polyvalent means of securing victory or gaining consent without needing to know anything ultimately about what the other is after.[24] Ultimately there is nothing to interpret in this art, because the set of stratagems that it offers only poses problems of meaning as a preliminary to a more efficacious problem of use: it is a machine for exerting influence, or "getting things done."[25] In Schopenhauer's world, even if you do suspect some hidden intention or meaning behind the operations of your adversary, the aim is not to disclose it but to create disarray and confusion, knocking your opponent off his or her guard, forcing his or her hand, destabilizing them and setting them spinning, perhaps into your arms.

The point we are making is the simple one that what a book says must also be understood in relation to what it does. The giving of advice and guidance, the laying out of sets of rules, the exploration of strategy and tactics of the kind that we can find in the writers we have mentioned, are eminently practical and indicative of the surreptitious agency of the text. But a book will only retain its practical value if it can take into account and address the allies, the networks of agents formed in and by the myriad techniques, technologies, objects, and so on, that give form to social relations today. As Schopenhauer notes, winning hearts and minds is not something that can be accomplished by means of words alone. A sensibility to more than just words and the ruses they accomplish is required. Gadgets, devices, objects—media that draw together or push apart, that operate along with, order or disorder, remove and shift boundaries—are crucial elements in producing consensus, however artificial or artifactual such agreement or assent may be. And if, as has been claimed more recently, consent is indeed something that is engineered,[26] the sociotechnical twist we are proposing here, when the ruses of power depend on the effective manipulation of black boxes and gray zones, will have to form a kind of reverse engineering for the fabrication of new moves in the negotiation and control of media systems.

To ensure its hegemony, unified, organized power entails books, documents, and even simply paper in its multiple forms, because these are dynamic, multivalent technologies that provide myriad affordances for the organization, distribution, and coordination of the explicitly or implicitly cooperative practices through which alliances and networks are assembled. They produce tacit solidarity, knitting millions of people together in a manner not unlike the vast "idiotypic" networks whose ongoing interactions provide an organism with its ability to resist infection. Problems arise for such networks when they lose their plastic, polymorphous versatility. Antagonisms and differences that cannot be tamed and pacified proliferate when networks of actions and reactions lose the material objects, the paper technologies, around which they cohere. Paper forms: Post-it notes, reminders in pigeonholes, reports, and minutes of meetings are embedded in formal or informal organizational practices and betoken types of cooperation and coordination that are lost or destroyed with certain strategic cost. It is not unreasonable to posit a similar kind of material effectiveness for the book itself, so often studied from the point of view of the meanings it yields.

The adventurous theory that the steady poisoning of the population of Rome by lead carried in the city's drinking water ultimately caused the downfall of the empire offers a salutary lesson here in thinking about the variable role of nonhuman objects in the pragmatics of power. According to this view,[27] it was not the bluff and bluster of the twelve Caesars, or the rise of Christianity, or even the military onslaught of the barbarian hordes that was ultimately responsible for the collapse of the Roman Empire. Rather, the steady, drip-drip impact of an unperceived factor in the environment weakened the physiology of the population to such an extent that resistance to any threat became impossible. As with the viruses transported to the New World by the conquistadores, the construction (or destruction) of a hegemonic form is accomplished in alliance with unforeseen or unacknowledged environmental factors.[28]

One need only refer to the leaked memos and exasperated journal articles of junior officers in the American military, pointing to the significant loss of information inherent in the rapid mutations of an organizational ecology of media, for confirmation of the hypothesis advanced here.[29] Of course, any well-designed media form can give its audience the illusion of knowing more than they actually do, but in its alternately bullet-pointed concision or its spaghetti-connection complexity, digital presentation software develops this illusion to a color-coded extreme, even as the ironies of the admission that not every strategic problem of geopolitics is "bulletizable" start to dawn. But the technology itself is inseparable from the practices of which it is a part, and it is in the way that aesthetic qualities conjoin with organizational practices, roles to play, appearances to manage, and so on, that the technology perhaps accomplishes its most powerful effects. Skim-read in the helicopter on the way to the board meeting, posted after the event as an e-mail attachment, the executive summary or the

PowerPoint presentation offers a saving or compression of time through substitution for more time-consuming—and more traditional—briefing documents. Why concentrate now? If you have the slides, you have the knowledge.

Books, like every other kind of media form, have to be situated in the complex ecology of which they are a part, and it is from there that their relative merits can be evaluated. Machiavelli, like the theorists of science and technology studies after him, emphasized the importance of making alliances—it is usual to lay foundations before one becomes a prince—and one should always want to know how stable or reliable some new force might be. If consent, or its opposite, is to be engineered, then the wise engineer will have a sense of how reliable the materials he or she is working with actually are. Reading a book presents a wager to the reader as a medium to be so tested, writing one, a gamble on the moment of interpretation.

Grayness

Grayness marks the breakdown of clearly defined contrasts: a Monday morning feeling, a certain blankness that is not indifference or affectlessness but something approaching what Roland Barthes theorized as the "neutral," a fading and withdrawal rather than an abolition of contrasts.[30] The gray zone—an expression coined by Primo Levi[31]—denotes a space of activity that is ethically ambiguous, with "ill-defined outlines" and a "complex internal structure." In a gray zone, everyone is sullied. But gray is not always and everywhere a variable proportioning of black and white, for example; it can be equal proportions of red, green, and blue in the RGB color model. Gray can be warm or cool; in addition to neutral or achromatic, there is gunmetal gray. On a gray day, the horizon is often difficult to perceive through the haze. Without precise contrasts, grayness gives rise to an experience of the vague, to fuzzy experience. To escape the bland feelings that blend into the background like steam into clouds, a little clarity, definition, or even friction is required. Procedures, protocols, formal rationality: algorithms and routines can be used to attenuate difficult contrasts, or damp down surfeits of perceptual and affective intensity or information overload. Grayness is a quality that is easily overlooked, and that is what gives it its great attraction, an unremarkableness that can be of inestimable value in background operations.

In the novels of John le Carré, the retired British intelligence officer George Smiley is generally presented in the unassuming tones of a person who would go unnoticed in the streets. If the intelligence officer is thus a kind of gray inversion rather than an eminence, his effectiveness must pertain to his prodigious memory and adroit way with the historico-political archive. Toiling away on intelligence files with the same fine-grained attention to detail that he would accord to the German literature that his scholarly ambitions once propelled him toward—as if the file were a text or vice versa, as in a gray zone it is difficult to tell—he applies himself with great, but measured and sensible, dedication to warding off the threats of communism. It is as if the great machinations of geopolitics, the strident declarations and grand oppositions they betoken, found the conditions for their appearance in a zone where nothing was really clear. Equally, in mist, fog, and the darkening cloud of atmospheric variation that announces a storm, grayness also yields drama and dynamism. Condensing into a precipitate, as "drops of experience"[32] the meteorological movements of gray feelings they assemble point to the atmospheric qualities of affect, a changeable but often unnoticed background—unnoticed until an environmental shift occurs, a change of pressure or temperature. Grayness is an affective *and* perceptual condition that is pervasive and all the more troubling for it because one never quite knows if a storm will break or the unremitting gloom will just continue indefinitely.

For historically understandable reasons, media studies has tended to focus on large-scale agglomerations, the starkly evident forms that, for want of a better expression, the discipline calls *mass media*: newspapers, radio, cinema, television, characterized as tendentious, one-way, but sometimes two-step, flows. More recently, with the growth of the Internet and the development of so-called participatory technologies, media studies has developed a taste for examining *social media*. But neither mass media nor social media exhaust the ambit of media, any more than historically specific technologies and practices give us the standard by which to define, and hence to understand, processes and practices of mediation. So while it might be true to say, borrowing from Whitehead, that in matters of mediation, "civilization progresses by the number of operations it manages to carry out by habit,"[33] it by no means follows that those operations should be exempt from analysis, exploration, and experimentation.

The unobtrusive grayness of so many types of media practice, from system administration to data gathering or the control and verification of all sorts of qualities and attributes, calls for a kind of suspicious attentiveness, the cultivation of a sensibility able to detect minor shifts of nuance, hints of a contrast where flatness would otherwise be the rule. Not that gray media are the bearers of some sort of hidden meaning that might be brought to light (they need not be the object of a hermeneutics), but a certain recessiveness is often a crucial aspect of their efficacy, and that recessiveness is what makes them of practical interest here.[34] Outside the realm of systems design and administration, it is difficult to excite any interest in the finer details of database design, for example.[35] Ethically and politically, the "black boxing" whereby mediating processes are stabilized to form part of the environment of habits—a sociotechnical habitat—involves a critical threshold of perception, one that enables the dependencies of objects, abstractions, representations, or systems to go unnoticed. But black boxing is perhaps too clear a term—boxes are rather too sharply edged to describe all kinds of operations or practices of mediation. Working away in the background too, science and technology studies in recent years has excelled in analyzing the myriad devices used to construct markets, for example, and has, in particular, generated a detailed analysis of the cyborg qualities of economics.[36] Such a context is important, since much of what passes for politics in the present era has already had to be parsed by a filter composed by a correspondence to ideas of good management and of the economic. There's a deferral, a passing off, from politics into fiscal reason, and from thence into problems of implementation, since nothing can be done for a political or "ideological" reason. Such implementations are themselves mediated by abstractions, operative layers with different degrees of resolution and scale, overlapping each other, clearly obscure. The grayness of much media and mediation here points toward the sociotechnical conditions of contemporary democracy and the bleeding in of bureaucratic technologies into the operations of power.[37]

It is nevertheless difficult to subtract oneself from the logic of representation that has proved so definitive for the way in which media are thought of and analyzed. The Cartesian heritage of modernity, in which this logic is so prevalent, and the "bifurcation of nature" of which Descartes's writing is a symptom dissimulate what has been called a "gray ontology," an ontology that remains undeclared in an epistemology that focuses on clear and distinct ideas and transforms *things* into *objects* or "gray shadows of things" submitted to the categories of knowledge.[38] Secreting an ontology of things that types them as submissive objects, the representations by which the ego gains a knowledge of the world involve a shading off into the background of the obscure and troublesome materiality of things.

If Primo Levi's work points toward the distressing and shameful nature of the gray zone, Paul Klee's pictorial invocation of a "gray point" as a multivalent nucleus that oscillates between chaos and the emergence of an order is indicative of the nuanced and muted tensions that the processes and practices explored here are inhabited by.[39] Problematic not just ethically but also aesthetically, the different valences and values of grayness (if not of a gray ontology per se) are explored here in terms of what is best called an ethico-aesthetic paradigm.[40] Gray immanence for gray media: there is an aesthetic that is indiscernible or inseparable from the technologies, techniques, practices, and devices that make up much of the abstract infrastructures of contemporary societies. Unobtrusive processes are working away in the background, giving shape to activities and events. Processing, in the sense of transforming (with the banal discretion of the technocratic), is grayness par excellence, achieving a withdrawing or minimization of perceptual and affective contrast, yielding the low-intensity presence of uniformity. Such muting of intensity characterizes much of what we are exploring here: forms of governance gain ground because no one sees them coming.

While gray media and the affective and perceptive sensibilities to which they give rise tend not to excite much commentary, they are often spectacular in their consequences: the rolling disaster that is the large-scale IT project; the billions knocked off share prices through the convergences of automatic trading algorithms or added to them by the deft manipulation of a new accounting rule; the unfathomable opacity produced by a new protocol for corporate governance. But grayness demands that claims made for the centrality of the spectacle, as too the undue focus given to media messages, reception, or participation, be nuanced by an acknowledgment that the listlessness and boredom of the more sociotechnical aspects of mediation have far greater importance than one might have imagined. "In the beginning was boredom, commonly called chaos."[41]

Sophistication

Being sophisticated is the fruit of a technosocial and geopolitical imperative as much as it is a description of a practical state of affairs such as the possession of a certain style or degree of savoir faire. For the purposes of communicating, making connections, having one's finger on the pulse, inscribing oneself and one's activities in the knowledge economy, it is difficult to avoid the necessity of organizing one's thinking, speaking and doing in terms of their fit with highly complex, technologically advanced registers of discursive and nondiscursive machinery. It is not just a matter of vocabulary, as if being sophisticated were simply a question of using clever words—although jargon can excite, bamboozle, and solidify alliances. Nor is it just a matter of being able to compete in the ramified race to be an early adopter or to acquire a high level of literacy in a new technology. To operate adeptly with things means getting a feeling for what makes them sophisticated in the first place. Sophistication does not rule out brute force and vulgarity, but it extends, complements, or substitutes for approaches based on bludgeoning persistence with a kind of durably efficacious calculus that entails crafting and more than a little finesse.

The assortment of stratagems contained within this book are themselves written under the sign of the imperative to be sophisticated. It is an injunction that is conveyed in the volubility of discursive interactions, the mutating structures of technical means, the ordering devices of everyday banality, a plethora of forms of mediation and of media forms. Spreadsheets, e-mails, smartphones, GPS, and the even more sublimated gray media of project plans, workflow algorithms, and the like: the communicative fabric of social relations is not straightforward. To make a telephone call is to become an element adjoined to a vast network of more or less effectively coordinated and stabilized actors, from billing practices of service providers, through routers, switches, telecommunications protocols, satellite dishes, and the balance of geopolitical forces, down to knowing the modus operandi of successful forms of communication and address. Such networks are part of our sociotechnical infrastructures, and operating effectively within them entails a kind of sociotechnical sensibility, an adroitness in the practice of social relations that articulate the pragmatic forces, actions, and actions on actions that bring them into being, stabilize them, and make them permeable to intentions. The abstract materiality of these infrastructures is labile and mutable and offers diverse opportunities for manipulation, modulation, and control. Hackers excel in exploiting the cracks in programmable systems, but a practical knowledge of how a pricing structure operates, for instance, can also let you run circles around your service provider, while it runs rings around you. Understanding the interplay of such manipulations, establishing the means of operating, evading, or going with them, becomes crucial, and doing so presupposes a heightened sensitivity to their operation. The myriad technical devices, formal protocols, and material structures with which our activities are more or less successfully calibrated,[42] and by which they are ordered and configured, should be viewed in terms of the displacement and condensation of quanta of power,[43] because while making a machine do something you don't want to do yourself can save time, it also shifts the initiative and the operative focus of control. Understanding a data structure, for example, in the same way that an orator understands his or her audience—its sensitivities and concerns—is prerequisite to its adept manipulation. The utility of a tool or a device presupposes an assemblage of relations of which that utility is a part. Techniques and practices that work with gadgets, widgets, bureaucratic procedures, numerical protocols, aside from, and perhaps because of, their association with modern knowledge practices, are thus able to articulate and order, shape and transform, the fluctuating multiplicity of forces that are conjured up for the demands of specific kinds of activity—productive or otherwise. The question of how they are, or might be, so enabled is one that is pursued in the pages that follow.

Such practices are explored here under the imperative sign of sophistication in homage to the much maligned "masters of Ancient Greece" (as Hegel once called them): the sophists. When talk gets to sophistication, and thinking turns to language and the virtuoso performativity of contemporary production, as it does in the work of autonomist thinkers such as Paolo Virno and Christian Marazzi,[44] what often gets forgotten is the ruseful cunning, the artful cleverness, and the challenge to presumptive moral judgment exemplified by the sophists. It is not Aristotle we should turn to for a better understanding of the artfulness of productivity or the political nature of communicative action, as Habermas puts it, but the sophists. These mischievous technicians of the word—for whom being right or being just was something to achieve through an artful exploitation, performance after performance, of the opportunities and affordances offered by language in situ—acquired as a result something of a mixed reputation (bad faith, cynicism, and demagoguery, for starters).[45]

While the contemporary economy is certainly one in which language, communication, and symbol manipulation, among other forms, occupy an important role in productive processes, the situation in which language becomes the primary form and material of production may be some way off. However, the voluble bulks of excited media commentary, the immense harvests of data generated by social networks, the centuries of low-res digital footage making up the archive of audiovisual surveillance practices, or, indeed, the billions of lines of computer code, the myriad forms and endlessly recessive caves of document storage full of records, policies, and procedures, all point toward the infrastructural place of language in its many varieties. The structural logic of semio-linguistic thinking that has been so popular in media and cultural studies is either too crude or too excessively refined a tool to dismantle some of this discursive machinery, and in its usual contentment with the formalized abstractions of structure, it misses the slippery, transverse, or sometimes all too blunt connections between language and things and the varying degrees of stability, coherence, and consistency that are to be found in the devices, technologies, techniques, and practices—in short, the *machinery* of media.

The reference to sophistry here is not made as part of a historically exacting genealogy of the linguocentric, logocentric proclivities of the contemporary, but the link is more than a picturesque analogy. It is not just that recent explorations of the politics and ethics of communication, in their Aristotelian inheritance, imply an unthought stance with regard to sophistry.[46] Within the history of the development and study of media, early theories of propaganda and of the political role of the PR counsel, for example, replicate much of the position and presumed functioning of the sophist.[47] Historically the critical response to such a position, on the basis of presuming the sovereignty of reason, likewise conforms to type by replicating the dichotomous arguments about autonomy and manipulation characteristic of much contemporary critical thinking: don't be swayed by the song of the Sirens.[48] And yet, as the recurrent criticisms of politicians for their hypocrisy and cant (by journalists who themselves hope to excel in the manipulation of opinions) or of mumbo jumbo (by commentators in the name of a presumed common sense) show, such positions, in their own artfulness, owe more than they might care to think to the garrulous ability to exploit, twist, and stretch out arguments and the meaning of words for pragmatic effect. Let people make up their own minds, proclaims the hack, in an appeal to the sentiments of his audience as artful as any of the hypocrisy practiced by his opponent.

The understanding of, and response to, the injunction to be sophisticated that is proposed here takes particular inspiration from a writer like Schopenhauer, who recognized that rationality by itself was too fragile. In *The Art of Always Being Right*, he offered stratagematic counsel to the reader looking for ways to win arguments in the face of an adversary who would do anything to win, regardless of the strength of his real position. A range of stratagems flesh out his advice that attack is the best form of defense, and they give rise to a humorous reframing of dialectics as sophisticated and badly intentioned dueling. The counsel that Schopenhauer offers is reminiscent of the advice offered by the seventeenth-century Jesuit Balthasar Gracián and, in a rather different context, by Machiavelli, especially in *The Prince*. Like these earlier writers, Schopenhauer tends to be somewhat ambiguous. Gracián's art concerns parsimony of effort, obligation, and appearance, the playing of a long game, but it is also one of positioning, of maneuver in relation to other forces such as luck, norms, rules, and apparition.[49] This is not so much the stance of trickery as one of maintaining the grace to avoid being hampered by overcommitment of resources, principle, or information. Machiavelli's position is doubled too, often interpreted as being a stage whisper, a leak about the games played by princes as much as an advisory document. But it also has the character of the manual, a means of getting to the nub of problems by engineering them.

In any case, before the ambiguous attempts at domesticating the unconstrained performance of language, at codifying sophistry through genial inventions like that of disciplines such as rhetoric and principles such as the Aristotelian one of noncontradiction, what is at work is a sort of accursed share of language. Historically, through the tools and techniques that it has developed—logic, rationality, principles, and less explicit forms of codification—philosophy has been quite successful in transforming this unruly matter of language into faults, cracks, and disturbances in the matter of communication, or, indeed, the glitches, bugs, and paradoxes that haunt and form mediations of all kinds. In short, into everything that makes up what, from a transcendental point of view, has been thought of as the radical evil that ought to be expunged from language and communication more generally.[50] More virtuoso than virtuous, sophistry's beyond-good-and-evil ethics can be captured in the loquacious idea of speaking for the pleasure of speaking, a sumptuary, wasteful form of expenditure in which power, skill, and expertise accrue to the incalculable joys of utterance unconstrained by the normative presuppositions of right language use.[51]

But an obvious objection arises to the value of the inspiration we are drawing here from the likes of Gorgias, Callicles, Protagoras, and Antiphon. It is that sophistry is a practice or set of practices that operate with natural language only. It is the hopeless ambiguity of natural languages, their propensity toward the proliferation of homonyms (Cassin's "radical evil"), calling for endless procedures of disambiguation (did you mean x or y? etc.), that impelled the development of formal logics of various sorts in the first place. Indeed, Tarski's comments about the evil of natural language is a precise expression of this concern.[52] Yet in logic, mathematics, computer science, and so on, processes of formalization generate their own inconsistencies and incoherence, and the history of efforts to implement formalisms in programming languages, system protocols, and technologies of all kinds equally is by no means seamless or without fault lines of its own, albeit of a kind that provide the pretext to endless upgrades, patches, rewrites, and technology shifts. A software engineer cannot avoid making assumptions about how an application or a tool will be used, and such assumptions are ripe for exploitation in more ways and more senses than one.[53]

So it is not just through rhetoric, grammar lessons, and discursive conventions but also through formal logics, technical protocols, social proprieties, and the like that the babbling sonic matter of speech, the transcursivity of glyphs, and the hypnotic allure of electronic light are codified, linearized, rationalized, finalized, rendered useful. We thus have ample justification for considering technology to be sophisticated in the way that we are suggesting here. However, lacking a fully affirmed sense of artful cunning and produced on the basis of external finalities, sophisticated communication today rarely yields the innocent joy that reduces the adversary's position to the rubble of convulsive laughter. What it does yield, though, are voluminous mounds, layers, piles of used-up, dead linguistic matter congealing like hair gathered in a bath plug, data that are the digital equivalent of rotting offal, linguistic remains of the bodily functions of expression and the gray affective (dis)ordering of endlessly procedural and procedured communication. Being sophisticated today is about operating with media forms, techniques, and technologies that are excessively, absurdly, finalized as to purpose and utility, but whose seductive faces of apparent, personalized seamlessness, whose coded and codified bureaucratic allure, when regarded from the right angle, present multiple occasions (*kairos*) for crafty—and well-crafted—exploitation, provided that their sleek affectation to affectlessness is probed for the energy it absorbs. Alternately, when the rules of engagement go awry, when the organization encounters an event not in the handbook of procedures, or when chance itself becomes the manifest rule, a certain finesse may be found in collapsing, going berserk, or heading to the nearest exit without stopping to collect one's belongings.

Stratagem

The effectiveness of a device or gadget, administrative practice or form of thinking, is often understood or explained through an uneasy conjunction of technical and scientific categories, particularly when it comes to considering work or the ambient elements of the knowledge economy, its infrastructure or media of choice. Technological innovations are so routinely figured as applications of the disinterested categories of scientific knowledge that any critical consideration of them will prefer to assume that the founding knowledge is itself faulty, evidence of the workings of ideology, rather than address the technique or technology in its own right. But although it would be naive to assume either that all forms of scientific knowledge are what they purport to be or that science cannot explain some aspects of the technologies built in its name, sniffing out the practical, experimental possibilities that alternative hypotheses about the operations of technoscience and its artifacts provide has to have some significance here.

The distinction and hierarchy between the epistemic and the technical that this habit of thought testifies to is itself not new. In ancient Greece the proscription against sophistry resulted in part from a systematic discrimination against technique in favor of the epistemic values of knowledge, a proscription and discrimination that have resonated throughout the centuries. Our exploration of evil media displays something of a preference for considering media and mediation in terms of an understanding of technique that sees it as not fully subordinate to knowledge, as having an active value of its own. The way we frame our discussion of media and mediation—as stratagems —seeks to draw attention to aspects of such practices that cannot be, or are all too easily, explained or justified as a scientific application of technical principles, as an emanation from some global macro-actor or as the verifiable expression of some other kind of conceptual abstraction. Much of what is proposed here does not have the pursuit of truth as its telos, even if it often avails itself of a claim to truth telling. So while the book is not exclusively about technology or about technique, and while the notion of the stratagem through which the discussion is developed is not itself technical, *Evil Media* offers a practical exploration of ways of operating or doing, of the shape and scope of particular kinds of action and the consequences that can be drawn from them.

Stratagems do not point to unproblematic neutrality in the operations of the mediation they describe (among other things, this would take us back to a standard distribution of values between humans and machines, machines as ends to uniquely human specified goals). As already suggested, if neutrality there be, it is in the sense of a grayness in which qualitative patterns of contrast are muted or recessive, rather than simply nonexistent. The affordances or opportunities a stratagematic operation lends itself to give a shape to the broader actions or activities of which they are a part. The introduction of waiting-time targets in a hospital, for example, or the use of some other set of key performance indicators will prompt an institution to shift resources to avert the risks of a league-table slip, the use of a pricing mechanism will turn a student into a consumer, a vector in the application of market logic, all of which can be understood as accidental side effects which nevertheless have their uses.

Science and technology studies might provide an idea of what is involved here. Bruno Latour's statement that "there are only trials of strength, weakness, more simply there are only trials"[54] has to be understood not in respect of some pregiven set of entities—humans, for example—who would then enter into contest with each other. It is, as others have noted, a strong statement about things themselves,[55] and one that can, without too much difficulty, be given something of a stratagematic twist. Indeed, STS, in some of its early forms, displayed something of a Machiavellian inspiration, one that this book has also adopted and developed in its own way. The point here is that when we consider the pragmatics of power, then strength (or weakness) is a function of the allies one has at one's disposal, and virtue or wisdom is something that is exercised in relation to the alliances one has managed to build. "Machiavelli knew perfectly well that the alliances binding towns and crowns are shifting and uncertain. But we are considering much more shifting and uncertain alliances between brains, microbes, electrons and fuels, than those necessary to bind together towns and crowns."[56] Of course, one might want to contest this as a view of the way in which scientific knowledge is produced, but that is not the focus of this book; we are more interested in the murkier realms of media and media practices where the injunctions conveyed and the alliances they involve are shifting and ambiguous. The delegation of actions to the abstract materiality of contemporary media infrastructures is not unequivocal or without consequence for the exercise of power.[57]

As phenomena such as "lock-in" demonstrate, significant advantages accrue from these processes of building (or breaking) alliances.[58] Browser wars, the bundling of software, and proprietary control over source code represent some rather obvious and conscious forms of strategizing in the economic sphere, in a way that might be considered analogous to the propagation of drug addiction among specific communities, along with the capacity for pacification and control.

But even such obvious forms of strategizing have their problems: the intensive targeting of youth by corporations eager for them to consume with alacrity can create blowback when the precise economic conditions for such consumption disappear; the very ease with which digital data can be collected produces significant problems of intelligibility for humans; the securitization of certain kinds of market operation generates wildly risky, opaque sets of liabilities; and so on. We might hypothesize, then, that some kinds of stratagem, figured in a pseudo-economic calculus—a hedonic or, better, malefic calculus—have a rapidly diminishing marginal utility. If a stratagem obtains its efficacy in part through the emotive or affective energy it succeeds (unbeknownst to itself) in mobilizing, reinvestment or displacement of that energy elsewhere will require greater outlay to achieve the same effect.[59]

As has been mentioned, the approach to media we are exploring here entails the cultivation of a certain kind of ethico-aesthetic sensibility that seeks to appreciate the ways in which objects—such as digital artifacts and practices, knowledge management, software design or audit, even theories and knowledge—can be manipulated and experimented with in view of the differential production of power dynamics shifting away from an ethics and aesthetics that implicitly or explicitly adopt the point of view of the spectator.[60] Agamben has underlined the disaster that such an adoption constitutes from the aesthetic point of view, and Alain Badiou has argued that in the field of ethics, such a position results in a logic of nihilism and the kind of quasi–a priori injunctions against evil of the sort we have already considered. We seek to inhabit the position of the productive dynamic of power here, albeit in such a way as to acknowledge the problematically open-ended, experimental position that this places us in. Stratagems in this respect, rather than simple recipes to be followed, might better be understood as *operative constructs* in the sense that they have to be taken up, used, worked with, although with a certain care or cunning lest they fail, collapse, or blow up in one's face.[61]

Stratagems do not cohere into a system; otherwise they could be treated as theorems or redistributed in terms of the time-honored distinction between strategy and tactics. Even if that were possible, it is not really desirable, because of the operation of reduction—this being explicable in terms of that—it allows. Rather, stratagems are better set out in terms of an extensive, open-ended listing through which they and their virtues might be enumerated and explored on their own count. What is more, they also display a certain undecidability because inevitably a stratagem does not describe or prescribe an action that is certain in its outcome. Cultivating a sensibility is thus not the operation of an aesthete but a practical element of the approach adopted here, a jogging out of habit-forming stabilities. As Foucault underlines in his discussion of the "gray, meticulous and patiently documentary" quality of Nietzschean genealogy, a certain attention to slight nuances of detail, to "disparity"—those attenuated or recessive contrasts—is crucial to the proper operation of evaluation.[62] Apropos of an algorithm, a technical invention, the informal mediating practices of a manager, say, this means an attentiveness to the precise latitude of operation within which that algorithm, invention, or practice will achieve the desired effect, what Gracián might have called *agudeza*—acuity, sharpness, wit. Like the politician who, observing the rules of contemporary oration, overdoses on the rule of three or on the pregnant pause when speaking in public, the pragmatics of a stratagem always risk misfiring,[63] especially when treated as a simple code requiring no artfulness or ingenuity in its deployment. Applying a rule or following a protocol does, of course, have a value, but the desire to form part of a mechanism to which such following testifies is itself a stratagematically helpful misunderstanding of the shifting operations of relations of force. Naturally leaks, queues, recursive structures, not to mention the time-honored practices of psychological operations or intelligence gathering, may be interpreted as component elements of a potentially formalizable system, and they are often thought so in certain conspiracies. However, to treat them as such has its risks, not the least of which is to overstate and hence underestimate their effectiveness. Similarly, to see tactics at play (where we see stratagems) is equally to run the risk of tacitly assuming, by contrast, the underlying coherence of a strategy, missing the critical operations of circumstance and the contingencies of the opportune moment.[64]

In an unclear but doubtless determinable relationship to sophistry, Schopenhauer's exploration of the "art of always being right" (he mischievously claimed for it the status of dialectic, rereading Aristotle against Hegel) entailed the elaboration of a series of stratagems for working with the propensities of argumentative language to fool, lead astray, trip up.[65] A stratagem in this context was not just a power play but a deliberate attempt at exploiting natural language and the opportunities that the temporal unfolding of discourse provides. Working on the other's susceptibility to enticement and entrapment by language and profiting at every moment from the advantage it might confer, the risk was always that one might oneself get taken in, hooked by one's own verbal dexterity, missing the sucker punch. However, as has already been remarked, this approach to, and cataloging of, stratagems had the relative luxury of operating within a highly restricted media ecology, in which one might plausibly claim that power operated in relation to forms of communicative action that depended largely on speech and writing. Such is not really the case today, when speech and writing are continuously remediated through ever longer chains or networks of people, devices, and protocols, in which "debate" occurs only in a limited subset of situations. So while the general principle of a stratagematic analysis remains in place, the task now is made more difficult by the proliferation of media, the range of materials and kinds of languages or semiotic systems at play. In any case, verbal jousting à la Schopenhauer is rather too evidently a spectator sport these days, such that if one seeks to capture the value of thinking with the stratagematic approach here, it will have to be away from the lights and noise of the front-of-house theatrics, in the "articulation work" that makes the fireworks possible. As we also learn from likes of Machiavelli and Gracián, a certain discrete unobtrusiveness is often the best way to shine.

The stratagematic mode of writing, then, offers a way of exploring the opportunities and affordances of media and mediation. The counsel it offers is regrettably not a set of recipes for success, even if we have a liking for the algorithmic or phantasmic tendencies of certain publications in the broad field of media operations.[66] Here again the approach takes something of its inspiration from Machiavelli, whose name has, in the Western political tradition, become a byword for naked advocacy of the values of deception. And yet, as the most studious of recent commentaries have suggested, there is a sense in which his writings actually take up a practice of *dissimulation*, an ironic approach that consists in dropping hints, helping readers to sharpen their own skills in the assessment of appearances: "dissimulation about deception," rather than its advocacy pure and simple.[67] But it may be too late to go back, to reconstruct the real Machiavelli underneath the many-layered versions and imaginary constructions of generations of scholars, politicians, and fabulators; and a potential for flattery and aggrandizement arises from the thought that one might be imitating such a figure from the past. As Erica Benner puts it, "He is well aware that modern princes and republics frequently mimic the names, maxims, and other appearances of antiquity in the hope of lending an aura of greatness to imprudent or *disonesto* deeds," a view that should itself be taken as a shrouded warning with current value, as "it is unlikely that Machiavelli wants his contemporaries to imitate ancient political works in this shallow way."[68] The lesson here is clear: anything other than a thoroughly authentic relation to the past, to the real Machiavelli, is a mistake. But the imaginary, fantasized, or crudely naturalized Machiavellis have value too, because beings of fiction have a value that is not to be underestimated, not the least of which is to point toward the pragmatic value of deception about dissimulation. The stratagem negotiates, plays with, and yields to the seductive values of the imaginary and the real in equal measure and as such provides an opening to evil media.

Intelligence

Brainwashing

And if the lambs say among themselves: "these birds of prey are evil; and whoever is least like a bird of prey, but rather its opposite, a lamb—would he not be good?" there is no reason to find fault with this institution of an ideal, except perhaps that the birds of prey might view it a little ironically.
—Friedrich Nietzsche, *On the Genealogy of Morality*

Evil media have a history. We have alluded to some elements of this past in the introduction, but such histories need not extend centuries into deep time or sport the names of famed scholars and diplomats; they may also exist in the shallow history of electronic media and echo emptily to the fame of nameless operatives. An example of such is brainwashing, characterized by indoctrination, mind control, the manipulation of thought patterns and brains, characterized as clumps of rewireable stuff. An imaginative construction from the Cold War era, brainwashing is always something that others do, your enemy does. The other, you convince yourself, is an enemy of autonomous rationality, a purveyor of cheap and manipulative ideologies, an ill-willed manipulator of the free-thinking individual. And if the other, in this way, is bad, malevolent, or evil, then we, you conclude, must be good.

Any orientation in the field of study of evil media necessarily pays homage to brainwashing. Arising as a polemical phenomenon in an era of acute paranoia, it fixes in our imaginary the panicky affect of the loss of autonomy to some malevolent other forever bent on subliminally directing our thoughts to alien ends. More dramatic and obviously politicized than the various bodies of media-effects research that were popular at the same time,[1] brainwashing tries to convince us of the existence of a geopolitical threat that would at the same time launder our thoughts and wipe clean this already too mischievous muscle.

But in the now tarnished hall of mirrors of the Cold War, the strategic accusation of brainwashing belies the many layers of manipulation and deception to which a public—and those who saw themselves as gaming them—trained to accept the credibility of an appeal to science in the face of totalitarian ideology was subject. Just as exposing the conjurer's tricks does not necessarily spoil an illusion, examining the effectiveness of brainwashing techniques and polemic does not preclude the continuing exploitation of the creative possibilities of low-level manipulation and mind control: on the condition that we understand the manipulative suggestions of the brainwashing process as so many germs of thought with which to infect their hosts. As with hypnosis and sophistry, what is put into play with brainwashing, when we review its emergence and strategic operation, is an ensemble of forces that no one can pretend to master, short of being taken in by their own dissembling.

Shorn of its luridly sensationalist trappings, the polemical and strategic unity of brainwashing as a phenomenon discloses some of the epistemo-technical ruses of modern reason. Brainwashing not only links a set of practices and techniques but also and inseparably offers a tacit commentary on, and an image of, those same practices and techniques and their relationship to the mechanisms by which they may be proved. The real effectiveness of brainwashing as a historical construct lies in the way that it dissociates science from politics within the kingdom of representation, situating good science on one side and the malevolent manipulation of science and reason on the other side of a heavily politicized divide.

This dissociation testifies to one of the simple and time-honored rules proposed by Schopenhauer: "The discovery of objective truth must be separated from the art of winning acceptance for propositions."[2] The specific stratagems that one must follow in observing this rule, of course, are as varied as the practices, techniques, and technologies in question, but *that* the rule is followed is a practical imperative, one that is usefully contrasted with the categorical imperative of Kantian morality, with its universalizing test for actions that respect the autonomy of humanity as an end. Purporting always to be right is crucial, especially in an economy in which cognition, knowledge, and science are central. For the sake of appearances, it is your *duty* to pretend to truth: respect for the spectacle of purely autonomous rationality demands it.[3]

Following Schopenhauer's lead, any study of brainwashing keen to press its techniques into the service of some other form of mind control must accept as a prerequisite that the initial presentation of brainwashing as the malign external perversion of otherwise sound science tells only part of the story. Indeed, the symmetries in the narration of brainwashing are too obvious to ignore: the mind is manipulated against its will by an external force; science is perverted against its essence by an external force (as if scientists themselves never invented fantastic trials of strength in their undertakings). A more interesting image of brainwashing emerges from taking the opposite view: not of a cynical manipulation of science but of its erection into an all too credible ideal. Why would the NKVD officer manipulating a prisoner using the concepts of Pavlovian psychology be any different from the CIA operative drawing on the Freudian concept of transference to rationalize his own practices? Or experimental treatment using an erstwhile "lie serum" be any less scientific than the considerably more widespread belief in the efficacy of frontal lobotomies?[4] Borrowing from the sophisticated musings of Jean-François Lyotard, we might say that when the scientist waves his magic wand, "It is not the addressee who is seduced by the addressor. The addressor, the referent, and the sense are no less subject than the addressee to the seduction exerted."[5]

The theatrical spectacle of people not fully in control of their mental processes did not emerge for the first time at the show trials of the Stalinist purges, with the confessions of Zinoviev and company. The asylum in the hospital at Salpêtrière in Paris formed the setting for Jean-Martin Charcot, a real P. T. Barnum of nineteenth-century science, to display his hysterics in the service of scientific inquiry. The context is different, the mechanism and the ends, too, but Charcot's hysterics performed for audiences (the real one in the Tuesday lectures, the virtual one in the photographs of the *Iconographie*) as did Stalin's opponents.[6] The difference, of course, is that the neurologist Charcot's showmanship created a science (psychoanalysis), while Stalin's created an intelligence agency (the CIA). This sort of technological *epideixis*, this showing (and showing off), in both instances had a remarkable impact: a heightened sensitivity to the presumed remarkable powers of science and technique.

Some interesting symmetries connect these different situations: Charcot makes his patients perform so that offstage the genius can reinforce his scientific credibility; Stalin makes his victims perform so that offstage the Kremlin can reinforce its political power. The journalists and intelligence experts weave together a narrative making Stalin a performer in a new theater of images so that the genius offstage—actually, we don't want to overemphasize these similarities or make the situations appear more clear-cut than they really are. It's not quite certain who is performing, who is acting or acting out, and for whom. When brainwashing was invented, was the real monster, the evil deus ex machina pulling the strings, Stalin? Or was it Allen Dulles, whispering in Truman's ear? The journalist Edward Hunter, breaking the news about brainwashing in Red China?[7] Or perhaps it was just the television set in the corner all along? The point is that in Salpêtrière, as in the United States after World War II, an apparatus that produces something as "self-evident" fact is required. A whole chain of events, a whole network of actors, is required to give brainwashing the amplifying power that it possessed as part of a moral panic. The polemical phenomenon "brainwashing" doesn't emerge in a void, the result of some purely ideological fantasy, any more than it refers unproblematically to a set of unequivocal facts.

In the immediate aftermath of World War II, the strategic situation between the Soviet Union and the West resembles nothing if not the epistemic hell of the analytic situation of transference and countertransference: What does Stalin want? What does Truman want? If he says x, it's because he wants me to believe y, but he knows that I know that he wants me to believe y, so there must be a z. Every suggestion spirals into a sump of strategically deployed signs. Perhaps it is not so surprising that one might invent a theory (game theory)[8] that effectively formalizes and rationalizes this endless, double-handed interpretative delirium—and equally unsurprising that this kind of formalism then makes it into the scientific study of unconscious processes.[9] But least incongruous of all perhaps is the growing awareness of no longer quite being in control of one's thought processes. In this context, the real genius of the heteroclite construct "brainwashing" lies in the remarkable diversionary tactics it inaugurates for wayward psyches: capture and displace the attention of your audience so that it focuses on what is happening somewhere else, on the other side of the Iron Curtain, or the other side of the room, where the television innocently beams away.

The shimmering multiplication of images, reflections, and refractions aside, the accusation of brainwashing stabilizes around a credulous staging of the authority and power of science. The Manhattan Project had already detonated its own payload of scientific power, and *Sputnik* was about to project an image of technoscientific advance into the stratosphere; and in the absence of the other (the so-called Red Menace is a weakly imaginative construct that fills a void), the very real ignorance at play at the dawn of the postwar era readily appeals to psychology to somehow crystallize and stabilize the "intuitions" of those at the controls of strategic policy. In a way, the intelligence agencies could do little else: in the absence of a real object of study, or of those "reliable witnesses" that are the hallmark of any science that has managed to turn its artifactual, experimental constructions into conductors of the real, one could only ever appeal to a speculative construction, and a fetish of scientific method.[10]

The crucial point about brainwashing, then, is not that it needs to be grounded in some set of references to science or technology. It is the appeal to science and technology to explain brainwashing (and hopefully manipulate to one's own ends) that gives this polemical phenomenon the ability to assemble hearts, minds, and federal budgets. And like any kind of weaving together, such operations prompt other movements, in this case providing something of a rationale for torture, given the way that CIA investigations into brainwashing quickly became a laboratory for studying interrogation techniques.[11] At a historical point when such large-scale sureties as the Cold War have not so much collapsed as been dissolved, the permeation of such dynamics into new lines of alliance is worth scenting out. Everyone feels happier if he believes he has science and not just ideological manipulation on his side: the populace at large, the torturers, the policy wonks, the politicians. And if you can't directly control the thought patterns of these others, you can at least suggest through inference that if the other is bad, then I must be good, or at least realistic.

Systemic Ambiguity

With most species of orchids, it is not the fittest but the most deceptive ones that survive.[12]

In a world in which a primary economic horizon is one of war in its various modalities (conflict with the irreducible other, the perpetual struggle of all against all, or asymmetric warfare), the kind of practical criticism traditionally carried out by intelligence and counterintelligence operatives becomes a vital necessity. As has recently been noted, the surprise conjunction of literary criticism and geopolitical strategizing represented by Cold War intelligence practices at senior levels of the CIA and its forerunners allowed for an attentiveness to, and cultivation of, ambiguity that presented an invaluable means for monitoring, evaluating, manipulating, and deceiving the other.[13] Ambiguity, along with the mental conflict it discloses and creates, is at once a diagnostic tool, to the extent that it symptomatizes potentially antagonistic or threatening intentions, and a critical weapon, to the extent that it creates doubts, uncertainties, and the possibilities for divergences in the field of action in which it is at work. For the assiduous operative holed up in an office in Langley, Virginia, in Ludovisi in Rome, or in St. James's in London, applying the same scrupulous attention to textual detail and the nuances of phrase in a covert operation such as HT/Lingual as would once have been applied to a poem by Ezra Pound or a letter composed to e. e. cummings appears as a geopolitical imperative and defense of imperiled imperial values.

The movement is from the file to the document to the text and from there, through close reading, to the other and their intentions. With suitably muted ambiguity, William Empson argued that "the fundamental situation, whether it deserves to be called ambiguous or not, is that a word or a grammatical structure is effective in several ways at once."[14] Acknowledging the claims of his critics, that almost anything could be considered ambiguous given the expansive understanding of the notion that *The Seven Types of Ambiguity* exhibits, Empson defends his position on the grounds that its more encompassing vision would be better able to find causes for "so straddling a commotion and so broad a calm" as a reader is moved to.[15] Enter New Criticism and the strategy of close reading. Enter James Jesus Angleton and the newly minted position of the CIA's head of counterintelligence.

For the gray eminence determined to exercise the strategic calculus of statecraft, it takes but a small permutation of the terms involved in Empson's claim that "the machinations of ambiguity are among the very roots of poetry" to find an artful beauty in deception and dissimulation.[16] However, for literary critics and intelligence operatives working in the nascent era of mass media, with the still unchallenged cultural hegemony of the book and an education in literature as yet untroubled by the tensions to which the presence of so-called minorities would expose the canon, the kind of ambiguity to which their eyes and ears were sensitive could be seen to arise from the intentionality and mental conflict of individuals immersed in a single language, and what is more, a language that could be considered the bearer of largely consensual, but somewhat threatened, cultural values. While for Empson the concern was one of bringing language "under control,"[17] exploring and exploiting the covert action of ambiguity, practicing New Criticism CIA-style depended on the idea that cracks and faults in the use of language symptomatize an intention that is often undisclosed, betraying a form of mental conflict, the disclosure of which matters for the sake of national security. Little matter that the intention could be a much-fantasized threat to world-historical destiny; ambiguities (manifest as a detail effective in several ways at once, alternate meanings resolved into one, unconnected meanings given simultaneously, combined meanings indicating a complicated state of mind, fortunate confusion, irrelevance provoking interpretation, full contradiction) are indicators of deception and thus indicative of a forthcoming action that must be thwarted, turned, or inhibited, influenced by the production of material that selectively guides. The conviction of Angleton's practical criticism is that the other is always the bearer of a hidden message that close reading can disclose, and if it cannot, if ambiguity cannot be resolved, then other techniques are available for disclosing or producing hidden truths.[18] Naturally, if the other isn't behaving deceptively before the adoption of countermeasures, you can be sure that he will afterward, as the myriad forms of blowback attest.

Parallel to Angleton's rise began the long career of the computer in the unveiling, encrypting, and sifting of signals intelligence. Perhaps one might see his emphasis on literary skill as a preemption of its negation in the machining of language (analogous to the way that, in media theory, photography is often said to have purified painting). As such, the world today is also one of scripts, of databases, of data structures and algorithms, a world of machines as much as of texts or documents. Equivocal language includes not only the semantic richnesses of Shakespearean diction and the stutter-phonics of Gertrude Stein but also the aridity and obsessively repetitive ordering of assembly language and the fastidious deductive hierarchies of first-order predicate calculus. Likewise the intentional action of an individual is only a limit case of a more general and dispersed array of forms of agency, of kinds that are always agonistic: humans talking to machines, machines talking to humans, machines talking to machines, and so on. In such circumstances, ambiguity is more helpfully understood as something that arises not from conflicted or covertly oppositional intentions but from the jarring and clashing, the mutating modulations of systems and mediations, in which problematic zones of indeterminacy arise because no system is ever truly "closed." It is never quite possible to eradicate the interaction of formal systems with natural languages—whether that be in the "object" languages that formalisms seek to ground and explicate or in the now mundane interactions between programmed machines and their human users. When systems interact, the patterns of behavior that they exhibit, their potential for mutual misinterpretation, grow from something arising between them, a crack, a fault, or a translation failure, which then becomes a critical factor composing their subsequent internal states and mutual change. Gilles Deleuze, borrowing from Leibniz, the genial philosopher of mathematical systems, theorizes the central role of "ambiguous signs" in their relationship with the bifurca-tions that emerge around the singular points of a system. "We are, he says, no longer faced with an individuated world constituted by means of already fixed singularities, organized into convergent series. . . . We are now faced with the aleatory point of singular points, with the ambiguous sign of singularities."[19]

But far from reducing the opportunities for manipulation and deception, the new situation of systemic ambiguity opens up and extends the scope of intelligence and counterintelligence operations for the astute media operative. Of course, under such circumstances, maintaining the prerogatives of a dominant imperial center becomes a considerable challenge, which is perhaps one reason to be thankful that many of the tools and techniques for detecting and tracking the ambiguities that portend mental conflict *and* social antagonism can be provisionally conferred on the algo-rithms and data structures of dataveillance and forensic computing technologies.[20] Nevertheless, in a period in which it is difficult to trace patterns of conflict and the emergence of antagonisms back to a single binary opposition with any degree of plausibility, the gray zones of gray media call for new forms of investigation and a nuanced approach to the kinds of tensions and patterns of interference that arise. If the operatives of the Cold War could reserve for themselves the position of gray eminence, the distant adviser to the executive power, the new spaces of collectively intelligent networks and the asymmetrical relations these put in place demand instead the more difficult position of gray immanence.

Objectify Indeterminacy

Understanding that ambiguity is as dispersed as the forms of mediation that make up agency and that confer a consistency on the links and connections of power is crucial to developing an adequate stratagematic calculus. The best course of action in many circumstances is to condense these links and to focus on the ways that they sometimes converge in and on individuals, since the proverbial hypothesis of the weakest link in the chain is often valid. But it is too easy to mistake the patterns of behavior of nodes in a network for the intentions of a subject: pattern recognition provides a comfortable resolution to the problems that systemic ambiguity poses. However, if all that is yielded vis-à-vis others is the undisclosed intentions of subjects, then the collective, the machinic, the workings, may be missed—risking turning the ambiguities of the other to the balance sheet of the moral account.

In the most banal of interactions, systemic ambiguity typically manifests itself as "user error."[21] The erroneous ways of the user, like the bugs that our immersion in natural languages produce when brought into conjunction with formal systems, testify to the evil that an open semantics, a semantics that cannot be parsed in a finite series of deductively closed steps, bears within it.[22] The explicitness of the rules according to which formal systems operate, in this way, work to pass judgment on the transparency of the actions and statements that those systems are brought to bear on: whether that occurs in the form of the quantifiable cataloging of actions in an audit trail, the policy and procedures painstakingly and minutely enumerated in the documents of corporate governance, or the more mundane actions involved in producing an electronic document.[23] The script that is followed in a call center confers a metric on the movements of persuasion and influence in a conversation, providing an external measure on the pleasures, operations, and meanings of speech, and works its way into the mental devices used to parse language. The caller takes a new tack, and the pragmatics of the speech situation twist subtly: "Have a nice day" now means that the supervisor can stop listening in on the conversation. Actions that might once have been performed as if they were second nature, judgments that may once have been formulated as a routine element of local knowledge, are accomplished haltingly; the uncertainties that emerge where one system decodes and recodes another generate patterns of behavior that conflict and bulge with the newly framed norm.

User error increases to the extent that divergences from the norm increase: it may be the symptom of a conflicted mentality, easy to blame on stupidity and a failure to internalize new norms of production (What do you mean you haven't read the manual?), but may also be a sign of the tense bifurcations brought into play in a shifting ecology of media forms. Beyond a certain threshold, persistent user error may be cast as deviance, motivational deficit, a lack of adhesion to the creed expressed in the mission statement, a failure to meet the requirements specified in the job description, a failure of the education system, a weakness in the labor market. (You just can't get the staff these days . . .)

The resolution of systemic ambiguity through the attribution of user error is itself fraught with anxiety. It is difficult to escape the assumption that the "shape of actions" taking form in media systems must ultimately be understood in terms of what computers still cannot do,[24] implying that a human element ultimately takes responsibility for the warps and shifts in a technosocial environment. Likewise it proves difficult to conceptualize formal and natural systems without introducing some hierarchy between them. The "3C" thinking (command, control, communication) that pervades the architectures of corporate accountability offers the classic double-edged sword here: to be in charge of, and take responsibility for, a system equally means accepting a level of responsibility for its failure; if your staff really are that stupid, the suspicion may arise that you are a cretin, too. But equally (and the recurrent "surprise" problems in the financial markets offer the most obvious example here) the most catastrophic stupidity arises from the sedulous dedication to conform one's actions and judgments to the letter of what complex technological support systems tell you. Once again, legacy systems from an earlier era of conflict provide useful pointers. The case of Kim Philby, the British-Soviet double agent frequently thought of as the "perfect" spy, shows that it is in the most exemplary, least ambiguous behavior, the most dedicated adherence to norms and the most admirable professionalism, that the greatest danger lies, ultimately giving rise to the recurrent concern "who—or what—is running whom?" In a world where the problem has changed and ambiguity has become systemic, potent ambiguity lies perhaps in the willed closing of any gap between user and algorithm.

Somewhat late in the day, management theory discovered that ambiguity can have a useful strategic function within organizations. As a "strategy in organizational communication," ambiguity fosters "unified diversity" (what the ancient Greeks would have called *homologia*, meaning: "We don't agree, but it sounds like we do"), maintains positions of privilege, promotes plausible deniability, and facilitates orga-nizational change. Now, quite aside from giving the scheming executive an efficiency-based rationale for his or her power games—and the invaluable addition of an extra equivocation in his or her action (something rarely considered in communication and organization theory), management theory focuses somewhat exclusively on written and oral communication, precluding a more complete appreciation of the operative's palette.[25] Indeed, the research focus on linguistic communication can itself have useful strategic outcomes, since it removes attention from the shifting environment in which that communication operates.

But systemic ambiguity suggests that it is in the subtly shifting composition of the technosocial environment that the efficacious operations of uncertainty, equivoca-tion, hesitation, and other forms of deviation and deception occur. For digital tech-nologies, the introduction of a new piece of software produces a new enunciative situation, a style of statements and the engendering of particular forms of interaction. Not unreasonably, the perplexed user, at a loss to deal with a machine that does not easily disclose its intentions (it rarely says "work harder" or "think less"), frequently raises the question of what the machine wants, and in an extension of transferential dynamic, "repairs" the gaps in the discourse of the machine, ceding authority to a machine, which is thus assumed to somehow know better.[26] But as critics of both analysis and artificial intelligence have suggested, in such situations, giving the appear-ance of thinking that the other has some profound knowledge is itself a ruse, a game.

It is not surprising, then, in a complex ecology of human and nonhuman agents in which unstable mediators mediate unstable media, that systemic ambiguity is resolved by the injection of redundancy into one or other of the systems in a relation: the disambiguation of language through the insistence that one word must mean one thing at a time to both partners in a dialogue, for example, or the codification of the end user's relation to a software application through overly explicit instructions. But too prompt a resolution of ambiguity precludes an understanding of the machina-tions that it accomplishes. For philosophy, that meant a decisive misunderstanding of the ways in which consensus could be formed or consent engineered, leaving the politicking of language to continue in its sophisticated ways to the dismay of critical rationality. Stabilizing the place of digital artifacts as known, determinate quantities similarly blocks off an exploration of the transformative possibilities they might introduce.

Crucially, systemic ambiguity is as much about the *production* of signs as it is about their deciphering. Becoming able to read the shifting balance and distribution of forces in fluctuating patterns of uncertain signs is one thing. Being able to produce such signs, to turn them to your advantage, is another. Granted, the introduction of a new technology in the workplace or the home often gives unintentional rise to the ambiguities inherent in uncertain translations from one language, technology, or coding system to another. In these circumstances, actions that might otherwise be interpreted as a malevolent power play can easily be recast as something else. A workforce can be reskilled or modernized by exploiting the hesitations that arise over the interpretation of a new system (get rid of these expensive, technophobic old-timers). Equally, a more adaptable, more flexible generation, anxious about the cultural privileges that accrue to older media systems, might be persuaded to find in the imperfect translation from one system to another a failing and a weakness of a code or language that lacks the familiarity of the easy acquisition. What appears truly difficult in such circumstances is to maintain and affirm the ambiguity as such. This is because the risk associated with operating with and within the ambiguous is the risk associated with the instability and reversibility of power relations as such.[27] Uncertainty can communicate a perceptible lack of power and an inability to act decisively. Prolonging the indeterminacy that ambiguous signs express means, almost by definition, increasing the likelihood of contestation. When one system does not succeed in subordinating another, the translation failures that symptomatize this fault or disturbance, whether glossed as user error, bugs, bad design, or system unavailability (or indeed something more insidious), point to aberrations in the mediation process and a trial of strength gone wrong.[28]

Leverage Anxiety

In a world of ruseful cunning and manipulation, nothing is straightforwardly unambiguous or unproblematic; everything is pliable, biddable, suggestible. The question of the tools one uses, the forces one has at one's disposal, and the ways in which these can be made to work to one's advantage is thus permanently open, including the sleek facades and seamless, transparent interfaces that seem to tell another story. In the multiple fields of knowledge production, the exercise of strategic or stratagematic intelligence requires an attentiveness to what would otherwise remain irredeemably obscure epistemological discussion, hairsplitting conceptual distinctions, even throwaway comments and off-the-cuff remarks. Chairman Mao knew this only too well, pointing out that in the field of politics, trouble is an excellent thing: "There is great chaos under heaven—the situation is excellent."[29] Even the emergence of a controversy in a scientific field can furnish crucial indicators for otherwise imperceptible shifts, geopolitical impasses, and social problems, offering a toehold for the astute media operative. In this way, the faults and disturbances marking our mental universes offer the same kinds of opportunities for exploitation as do bugs in the algorithmic universes of software, and one stratagem is always in the position of being able to turn another to its own account.[30]

The domain of the psy disciplines—once a favored epistemo-technical resource for PR gurus, cold warriors, and wizened imperialists, and drawn on pell-mell in the development of strategic ambiguity—yet again proves a crucial resource for following the shifting configurations and shadowy actions of mediums. While "spychoanalysis" would have been a good name for the fantasized practices of mind control, part of the genius of psychoanalysis was to have linked what it does as a set of therapeutic practices to a conception of knowledge and truth that would exonerate the field of any suggestive wrongdoing. Its promise to uncover hidden truths, its use of the concept of the transference to break down the unconscious resistances of the patient and mitigate against the possibly distorting effects of what is usually thought of as suggestion, and more generally to detect and disclose things that a patient could not or would not admit, has, one will admit, a certain strategic allure. For the squeamish, psychoanalysis certainly has a more seductive quality than torture, at least if it is a question of getting people to speak. More refined than the salivating hounds of behaviorism, in the context of social power and geopolitical conflict, the theatrical mise-en-scène of its conceptual framework, psychoanalysis's learned allusions to ancient Greek culture also give added value and a hefty payout of cultural capital with which to speculate and scheme. As with the resonant connections between counterintelligence practice and literary criticism discussed earlier, mapping furtive and clandestine dynamics into textual structures and theatrical scripts offers an ornamental handle on the resolution of geopolitical problems. The stratagematic value of concepts of analysis is worth exploring here, then, even if now only diminishing returns are to be gained from slipping a little Freud into one's daily briefing.

The double reference to knowledge and to therapy within analysis exemplifies the possibility of a flip-flopping move that can be used with impunity to avoid unwelcome accusations of trickery and manipulation. On the one hand, the therapeutic claim—we're only trying to help alleviate the suffering of psychological disorders—can be used to sanction any manner of improper suggestiveness in practice. On the other, the knowledge claim—that in analysis patients disclose the truth of their suffering—may countervail the criticism that the analyst puts ideas into the patient's head, constructing the problems that analysis then claims to resolve. Unlike behaviorism, which quite openly acknowledged its debts to the model of reflex action by siphoning off the excess produced in expectation of reward, the implications of the suggestive stimulations of reflex action were historically cast aside on the royal road to the unconscious.[31]

Thus one might say that in spite of the well-meaning therapeutic intent of analysis, its appeal to science offers a cover, an alibi, an air of benevolent neutrality and cultural sophistication, a confident feeling of being in the right, to what others might see as a technique of influence.[32] We have already seen the value of this in the polemical construction of brainwashing. So when Jung, breaking with Freud, remarks that in the transference, that imprimatur of scientificity, the analyst can appear as a devil, a god, or a sorcerer,[33] it is not difficult to laugh such things off as the obsessions of a mythomaniac. (The archetype? Not a scientific concept, I'm afraid.) But when we add to the balance sheet the systemic downgrading of fear in favor of an endogenous logic of anxiety,[34] and factor in the findings of recent work on the psychology of torture (difficult to attribute those anxieties to the subject in question),[35] we cannot help thinking that Jung might have had a point. Perhaps the reconstruction of the unconscious might have been at the service of other forces than those of pure science all along? Maintaining plausible deniability for the hex you've placed on the terrified libido is made considerably easier if you can excise in advance any connections that the unconscious might have with the outside world.

Part of the opposition that psychoanalysts, stalwarts of the Cold War of the psyche, have toward initiatives developing elsewhere—psychopharmacology, cognitive science, and neurobiology, for example—stems from the complications that they bring into the dynamic of transference (whose operative structural fantasies are rather homologous to brainwashing and mind control): what strange, active, and possibly empowering effects might an anxiolytic or an antidepressant have on a patient's unconscious resistances to the outing of the truth? The medium of psychoanalysis is speech, but a powerfully motivated forgetting must be at work to make us ignore the possibility that the psyche is constructed through other media, too. Irony fading, the analyst comments that, in one such effect, "Addiction opens a field where no single word of the subject is reliable and where he escapes analysis altogether."[36] Fearing the spiking of the psyche, the analyst insists on the exclusion of any other agents than the medium of language.

What we are getting at is that a certain doctrinal (or theoretical—the difference is slight here) rigidity renders a practice open to the classic counterintelligence scam and ruse of power: the turning of an agent. Given the wilderness of mirrors in which analysis finds itself, a strong possibility exists of no longer knowing who or what is running whom: we can ask in all seriousness whether Anna O., right at the inception of the analytic movement, was humoring Breuer and Freud all along? In any case, one cannot ignore the hypothesis that the unconscious might be *simulated* in particular situations any longer.[37] What becomes of your intelligence-gathering operations if the other you think you are controlling is ironically conforming to your demands or imitating you in a game of sly civility?[38]

One can always find a use for someone or something that so adamantly holds to doctrinal purity and the universality of its judgments, maintaining a haughty disdain for anything even moderately pragmatic: the fabrication of a terrain predisposed to certain kinds of affective configuration (anxiety, a disposition considered to be universal); a willing ignorance of the myriad other mediators by which an unconscious might be constructed; the belief and expectation that politicians, strategists, and marketeers will respect the autonomy of the scientist. Analysis, we might say, prepares the ground for depressed, anxiety-prone subjects and offers a remarkable set of tools for welding subjects to their symptoms. All the misery of the world, miraculously transformed into the exasperated comments of the parent to the child: You'll see, just wait until you're an adult . . .

So what was it that Jung glimpsed? Devils, demons, gods, sorcerers: mythic images going beyond the family, sure, but also something properly *frightening*. Castration anxiety? Perhaps. To the great benefit of already well-stabilized forces, analysis didn't really want to have that much to do with fear. Freud himself sometimes seems to say that by virtue of its connection with external objects, fear is unanalyzable.[39] Anxiety, by contrast, is not only susceptible to analysis but performs socially useful work in preparing us for the kinds of shocks that frightening situations create. Anxiety may in some circumstances deliver a high stratagematic yield. But if this distinction seems uncertain to us, we cannot ignore the inestimable value of focusing on what happens *inside* a subject, as part of the more general process by which zones of secrecy, culpability, and shame can be fabricated. With the cognitive sophisticating of behaviorism through algorithmic models giving this approach a new lease on life, the days of the use of analysis in the games of intrigue and intelligence may be numbered. Indeed, the color-coded lure of mapping brain activity seems to imply that nothing can ever be kept truly secret any longer, as if the experimental setup were simply transcribing deviant neural activity with perfect transparency and had no power to intimidate of its own.[40] Techniques for turning the other to your cause are always welcome, because even if, deep down, they are afraid of you, it's always good to have people who can keep a secret on your side.[41]

Speak the Metalanguage of Metabolism

The invention of psychopharmacology, following Loewi's experiments in the 1920s demonstrating the chemical basis for the transmission of neural messages (while not definitively ruling out the previously reigning hypothesis of electrical transmission), and the commercial sale of psychotropic drugs such as chlorpromazine and the invention of benzodiazepines in the 1950s, along with the publication of manuals such as the ever-expanding *Diagnostic and Statistical Manual of Mental Disorders*, has had a powerful effect on the constellation of forces making up "the social." If the irrational exuberance of psychosurgeons demonstrated that social relations and the imperatives of the state could sometimes be fabricated or repaired with ice picks and scalpels,[42] favored tools of the lobotomist, the pop-cultural mythologization of mother's little helper, the barbiturate, not only confirms, as McLuhan has it, that the medium is the message,[43] but also acts as an index of complex shifts in the ecology of media as nervous systems, metabolisms, and the capacity to cope and to compensate become integrated, unevenly, into it. Drugs, as mediators, initiators, and attractors of changes in bodies, as means of coping with relations between bodies and other elements in media ecologies, become handleable as media. Indeed, as under certain interpretative regimes the body is but a vehicle for the circulation of information, what else could drugs be imagined to be?

The development of psychopharmacology and its steady infection of the social generates new media spaces, new media with their own messages. These new media are no longer simply electronic technologies working at a distance in extended space but chemical technologies creating distances in intensive space, keying social relations into the biochemical strata of organic material, targeting and mobilizing populations of neurons, not through the electronic messaging systems of mass media but through the facilitation of neuronal transmission systems, meshing with the loops and hits of online connectivity, catalyzing circulation through the topologies of networks linking synapses, minds, emotions, technoscience, geopolitics, creating gray media for gray matter and vice versa. While no simple one-to-one mapping may exist between the use of pharmaceutical substances and widespread patterns of thought, in matters of mind control, we should at least be receptive to the idea that new substances generate new stratagems.

Research programs originating early in the post–World War II era already testify to an interest in the manipulative potential of psychopharmaceuticals.[44] And the question marks that still hang over the funding of Timothy Leary's research, not to mention the propping up of a charismatic leader (John F. Kennedy) by amphetamines, that famous smile holding back the strung-out grinding of teeth, are good indicators of the strange connections that become possible when active substances become a significant component of the clandestine relations and alliances of the polity.

Psychopharmacology alters the distribution, and thus the balance, of forces political, technical, and chemical, factoring in new agents for consideration in the strategic calculus of populations. Downplaying the strictly monitored conditions of the séance, the couch, and the fifty-minute hour in the ongoing battle for hearts and minds, since they are frankly too time-consuming, and embracing instead the gaseous dispersion and nebulous clouding of chemical media allows for unsupervised processes of self-medication that bring about the confusion of therapy, governance, and pleasure (albeit at the admitted cost of having to find uses for new kinds of "small [saleable] addictions"),[45] even if such measures require in turn a shift into the multidimensional spaces of nonlinear thinking. The slow metabolizing of power through a new alliance with chemistry and a corresponding molecularization of conflict, where negotiations are now contracted through the prescriptive regimen of the dose or the illicit one of the hit, requires an acceptance that bonds (both chemical and social) can be covalent as much as they can be ionic, in spite of the ionic's oppositional attractions.[46] Recognizing the pharmacological dimension of media implies an acceptance, then, of a troublesome shift in the characteristic operations of domination and control, to say nothing of communication, the problematics of which then play out at a molecular level.

The mathematical certainties of the causal chains of physics and the precision engineering of lock-and-key biological specificity might convince the untutored that the identification of the neuronal apparatus productive of affect could henceforth be played like a keyboard.[47] But if the hopeful hyping of drug design plays on a well-entrenched and neatly rationalized model of pharmaceutical practice, in reality, the chemical orchestration of inhibition and disinhibition and the corresponding dynamics of control requires much greater forms of artfulness. More specifically, it calls for a reckoning with the significant difficulties in making determinism—a useful hypothesis for the laboratory and a resonant aspiration for marketing—scale up and into the variegated territories of the social.

It is here, in the social, that the trials and tribulations of the weaponization of chemical agents help demonstrate some of the new possibilities, risks, and limits of control. The cartoon capers of government agents and scientists finding ways to break down enemy combatants using cigarettes laced with marijuana is one thing (as are the bigger-budget giggles of the exploding cigar as highly targeted assassination device),[48] but developing precision delivery systems for chemical weapons is quite another: the Moscow Theater siege in 2002, for example, was neither a well-orchestrated nor a precise military operation.[49] Controlling the impact of something that has to be dispersed by aerosol, as a mist in the atmosphere or through thermal bomblets (as is the case with BZ),[50] plays havoc with attempts to make the determinist logic of linear causality work beyond the level of the individual body. Material intervention at the level of gray matter was supposed to offer this. Doping up or doping down neuronal receptors is a tricky proposition once the subject is out in the open, and the user must overcome both the blood-brain barrier problem and the targeted-recipient problem. In an interrogation room, you can strap a suspect down and tease up a tender vein, but for battlefield ops and crowd control (CS gas and tear-jerking lacrimogens notwithstanding), the aerosol effect either disperses chemicals too quickly or concentrates them too indiscriminately. This creates obvious public relations problems and makes the development of tried and tested battlefield doctrine a complex task.[51] The propensity of unstable and unpredictable mediators to generate uncontrollable forms of blowback here presents a world historical, and possibly biohistorical, challenge for crisis management.[52]

Psychopharmacology is not exactly chemical warfare, however (even if pharmaceutical companies eagerly play on both sides of the military–civilian divide), and the displacements that pharmaceutical products accomplish in the ongoing production of the psyche still offer a latitude for maneuver worth exploiting. It may just be that psychopharmacology, especially in the gray area between (failed) covert military and (successful) overt civilian guises, offers the possibility of a more intelligently negotiated alliance with chemical agents. The use of pill technology for self-administered domestic consumption, for example, as opposed to the unpredictable mediations of weaponization, or the complex localized institutional apparatuses of lobotomy or ECT, allows for more accurate delivery (even if it does depend on a less tightly controlled chain of mediators). A pill embodies a strategy with much more tangible reliability than the shaky practices of quacks, headshrinkers, and other shamans, to say nothing of the eye-watering intrusiveness of the transorbital ice pick.

The definite preference that the psychopharmacological machine displays for the production of short-term effects is as critical here as is the media form, and can be of great value, especially if tied into other apparatuses reliant on the up–down, high–low movements typical of machinic junkies (even the stock exchange needs a stimulus package from time to time).[53]

While the poor adaptation of double-blind clinical tests—which allow for the marketization of drugs—to the evaluation of long-term effects may compound the problems of blowback over time, the molecules on which such tests focus are actually highly effective recruitment devices. Kingmakers of a new kind, they have sealed the ascendancy of a new macropolitical actor, the pharmaceutical giant, and while they may not possess the diagnostic power of a good doctor or psychoanalyst, in a highly pragmatic way, they do not require that a new recruit reveal the truth about himself or herself. The massive success of diazepam (from the family of benzodiazepines)—the most widely prescribed drug in the United States between 1962 and 1981, according to some sources—is exemplary in this regard.[54] While the curative effects of such a substance might blur the difference between a symptom and a cause, the molecule has no real need for secrecy, guilt, or shame. Look how quickly user groups set themselves up on the Internet—doctor–patient confidentiality doesn't enter into the equation. Anyway, anxiety offers a useful cover story for dealing with harmful or fearful incursions from the outside world, and in the worst-case scenario, under conditions of addiction (or influence, but for different reasons), as we saw earlier, the subject is easily discredited as an unreliable witness.

More significantly, perhaps, one of the invaluable side effects of benzodiazepines, cyclopyrrolones, dopamines, and SSRIs (such as Fluoxetine, i.e., Prozac) is to have accelerated the process of reforming and recomposing the very field in which and on which they operate. From an initial position where they complemented the medium of speech in the talking cure, pharmaceuticals have ended up taking over completely. Cognitive behavioral therapy would not exist if not for the reorganizing effects of drugs on research in psychology, creating the possibility of positing a comforting, if not exactly sophisticated, physiological basis for mental disorder.[55] But equally, liquidating the "dependency on authority" effects characteristic of therapeutic speech, the biochemical end of deference creates an ambiguous situation. While existential dramas of anxiety are replaced by effects of disinhibition that can, it is true, minimize the lacerating effects of the group superego (a distinct advantage when trying to operate in the amoral zone of strategy), a complete shift of affective investments with group identities is forming around the molecule.[56] Harnessing complex metabolic patterns and turning agents when the theatrical tragedy of the primal scene has been vaporized becomes a multimedia operation, and in the peculiarly interstitial spaces that are created when linearity does not scale up, negotiation, ruse, and cunning are open even to the most wilted of addicts.[57]

Proliferate Psychological Operations

There's no food in your gut, your sex is being had by someone else, your leaders are betraying you, your equipment is breaking. Bombing will begin in twenty-four hours. All those that have not left the area place themselves in danger. As you turn your back to your front door to go to a day of honest work, a family of strangers has moved in and displaced you.

Ostensibly, psyops, psychological operations, are an aspect of media that lacks virtue. It is often without the virtues of finesse, nor can it display the extremes of pitilessness or dishonor that can sometimes appear as audacious or necessary. Dropped from the air as shoddily threatening or exhortatory leaflets, "revealed" by other media as anonymous fakes, operating at arm's length as misattributed documents, radio programs, or Web sites, psyops forms a part of public relations that operates by novel means. Some of the best known of these are hoaxes, but another quality is core to the objects produced by psyops units. This, in short, is that they appear to be of deliberate shoddiness. Rudimentary drawings, sloganeering text, and ludicrous offers of brotherhood and peace are all brought to the fore. They insult the intelligence of their recipients, the enemy, and aim to trigger in them a significant margin of overconfidence. While on the surface, black propaganda hopes to extend the production of doubt, the encouragement of turncoats, or estrangement from familiar sources of information, it also functions to lure recipients into the idea that their enemies, the senders, are more stupid than had previously been thought. This margin operates in two ways. First, an overconfidence is achieved in the heart of the enemy. This encourages them to act without sufficient care and diligence, to rush. Second, the implied lack of sophistication also suggests that enemies understand their opponents as being less capable of thought. In most cases, psyops material is disregarded as something equivalent to the leaflets of pizza delivery companies or of palm readers dumped through the letterbox. In periods of crisis brought about by stupidity, social turmoil, or war, however, when the leavings of psy-warriors may be seen as a crucial and rare insight into the mind of the enemy, they may be tightly held on to by recipients.

A different approach to psychological operations comes through various techniques that aim to enhance the self-esteem, willingness to experiment, and collective participation of the recipient subject. The manuals produced in the 1980s by the CIA for use in supporting illegal anticommunist militia are useful to read in this regard. One manual aimed at Nicaraguan citizens, the famous "Freedom Fighter's Manual,"[58] sets out in cartoon form some of the basic forms of sabotage (dropping or losing equipment, letting resources or time go astray). It does so, however, without considering sabotage as one of the fine arts.[59] The manual merely presents a set of techniques of sabotage without presenting their psychological dimension, a dimension that could lead to the extrapolation of new kinds of sabotage. The psychological dimension is, however, fully present in another manual produced by the CIA, "Psychological Operations in Guerrilla Warfare."[60] This publication aims to steer death squads toward a more community service orientation, with extensive guidance on appearing to be accountable to the desires of the population and on turning combatants into a kind of fighting focus group as a basic unit of liberation. The techniques of group dynamics and self-empowerment through discussion, leading to decision making guided by the cadre, are presented alongside some basic techniques of guerrilla fighting. In this document, the correct moral and political development of the armed propagandist is crucial both in understanding the struggle and in interacting with members of the wider population. In such a way, psyops moves on from being a medial equivalent of the *ribeaudequin*,[61] the medieval war machines consisting of giant wheeled metal representations of the faces of terrifying creatures, from which massive blades jutted forward to be thrust into the enemy. (These extremely unwieldy weapons were almost useless, but all the more terrifying for the flagrancy of the carelessness they displayed.) It passes on to the development of psyches and further into the process of their constructive self-actuation.

The wider question of enhancing the active capacities of the subject of psychological operations and using those capacities as the basis for wider collective phenomena provides the foundation for a number of historically significant currents. Perhaps most salient in a psychological sense is the current declared by experiments that attempt to break the passivity of contemporary processes of subjectification, particularly in regard to the experiences of media. This is to say that while numerous tendencies throughout history work to incorporate psychological, emotional, or spiritual dimensions into medial processes, explicit programs of this kind are more recent and even come with a rejection of mediation as a pretext. An early announcement from the Situationist International declares that "the most pertinent revolutionary experiments in culture have sought to break the spectator's psychological identification with the hero so as to draw him into activity."[62] There is a curse on passivity, vagueness, the inability to commit, on pleasure in submission and time wasting, in this and related texts, an operationalization of psychology to produce desires in excess of capitalist possibility. Whether organized by teams of situationists led by an appointed director[63] or through "collective action to detect, express and realize,"[64] new desires in which individuated psychological structures or formations are not of as much interest as the creation of conditions in which such elements are dynamized through the design and implementation of specific mise-en-scène, "décor,"[65] or events. Psychological operations in this sense exist as the "setting up, on the basis of more or less clearly recognized desires, a temporary field of activity favorable to those desires"[66] as a means for the dialectical development of new desires as a basis for the reconstruction of reality. Here psychological operations become recursive.

This panoply of means—from the injection of information in deliberately shoddy formats; through to white, gray, or black propaganda; toward an increasing emphasis on the psychological dimension of the morale of the combatant and citizen as crucial; not simply as the key resource or means in the operation on reality but as a site of reality construction itself—traces a differential understanding of intelligence, running between ostensive stupidity, a narrative of empowerment, and the unleashing of desire as sites where the psyche is invented and, in turn, invents its own theater of operations.

Togetherness

Social Engineering

It can be difficult to get people to cooperate. It can be difficult to get technological artifacts to cooperate. To excel at the hackerly skill of social engineering, "you have to understand how people think and to see where that intersects with technology."[1]

In this sense, social engineering—as the means of blagging your way through a rule set and its lackeys and their equipment—is always one of the crucial components of accounts of army, prison, or camp life, the means for a bit of unfettering, a little back channel. In such cases, social engineering is the essential lubricant of a disciplinary society or a total institution, although calling it engineering is a little grandiose; others may call it a work-around or persuasion. How, though, does its position shift in a context whose governance is actuated by scripts? Whether read by people at the other end of a phone line or run as software, the script is crucial in getting everyone and everything to play a role, and in the way that is required. As Herbert Simon notes, "Administration is not unlike play-acting. . . . The effectiveness of the administrative process will vary with the effectiveness of the organization and the effectiveness with which its members play their parts."[2]

We can also understand social engineering as the reverse of the problem set by John Searle's famous Chinese room argument. Here the philosopher of language proposes that a computer that produces ostensibly intelligent results may not have any understanding of what it processes but may simply possess an adequate rule book for symbol manipulation. His argument is against the approach to artificial intelligence known as computationalism, the proposition that computers have mental states sufficiently analogous to those of a properly formatted human to be considered a phenomenologically registerable "mind." As Mark Bishop notes, this position can be held by any form of AI research, not simply those clinging to the transubstantiation of minds into sequences of symbols but also the more apparently affable connectionist and "bottom-up" schools.[3]

But what if there is a complication in the Chinese room? The operator sits in a box converting symbols in one language to their apparent equivalents in another by following the instructions. The operator does not need to understand the statements being made. What would occur if something outside the box started to use the system of symbols, not to generate a direct translation from one language to another, or to prove or disprove something about the nature of thought or computation, but to play with the system—perhaps to introduce some other qualities of the translator into the workings? By making certain conjunctions of symbols, it could be hoped that statements in something akin to a language understood by the translating worker might be arrived at. At this point, the person inside the box may be induced to laugh, get annoyed, rush, or answer in what they imagine to be a joke, or respond to a cry for help to something happening outside the box. In the original formulation of the Turing machine, the "state of mind" of the computer, the operative carrying out the work of symbolic transactions is bracketed out by the rule book or the "note of instructions," allowing them to act properly as a machine until they are indeed abstractable as such. Social engineering often relies on gaining access to this state of mind or tricking it into being.

As Searle writes in the mode of a thought experiment rather than in the empirical mode we use in this book, one thing that he downplays is the labor of the operator. The translator might get bored, might start to imagine a reading or become suicidal. The position is similar to that of soldiers stationed in nuclear silos, where command imagines that they should be bunkered together in pairs in case one should become crazed, refuse to fire, or start imagining the desirability of the end of the world, or even of communication. Perhaps the former is thought more likely than the latter, since it is assumed there will be no persuasion between the pair. The translator, like a call center worker, should certainly be subject to recording for training and quality control purposes. It is this empirical detail that makes access to the contents of the room potentially open to manipulation.

Social engineering proliferates with every black box, the putatively stable contents of which include an operative that makes it possible to turn the box inside out or to work both or either to a satisfactory degree of accuracy. Sometimes it suffices simply to ask people to do something they are trained to do, or want to do, or just because they don't have anything else to do, in order for them to do it. Here the right tone of voice, the use of jargon, references to keywords, and an understanding of the working atmosphere are all useful scene setters. As Stanley Milgram, one of the most admirable adopters of psychological experimentation in the wild, discovered, some-times all it takes is a white coat, a clipboard, and the right tone of voice to assume an effective position of authority.[4] While the naturalness of acquiescence should be assumed as a matter of politeness, etiquette demands the assumption of confirmation bias, the registration of the occurrence of what is expected.

The Chinese room, Milgram's test of obedience, and the Turing test are cases in which control, agency, and intelligence are functionally partitioned by the use of a sealed container and the introduction of a means of communication between inside and out. Arrayed around the container are different factors—curiosity, translation, eagerness to please—angled toward the activities inside the box. In the initial models of such classic cases, social engineering is a one-to-one operation, involving the use of a craft skill of context-aware persuasion, but they also presage something that is repeatable and capable of being conducted on a mass scale.

The requirement for social engineering arises because of information asymmetry. The thinking person intersecting with technology, the operator, the call center worker, the recipient of spam, the funding agency, all require certain lexical and technical operations to be carried out: proofs, persuasions, special pleadings, emergencies, threats of the consequences of failure, potential breakthroughs, the chance of great wealth or the chance to disburse a little bit of justice, to throw some light on things, to get through the day without too many errors of transcoding. Such asymmetry has its precedents. In his model of the stabilization of energy levels between two otherwise isolated chambers, James Clark Maxwell posited an operative, later called a "demon," which controlled a valve between them. The demon's job was to control the passage of molecules between the chambers, releasing more energetic molecules from one into the other, confirming—or contradicting—the second law of thermodynamics and the increase in entropy. The physicist Leo Szilard's contribution to the discussion on the demon was to note that the demon itself uses energy and thus also contributes to entropy.[5] Labor involves some kind of agency, and a capacity for disruption, variance, and improvement, all of which can sometimes be achieved by determinedly sticking to the rules of operation. Social engineering here is the skill of ensuring that inside the box, the instructions, from one source or another, are being followed correctly, no matter what they are.

Collective Intelligence

Collective intelligence is a means of forming a polity from a naturally occurring resource with variable degrees of purity. Various methods have been applied to its refinement and even synthesis. While collective intelligence has earlier manifestations as a noösphere or general intellect, few means of harnessing it at either massive scale or fine granularity existed until the conjunction of computation and media in networks.[6]

On the face of it, "crowdsourcing"—one of the characteristic means of such harnessing—is so obvious an offer, so legible in its grammar, that it becomes an almost perfectly transparent contract.[7] Its first aspect consists in the provision of thought, work, and content, at no cost, to a central repository that may sort it or provide mechanisms for such sifting. Its second is in its coextensivity with, and reliance on, the mechanisms that establish the possibility for such provision. These may be networks, languages, technical standards, forms of modularization of tasks, and the enthusiasm for participation that they mobilize. Third, it is differentiable on the basis of the mechanisms of ownership that it acknowledges and amplifies, a quality that in turn shapes the operations of the first two aspects.

Crowdsourcing shows its particular interest in relation to property. In *The Control Revolution*, James Beniger notes that the General Electric Corporation of the 1890s had a new information processor, "built of the collective cognitive power of hundreds of individual human beings."[8] The idea of collective intelligence here relies on the paid time of employees, a rather burdensome model for the present era. In the same way that financial crises, under certain conditions nameable only as natural, encourage the privatization of profit and the socialization of risk, the way in which such spreading or condensing occurs in problem solving characterizes the specific form of collective intelligence that emerges.

Collective intelligence operating through the conjunction of computation and media in large-scale networks takes on a number of different forms, several of which have been developed in specific relation to the development of software. We can broadly characterize them as either *permissive* (characteristic of the BSD licenses that allow publication, distribution, and modification of code while not restricting whether versions that have been modified must stay open) or *recursive* (characteristic of the licenses promoted by the Free Software Foundation, in which any further versions of the software must maintain the rights to use, read, distribute, and modify the source code).[9]

Since the development of software through such licenses, the fine modularity characteristic of their problem solving, and the impressive use such systems have made of networks as means of coordination, further means of organizing cognitive power along related lines have emerged; crowdsourcing appears as one of the key terms used to frame this shaping of collective intelligence.

The specificity of crowdsourcing lies in the construction of specific kinds of distributed labor networks that generate results for entities that have the capacity to set and adjudicate "challenges." It establishes a "new pool of cheap labor: everyday people using their spare cycles to create content, solve problems, even do corporate R&D."[10] The challenges may range from designing difficult chemical processes to participating in low-value data-processing tasks. Here the "spare cycles" of computers and of brains are conflated; work can be done by people with marginal economic value, by busier people in the margins of their days, or by networked computers when not in direct use. Like stuffing envelopes, seamstressing, or telecottaging, crowdsourcing represents a means of leveraging the slightest moments of wakefulness left in a body into transubstantiation as value. Peaks and troughs in demand can both be accommodated by working on the basis of a surplus. Such work can further be characterized in one of two ways:

Funneled   In closed crowdsourcing, the result is yielded to an entity that selects what it requires, if anything, from what is submitted, which may or may not provide rewards or incentives on that basis. Often this may consist of an agency mediating for companies that pose technical problems and set a reward for solutions or tasks actuated. Such systems are original in the way they may establish themselves as a service, not a product, and in so doing yield multiple levels of secondary products. An example of such would be a service that allows universities to upload student essays to see if they contain passages that match those from previously published work or previously submitted essays. With each upload, the value of the database increases, and thus students are working for themselves, for the university, and for the company compiling the database and selling the service.

Facilitated   Much of the energy generated by new networked forms of labor has gone into the imaginative configuration and tweaking of end user license agreements for services that allow you to work, to access the products of work, and offer the means whereby entities can "share knowledge efficiently in the course of online conversation without doing anything beyond having conversation" and that "could generate real power in scientific and business communities."[11]

The incorporation of collective intelligence in networks bears certain similarities to the use of worker-generated improvements in production often known as Toyotism.[12] Typical of some forms of production of the 1980s and 1990s, new techniques of stock control, logistics, and communication combined with flattened markets to build high degrees of customization of products, in which users specified their requirements more. Such forms of production also valorized the ability of workers to improve and speed up the production process through decentralizing the management of their work process (but not of the end results) to smaller, platoon-sized work teams. Such teams, incentivized by rewards and improved status, were able to yield better results, by internalizing production norms within themselves, liberating management from the need to carry out much of its historical disciplinary work. Elsewhere "quality circles" became means of airing problems and harvesting workers' insights into the operation of procedures.

Crowdsourcing differs crucially from this earlier phase in the ways that the current means of extracting, working, and distributing collective intelligence operate through computational and networked digital media. This is not so much an authoritarian or disciplinary means of making the brains run on time as a means of finding new grammars and techniques by which new things can collectively be generated and older things can painlessly be transducted into new contexts. This context should be understood in relation to other tendencies, namely, that the ability of capitalism to control the commodification of culture is in slow crisis, as epitomized in various forms of file sharing, and an equal but nonreciprocal crisis in which culture's ability to escape direct commodification is challenged by its implementation as tools to encourage, sustain, and format participation in social networks. In such a context, the figurations of collective intelligence are to be found as much in the anatomies of small conjunctions of synapses and gadgets as among the turbid dreams of a global mind.

Be Everything But Available

In the novel *Zoo, or Letters Not about Love*, the formalist writer Viktor Shklovsky fills page after page with a diastolic correspondence, which, while rarely echoed by the other side of the epistolary heartbeat, is drenched in the immolating rapture of love.[13] His letters to Alya provide traces of a hunger that consumes him, eats up all the mental currency of attention that he has in his pockets. This is a love, however, for a woman who—besides stipulating that he must not write to her about love—will not pick up the phone. Living in an era before the automated answer, Shklovsky feels the world reorganized. One of the many ways this is so is through the conjunctions of different spaces, but also of different emotional and linguistic intensities, squeezed along a copper wire. One of those spaces is absence. While the novel has numerous registers, devices, and ruses by which love is figured, one dimension that is rarely noticed is the story's mathematical content. Five times over the course of this short book, Shklovsky alludes to non-Euclidean geometry as exemplifying the world turned upside down by the magnificence of love. Although he does not name it, the figure he uses is the core to Nicholas Lobachevsky's hyperbolic geometry, with its possibility of infinite parallel lines arrayed around and surging through a single point.[14] Every experience of the world, every waking state, turns into an anticipation of, and hunger for, the beloved. The sensation of his adoration of her is compared to the moment in which a fine woolen scarf is drawn through a gold ring: every aspect of the fabric of the universe composed of lines converges on this one wondrous point and passes out through the other side, recomposed.

Shklovsky's problem is that the loved one may not feel reducible to this point of convergence—or may feel that it passes slightly to the side of her, a miss. In this condensation of the two figures of the loved one, the one who will not answer the ringing mechanism, who will not become a node, and the one who connects to everything, who recomposes the universe by simply being in it, we can see that network analysis is staged and prefigured: the loved one is the superhub of reality.

One of the conditions of love is the warping of time, the speed at which an endless embrace seems to pass, and the slow monotony of time spent unwillingly apart. However, another spatial effect of passion provides a recension of the evolution of networks and must also be used. That is the capacity for abundance, of being everything. Elsa Triolet, who plays the role of Alya in the novel, inadvertently takes on and trumps the role of the emperor as described in Kenneth Dean and Brian Massumi's *First and Last Emperors*,[15] to rule by being everywhere—to be everything, to saturate the lover's universe—and to be nowhere, unreachable, detained in the bath, in dalliances with fancy cars or dances with men decorated with earrings or a repulsive Englishness, with a million other things. The pain of the lover lies in the fact that the loved one is everything but yet is absent, following a different trajectory.

Writing on evolution, Henri Bergson compares the trajectory of a single life-form, the process of speciation and the development of a genus, with the trajectory of fragments from an exploding shell. The blast recapitulates its branching through a hierarchy of entities. Each species—one cluster. Each organism—only ever capable of being one fragment. Each mutation—one spin from true. Nature, however, has the capacity to encompass all—shell, explosion, and shrapnel—and is in no way bound to make the sacrifice of differentiation.[16] A special madness of love is an encounter with the condensation of all of nature in one being and a recognition of all one's prepersonal power unfolding in that universe, recognizing it not as a totality but as something that is also mutually unfolding. The figure of the fully graphed centralized network, the sum of all possible events or connections, is also that of the loved one, the universe. This is the tragedy of the single life, of mortality, when it is brought into contact with the reality of rejection or the apparent impossibility of not living an infinite number of lives simultaneously.

Just as "the probability of a global epidemic depends on the number and configuration of initial infectives,"[17] the problem of the lover, as faced by Shklovsky, is to saturate the imaginary of the recipient of the letters that are not about love with burning, enticing, or subtle reminders of the lover and the rapture the loved one might share in. Each ruse in the letters becomes a means of bending flat inattentiveness or bemused dismissal, of opening up a gateway to the universe of love, to the full force of its explosion. Each simple point swells in anticipation that it might be the one to draw the loved one in. The letter writer must hope for an absence of symmetry between the point of attraction, which is small, an observation, a joke, a copula of wordings, and the massively expanding universe that the lover anticipates being joined in. The writer's work is not to manipulate language to induce the reader into shedding perceptual habits, freeing the elements of the world from their mundane associations, but to suffuse the world with the inevitability of the reciprocation of love.

But more trivial passions can also be turned to account. We are told that in the interval between the saturation of connection of the superhub and the happiness of the isolate (the one who stays in the bath and refuses to pick up the telephone), new opportunities emerge for the harnessing of value.[18] In a market made smoother by the ease of connections between nodes, what was once detritus finds its buyer, a meager supply finds its true users, and amateurs of all sorts find their devoted fans. Every needle finds its necessary haystack. To put it another way, there is less excess that cannot be leveraged to a point of consumption. A difficulty presents itself, however: in making themselves available, the agents of these minor passions are compelled to compete with the proliferation of ruses, cons, games, lines, seductions, and choices of trajectory of all of those others who are also operating in this modality of space. The abundance of pretenders to superhub status can obliterate the possibility of choosing rather than submitting to the spatiality of absence. A great, roiling abundance of minor gateways, slight triggers into patches of the universe, get their hustle on under every stone and each mouse click. After all, one does not want to be reduced to a dot.

Economize Behavior, Scale Signals

The view that, after World War II, economics became a "cyborg science"[19] (by virtue of the inextricable connections between the developments of computer science, cybernetics, and economic theory) opens up a novel perspective for exploring the links between gadgets and the financialization of everyday life. And if (as has been claimed) the economy increasingly operates through language and the large-scale production of forms of credulity, a better understanding of the role of communications media in enabling that process seems worthwhile.[20]

It turns out that the kind of language through which this process of financialization operates is not really that of poetic eloquence or even that of prosaic discourse but a peculiarly behavioral brew made up of signals: basic forms of stimulus and response requiring little in the way of semantic elaboration. A discourse, if one can call it such, of minimal, time- and motion-optimized gestures, Skinner-boxing with the shadows of the hand-eye-brain—neuronal short circuits—a machinic discourse operating at the level of pulse-quickening nervous reactions, actuated by jittery, algebraic fingers and thumbs. It is a material elaborated for the purposes of just doing it, for acting without the need to have ideas. That is its great strength, because the result is impervious to reasoned critique: one doesn't need to think too much to point and click.

The slave trade and the extension of colonial powers into the East and the concomitant growth in trade of alcohol, sugar, opiates, and so on, made a dramatic precursor to the relatively stable organization of more and more areas of life under the rationality of the market. The extension of investment and extractive accumulation to areas previously not considered in economic terms can only occur to the extent that behavior in those areas can be formed by the habituated activity of stimulus–response shaping subjectivity into patterns of getting and using. Whims, fads, and fashions may be scoffed at by those with the defensive shield of a well-armored ego, but habits operate at a level to which egos are secondary: prereflexive behavior is a propitious domain in which to establish the relative stability of economic practice.

One could criticize the claims that behavioral economics makes in its statements of scientific fact, but nothing is ever quite so clear-cut in the world of economic theory, where fantasy, hallucination, wishful thinking, and a sometimes disingenuous aping of the experimental sciences are often the order of the day. It would be interesting to look at economic theories not so much as representations but as component parts in the production of particular forms of subjectivity.[21] In this respect, the recently popular field of behavioral economics might be considered not so much a theory *about* as a symptom *of* and a means of extending the impact of the permeation of market subjectivity into many areas of everyday life, a permeation of, and permeability to, behavior that can then be theorized in economistic terms.[22] A properly reflexive theory of behavioral economics would actually have to learn something from ethology (which advances a much more nuanced understanding of behavior than is usually allowed) to consider more directly its own role in the construction of animal activity.[23] Behavioral economics could then take some useful lessons from media studies, which excels in exploring the manipulative production of subjectivity. In fact, from the moment that economists start talking about signaling, asymmetries of information, and so on, the media are inherently involved—and even more so when ambiguity becomes central.[24]

The discovery among primatologists that the display of alpha-male behavior among groups of primates reflects the presuppositions of the experimental constructs of researchers, who thereby produce what they claim merely to investigate, brings ethological research into proximity with the findings of some recent critics of Freud, who argue that patients in some of the master's famous case studies simulated their symptoms so as to meet the clinical expectations of the august doctor.[25] This being the case, a comprehensive consideration of economics from a behavioral point of view might do better to turn its attention to the ways in which particular constellations of exchange are effectively configured to produce actors whose behavior develops in expectant response to the delirious presuppositions of market-based overproduction. Jean Baudrillard once called this "ironic conformity."[26] If markets produce agents who are irrationally exuberant, this occurs perhaps because the markets themselves are exuberantly irrational,[27] a point that one might be less than willing to acknowledge at a time when rearguard operations are being mounted everywhere to save founding economic dogmas.[28] The crucial issue here, though, is that for all its talk of "educating" people into more sensible economic behavior, behavioral economics points up the opportunities for the manipulation and control of subjectivities through suggestive operations of nudging, opportunities that for the same reason gesture toward just how little the artfully constructed mathematical models of the dismal science reveal.

According to the desired user scenario, you sit and you tap, you point, you click, you scroll, you drag, you drop, you flick. Walking into traffic on a crowded street, you busily thumb a text message into your phone (not for nothing do the Germans call cellphones "handies"). Speaking into thin air, you find yourself laughing out loud, alone. Actually, you are cackling, but no one pays you any attention, as they too are absorbed, distracted by high-res screens, gaming away on their handsets, posting data for dating, texting, tweeting, buying, selling, considering stock options as they follow the real-time 24/7 cycle. Buying. Selling. Buying. Selling. Pixelated stimuli yield finger-jabbing or caressing, screen-stroking responses as sophisticated media technologies cozy up to users modeled as simplified units of virtual reflex action. Stroking, clicking, and ticking represent action translated into the simplest of behavior, desemanticized and all but voided of gestural quality. Sophisticated technology requires users to be enrolled into an economy of minimal movement (except for gestural interfaces at the scale of games).[29] Icon-powered interfaces offer a regime of mazes and boxes operating at the level of the digit: thumbs up, thumbs down, the pleasures of the early adopters of psychically ergonomic new technologies shaping, en masse, the fortunes of hi-tech stocks and shares. Whoever said knowledge economy? From the point of view of the dexterous designs of digital media, Generation App operates in a manner more akin to a large-scale, highly distributed, mildly Pavlovian experiment. Maybe the experiment isn't deliberately designed to test a theory, but it at least has the benefit of being supported by a range of software-testing techniques, from registering keystrokes, through macro recordings, to iris scanning and webcam triggering: techniques that support, amplify, and confirm the production of the user as a behavioral unit and provide quantifiable test data to allow for this production to be optimized, whether or not anything is watching.[30]

When combined with the tools of cognitive science and psychology, software-based media forms offer a powerful set of devices for translating a range of background practices of everyday life into the new but deceptively familiar world of pointing and clicking, dragging and dropping, cutting and pasting. The point, click, swipe, and spread world at your fingertips is already a world of language, a world of "signaletic" materials input machinically and generated programmatically. Its stimulus–response patterns can be monitored and modeled obsessively, linked to statistical analysis packages, data mining, and pattern-matching techniques. They configure the nervous tensions of the end user into productive conjunction with new motor skills; the dexterity of thumbs and fingers are valorized for the production of more informational goods (and bads). It is a logic into which one comments, texts, tweets, likes, and dislikes one's way garrulously, anticipating the next device or killer app, seeking bigger hits of machine interactivity. It's not that one marginalizes the risky unpredictability of an interaction with a person, but that a seam is opened up into an intermediate condition between them. The broader significance of all the information that is consumed may not be readily known (who would even care?), but the reassuring familiarity of a glowing interface provides the comforting feeling that even if one is not in control, one at least has something to do.

But how do these micro-scale interactions turn macro? In the broader economy, wherein markets are made up of the millions of transactions of everyday life, and not just the operations of formal financial institutions, market devices are not just financial instruments, ratings procedures, or statistical models. They can also be online conversations, simple semiotic signals (correlating the stock market with homeland security ratings), and—in the logic we are mapping here—applications on gadgets with a high level of dispersal throughout everyday life, configured for the perpetual production and consumption of rumor, of data and information, of news. Market volatilities can be aligned and made to resonate with the paranoia and tension of the early morning commute, doubtful correlations that can be made between high-speed, high-volume market transactions, hastily tapped out texts or tweets, and the abbreviated highlights of a real-time news feed. Ambiguities are amplified or attenuated; confidence is bolstered or busted. Information convulses rather than flows. Market devices become operational at a behavioral level, permeating the psyche, when individuals reconfigure themselves as part of extended, society-wide data structures, when a practiced flick of the wrist allows a switch from e-mail to spreadsheet to bank account to news feed.

It is perhaps uncertain just how far behavior has been transformed into economics, and it is true to say that the conjunctions of mediators that we are sketching out here operate at best as highly unstable, fragile assemblages of elements. But that is hardly the point; the ritual appeal to science is de rigueur, and empirical states of fact obtrude but tangentially on the marketing value of hyperbole. Perhaps the cleverness of behavioral economics lies in the way that its statistical bent (correlations, not causes) has the potential to operate productively itself. The discovery, for example, that students at an expensive university experience a placebo effect from expensive aspirin offers a perfect rationale for the marketing strategies of the pharmaceutical corporation.[31] Giving the imprimatur of a scientific theory to pricing structures to entice or deter, for example, helpfully occludes the ethical ambiguities of manipulating as means at the service of the reinforcing or production of inequalities.

In fact, the financialization of everyday life will not be complete until everything has been translated into the semiotics of market signals. Capital movements, circuits of valorization, speculative bubbles—these depend not on highly literate disquisitions but on abbreviated snippets of information, rumor, anxiety, cognitively minimal, emotively maximal states, adopted by multitudes of agents. Gut feelings, bullishness, bearishness. This is where early adopters of theory, avid consumers of the latest news from the front line of modernization—politicians, spin doctors, marketing gurus, consultants, HR managers, journalists, and policy wonks—will all be able to play their part. We will all learn how to send signals. Politicians send signals to markets, consumers send signals to producers, prices are signals for everyone, all behavior is a derivative.

Stir Faith in Small Numbers

Small numbers can be decisive. One is reminded of the power of the few sufficiently many times to make the assertion suspicious. Look at how many members the

Bolshevik Party had in 1917, how many al-Qaeda operatives it took to bring down the World Trade Center, and how few people it takes to run the basic technical operations of Wikipedia. Parables and commonplaces abound with the power of tiny increments yielding a radical difference. Guerrilla warfare relies on the disproportionate effects that may be gained by the war of the flea and on the combination of precision, imperceptibility, and unpredictability of small forces accurately deployed.[32] The function of sainthood as an exemplary status of being relies on the rare yet presumable attainability of the ascetic holy life in a world of temptation. The effects of small numbers are pressed on us as exemplars of the instability of global systems and the power of the individual to effect real social change. Fantastic effects are yielded in such accounts through minimal but well-chosen or accidental acts that ripple through volatile systems. One should seek out the simple and then distrust it.

An important critical response to such accounts is to look for the background mechanisms, the popular support, subsidiary operators and alliances, technical preconditions, and conceptual structuration of things, that make a certain result more likely. The springtime of blossoming events has its own nameless natural history, but one that has only a loose relation to a proper phylogeny or to principles of identity by which it can be named or called to order. But equally, if a seeming miracle from nowhere is required, these background operators are the elements that must remain cloaked or established in such a way as to appear tangential. The stability of a system can no longer be said to be accurately reliant on its nesting within larger systems that guarantee it.

Another response is to turn to Poisson distributions (models of the probability of events whose averages are known) and discussions of the true nature of randomness, mathematical models of the ability of microscopically slight differences to effect significant results.[33] To this model one must add the factorial nature of recursive effects. Recursion again becomes a key everywhere life is experienced as a sea or stagnant pool composed of overlapping ripples, waveforms that are impossible to dismantle when they are both so dynamic and so tantalizingly modelable, seemingly predictable. But in becoming so natural, this fluidity of reciprocally enhancing constraints seems ripe for disaster and—coded as complex dynamic systems—makes the invocation of such disasters seem so pliant and biddable.

The experience of living in conditions determined by large numbers, of homogeneous populations of chance, while being ideologically entrained to focus on the opportunity of small numbers—whether the opportunity of winning the lottery or being immediately and inexplicably recognized for one's innate and unique talent in a televisual extravaganza—is not one that seems to have been predominant over the course of human history. However, it is an experience that contemporary media, cultural imaginaries, and the economic ideologies of self-affirmation and opportunity seem particularly proficient at generating as a state of ever-extensible hope.

We have yet to answer the question of whether, given the emphasis on the power of small numbers in the contemporary imaginary, the media systems that arise during the period of its popularity are configured in a manner that might tend to accentuate the effectivity of the small. The fantastic yields of computer viruses, worms, and bugs are often proffered as a state to aspire to, in which the smallest of operators reaches a magnificent climax for millions within days of being launched.[34] The yearning to be the bearer of such a difference, to be able to sense participation in such a moment, in turn drives the sales of sugary narratives that seek only to confirm such events as a possibility.[35] Redemption by an encounter with the nonlinear sublime replaces strategy in many minds, but as such it is also something from which stratagems can be derived.

Small numbers work because they do not exist in a friction-free environment. Whether such an environment is, at least rhetorically, said to exist at the level of a market, a conceptual smooth space, the noiseless environment of information theory, or a technology that implements it, such a condition tends to be difficult to identify. As such, the micropolitical event is able to use small differentiations in opportunity, event texture, speed, and the conjunction of forces and chances. Machiavelli uses the metaphor of a wildly flooding river to describe the propensities of fortune and recommends preparation and adaptation as ways of modifying and coping with the behavior of an aleatory world, and audacity as a means of bringing a mythically feminized luck to the point of subdual and consummation.[36] Somehow, in the present day, coupling preparation with audacity seems to translate into the expectation that minuscule variation, the righteous gesture, the personal disaggregation from the norm, the presence of a video or a document in a database, may be all it takes for something to change for the better.

The yearning for the significance of small gestures comes in part from a dismay at the effects of the large or monolithic. A citizen may hope to do something utterly innocuous, seemingly trivial, but in doing so to incidentally render the world perfect. Such expansive hopes are shared by those who buy lottery tickets, stir viral froths online, or determine that it is best to think positively. The idea of the small gesture that proliferates may be the Straussian "noble lie" of micropolitics or, in the case that it tends toward negligible results, its inverse.[37] It is a mode of belief, however, as we will suggest shortly, that is deeply suited to the naturally quantitative environments of networked and computational digital media, a mode of belief that also plays out at different scales.

Compared to the model of politics or socialization in which a degree of equal commitment to the cause, or of playing one's part in the wider social machinery, in which macrosociological categories entail strict orders of implementation and satisfaction at lower levels, such a model implies the possibility of the slippage of scale. But it also implies an important inverse. An action at the macroscale, that of states, intergovernmental bodies, standards-setting organizations, corporations, armies, or other molar entities, may ultimately dwindle to nothing, the full force of its signal decaying in the endless circuits it traverses and in the minor modifications and impossibilities it may succumb to as it tangles with the complications of the microscale.

In a further inversion, we can locate the reverse of this aspect of the micropolitical imaginary in the developing field of risk management in public and corporate governance. First-order risks, such as malfunctions, direct failures of task, or loss of property or revenue blur in relation to second-order risks such as loss of reputation and brand damage.[38] Maintaining good process at every stage and scale of a work cycle represents a means of minimizing the chance of minor problems turning into massive ones without any intervening passage points of escalation. The legendary yield that marks the transition from nowhere to everywhere—from mundane normalcy to utter collapse, from the pain of conformity to revolution, from unknown to stardom, from a sluggardly to an inspired economy—appears now to some to be as reliable as a train timetable, given the right throw of the dice.

As the preceding chain of switching perspectives and scales suggests, the problematic has no upper or lower bound. Nor does a condition of more or less contact with others of the same or different kinds or scales, whether structurally reinforcing or not, remove an entity from the condition of a probabilistic exposure to abrupt forms of change.[39]

One root of the awareness of the power of extremely small numbers comes in turn from computation's capacity to process many numbers. The relatively recent ability to work with the massively scaled computation of phenomena in complex geometries, to simulate nonlinear dynamic systems, and to engage in advanced forms of modeling renders such phenomena visible, apparently tractable, and open to interpretation and use. The ability to find hitherto unnoticeable or unproduceable disproportionate effects through the ability to sort through an exponentially larger amount of possible combinations inspires the possibility that any slight modification of behavior may yield spectacular results. In turn, the ability of programs to interpret, interact with, and actively inhabit such possibility spaces brings them closer to the surface of daily awareness.

The computational reinstantiation and acceleration of the power of small numbers resonate with their often promulgated relation to networks and their elaboration of a form that is at once continuous yet composed of discrete parts, with no limit of scale. The eagerness to discover networks as a form with ubiquitous explanatory powers (despite the limited nature of their topological qualities) reaffirms the power of small numbers and the ability to traverse scales while at the same time finding a means of explaining the function of such relations, a means of turning it into something rec-ognizable. One way of doing this is to make sure that networks are well integrated into other structures, such as hierarchies.

An affinity for the power of small things comes about most potently because of the recognition that at certain scales they can make the most crucial difference—the pos-session of a visa, word of a loophole, access to food, conditions that can be difficult, if not impossible, to arrange. These are trivial things, the matters of everyday life, the absence of which may yield death or its double, attrition. But this is a finality that stays within its own scale or place in the hierarchy of abstraction layers and thus, unless it is accidentally taken up elsewhere or benefits from the propitious generosity of an error, stays within its own proper domain, ending the process. In such cases, audacity and preparation speak different languages and cannot refer to each other.

Flirting Tips

There are no mechanically reliable paths to love, yet there is no shortage of contenders for the title of the most reliable technique in its pursuit. And while *The Prince* asserts that it is, in general, better to be feared than loved, certain cases arise in which excep-tions prove the rule. It would be easy to suggest that the more scientifically or pre-paredly that suitors array themselves, the greater their tendency to cretinization in the handling of such ineffable stuff; but one should not be blind to the possibility that—if promulgated in the right manner—such measures may maintain, if not deepen, the quality of mystery so keenly associated with romance. As with many of the stratagems presented here, the aim is not to present any one method as appropri-ate in specific situations, or as limited to certain actors, but to develop a sense of the range of explicitly sophisticated techniques in circulation and articulate their major tendencies. As an indicator of the relevance of this domain for stratagematic thought, little in the surviving literature of ancient sophistry broaches the topic. These early technicians propounded views and composed arguments on most other subjects, so we can safely work on the basis that they viewed love as fundamentally of a sympathetic nature, one so readily visible in its sophistication that to expound on it would be superfluous or would perhaps dilute the uniqueness of their expertise.

We live in times of a rather different kind. Like creativity and innovation, love appears today as something both immeasurable and bountiful, omnipresent and mysterious, amenable to policy and to both personal and governmental strategy. It is everyone's right and within everyone's capacity to perform love. In certain conditions, it may even be a duty.

At the same time as contemporary media establish new conditions for the arrangement of love, it also increasingly finds its echo in the proliferation of algorithmic approaches to romantic pursuits. These approaches offer particularly potent materials in which to find stratagematic activity. Algorithms require data to handle, and the tendency is toward increasingly fine-grained formats that are easier to process to meet this requirement.

Early ethnographic work on phone sex showed that a constrained range of signs, triggers, and responses is highly efficient at eliciting correct responses.[40] It is simply a step further to database such systems with basic response selectors choosing and delivering appropriate audio. Are you a screamer, a breather, a talker, or silent? Do you like to listen? Equally driven by the aggregation of particles of data, to each of which they add their own analytical twist, are matchmaking sites and services. These collect, correlate, and recommend potential partners or provide users with reasons to avoid them. Elements that are considered meaningful, such as gender, sexuality, sense of humor, caste, solvency, children, sect, hobbies, or user-authored categories and headlines, are listed in a table. Each characteristic is held separately in algebraic parenthesis. There is no limit to the number of kinds of data that can be held in this way. External to the parentheses, any number of functions or operations can be added. They can be used to represent people or to generate patterns that customers can identify with, advisory personae. An early recipient of cybernetic expertise, marriage bureaus, dating agencies, and contact sites share fundamental approaches in probabilistic determination.[41] Many will offer a unique spin on their analysis, the manipulation of hidden factors to find results that users didn't even know they were looking for. While eroticism spends too much time lingering and malingering to be fully efficient, romance is a matter of closing down the variables, optimizing an algorithmic function. Such sites therefore differ from the large swaths of the Internet consisting of pornographic landfill, the approach of which is largely to grow and occupy space. Similar multiply-and-conquer tactics include the massive volume of romantic advice available online in the form of dating tips and self-improvement or flirtation pointers.

Owing to the special nature of the data they handle, in which their users are also on view, some of the techniques deployed in other contexts are largely unsuitable for deployment here; recommendation systems based on the habits of previous customers would be among these, although such practices are not unheard of for more obviously commercial sexual transactions.

The highly abbreviated form of much Internet "content" is readily amenable to a regular churn of tidbits of advice that can be read for a few minutes while avoiding work or seeking an emollient to irritation. Women are advised on ways in which they can meld with their partner; on how to send signals, keep a relationship alive, look appropriate, have sex in a manner popularized in other media formats; on how to read a man for power, fertility, kindness, and compatibility while maintaining opportunity maximization. No stage of a relationship is left unadvised; makeup tips for postbreakup good looks are a great way of combining advertorial with advice. Men are instructed on how most effectively to recognize their fundamental predatory nature; to remember factoids about the relative nerve mass of genitals to lips, salival hormone transfer and trust inducement; to register and rank obscure indicators of interest; how not to appear teleologically inclined or to be daringly straightforward in the management of behaviors toward desired outcomes, but, where seduction is concerned, to always operate with staged damage-limitation action points. It's important to know how to gaze caringly and how to build muscle bulk where it counts in a dance of escalation and de-escalation. Back online, the narcolepsy of affirmative thinking is reduced to the lacing of data fields with enough triggers to yield a result through the effective execution of what is, after all, an algorithmic process.

Schopenhauer's thirty-eighth stratagem for winning an argument, the last one he proposes—being confessedly the most useless—is to "become personal, insulting, rude."[42] The question of whether the multitude of chat-up techniques, pickup artists, and dating tips ever becomes anything more than impersonal is moot, but the question of how to win at getting personal is crucial in the algorithmicization of romantic behaviors. The crucial aspect here is to lift actions out of the ensemble of behaviors of which they are a part, to detach movements, words, gestures, hormones, clothing, from a wider set of relations and to filter them in relation to a set of prepared and preferentially ordered triggers. This process of detachment allows bodily operations and linguistic behaviors to be interpreted and handled by the same set of tools: to be treated as media. So when a pickup instruction commends the sequence "gaze, approach, talk, turn, touch, synchronize"[43] as a means of homing in on and attracting a potential lifetime playmate from a well-stocked zone of other targets, the algorithmic dimension of such a set of instructions does two things: establish a procedure that can be used to shore up doubt and cowardice in the face of humiliation; and set a series of stages by which the data yielded by the target can be interpreted and responded to. Such an approach arms Cupid with a machine gun, leaving you to rescue the most heavily wounded with ease.

Pickup techniques are a more precarious freestyle version of the production line of speed-dating mechanisms in which a procedural armature is used to govern staged contacts between participants to protect, mollify, and encourage them in haggling for, or avoiding the attentions of, prospective sweethearts. As with all stratagematic approaches, speed dating encourages gaming, and numerous theorists have proposed means by which various cognitive abstraction layers analyze features such as scent, genetic differentiation, relative finger length, social dominance, and the ability to remove limited beliefs and replace them with unstoppable confidence. Rhetorical rather than biological gambits may also be in play, according to some accounts, and the ability to align the two abstraction layers is generally considered to provide optimal results.

One of the means of promoting the conditions in which this can occur is by cir-culating information about the latest research on the physiological bases of sexuality and mate choice. This is a process profoundly suited to media activity. The generation of factoids in media systems predisposed to their delivery is enhanced by the selection of research paradigms with a visible capacity for the robust production of explanation in short sentences. Simple causes get results. Sociobiology and its derivates are a reli-able source of resources by which the inner game of biology and the outer game of rhetoric can be combined.[44] Psychology, in turn, provides a useful set of tools for intermediation between the two layers. The whole ensemble, when turned into fac-toids, instructions for soul-merge, or highly motile explanations, may advantageously provide simultaneous feed for peoples' feelings of inadequacy and guides to a path to power that conveniently also require dedicated self-gratification.

A tricky maneuver here, then, is also how to mobilize different modes of intelli-gence as part of such stratagematic operations rather than as means of withdrawal from them. It is not simply that maze-solving abilities confer the ability to attract more voluptuous and fertile mates but that, in certain models of romance, intelligence itself also becomes a tool for displays of fitness.[45] The mind's ability to respond to the exponential demands both to recognize and to respond to manipulation, to mesh with and invent tools and techniques, and to generate means of displaying such wit and powers of interpretation, or to manifest the means of appearing to do so in an arms race of generative overinterpretation, offers a crucial coefficient for one's biological adaptation. The interpretation of the display of intelligence as a function of evolutionary success always risks simply recognizing only that which has settled out from the churn of events and lifetimes as appearing providentially so. What does not yet appear as intelligent perhaps here has an edge.

Mobilize Irritation

Irritability is a characteristic of all living organisms. Whether it is recognized as the capacity to move toward sunlight in plants, to creep toward a higher sugar gradient in bacteria, to respond to the traces left by conspecifics in ants, or to move away from a source of pain in mammals, the ability to adapt, even if only in minor increments, to a "positive" or "negative" stimulus is one means of identifying what lives and what does not. Irritability here means the capacity to adapt to a stimulus or a condition, but it may not be so easily resolved, as one may encounter a stimulus that does not have any direct means of being sated, neutralized, or avoided. Here irritation, rather than irritability, is perhaps a characteristic differentiation between animals with more or less sophisticated cognitive capacities. Irritation is the internalized sense or understanding of irritability, of being mobilized by something. This is not an occurrence on the grand scale but something minor, which occurs via the tickling of interests, detaching moments, senses, bodily feeling, attention. Nor can an irritation usually be said to be simply a wronging or a transgression or a violation of a body. Irritation may occur at the moment of the dehiscence of any of the scales of consciousness running from will to affect as they switch into an itchy attentiveness to something they do not intend but nevertheless find tricky to avoid. This is not to say that this moment of switching is by any means absolute; in general it cannot be, and as such, the situation does not resolve. As stressed attention flickers from one trigger to another, a state of futile partial engrossment in not quite achieving anything, like a priority inversion, opens the organism up to further irritation. Thus we see the annoyance of irritation, a source of its longevity as a phenomenon, and its usefulness as a point of entry to contemporary media, where it is an almost foundational condition.

Participatory social network software emerged after the dot-com crash at the beginning of the last decade. Most of the sites with high degrees of capitalization, saddled with having to generate expensive content, bombed. This event was often lauded as a reclaiming of the Internet for people rather than products as new services based on user-generated content came to the fore. These new services emphasized communication, community, and relationship building. The new model was to facilitate users to leverage the possibility of contact with one another and to support such communitarian action with incidental data-mining and advertising. Communication between people became more important than straightforward consumption. But these new sites also found a way to build on another result of the dot-com crash and the iterations of the far wider financial abyss of debt and obligation on which Western societies have built themselves. As Bifo has noted in *The Soul at Work*, the link between financial depression and its cognate other may be more than a simply nominal parallel.[46] Nervousness, time wasting, irritation, the ability to draw out or to dither the moment when unwanted but obligatory activities start, to combine idleness with something partially purposive, the sanctuary of the small gesture that has an even smaller result—all find their refuge, moment of forgetting, and therapeutic postponement in browsing, networking, fiddling. Indeed, numerous blogs and surf clubs undergo a purging of irony by an exultant harvesting and sorting, turning lives of clickwork into a yield.

As many forms of work now require the operative to be seated in front of a computer with access to the Internet, and many family homes are equipped with one or more terminals, and given also that phones now slip access into every pocket of intermediate time, the sites of boredom, obligation, and avoidance are multiple. This is not the boredom of blandness, of staring into space, at curtains or walls of nothing in particular so beloved of philosophers and artists as the moment when subconscious creation has a tendency to find itself getting done, but an itchy, iterative kind of boredom, an irritation against doing something pointless, onerous, and endless. Symptoms of this irritation can momentarily be alleviated by clicking on a link, casting an eye on some porn, twitching on some game, catching up on the news, making a status update. As Olga Goriunova notes in her study of the Russian "mate-lit" platform udaff.com, which specializes in brutally written stories of sex, drugs, and violence by and for a population of "office plankton," a quick burst of transgression and black humor can act as the necessary pick-me-up to get through the day.[47] However, while transgression and adrenalin are probably a high point in the broader tendency toward irritation, what is key is the possibility to instantly vary the degree of urgency, irritancy, and stuporousness of the material one treats. To be able to switch in an instant from something imperative but pointless to something genuinely meaningless but unforced, and then to something mildly attention catching and trivial, does not correspond to a flattening of nuance in interpersonal relationships or culture—it opens up, rather, a massive palette of irrelevance and pointlessness to be explored. Distraction without indulgence proposes snacking as a way of avoiding being eaten.

But irritability—as a characteristic abstractable from all living systems—offers, as a point of transition, certain movements to be expected, predictions to be acted on. Deep addiction to games and the Internet is a relatively minor condition in terms of scale compared to the epidemic of productive fidgeting that leaves logs, cookies, click trails, and identities in its wake. Here there is no state of information overload, or even one of absolute redundancy, but a sifting of options on the basis of the avoidance of resentment and obligation. Exhaustion is key to all aesthetics of combinatoriality within finite worlds.[48] Within the functionally infinite and untiring world of computational media, exhaustion is enhanced with choice.

Algorithms

Enhance Queue Formation

Economics is sometimes described as the discipline concerned with establishing the correct means of allocating scarce resources. In the context of digital abundance at least, what is often scarce is scarcity itself. Thus, paying attention to the mechanisms for the deferral of access, of gratification, for the arrangement of finitude, is repaid many times over.

In Vladimir Sorokin's narrative of the dialogue taking place in a line of people waiting to buy a pair of shoes, a Soviet queue in the early eighties, stretching several city blocks and lasting over a night, allocation of the purchase opportunity is made on the basis of timed arrival in the queue. As Sorokin states in his afterword to *The Queue*: "It was after the victory of the collective body that the phenomenon of the queue appeared in Russia with all its classic attributes: numeration (the person's number in line was usually written on the hand); the periodic roll call and ruthless elimination of anyone who stepped away for a moment; a strict hierarchy (those standing behind were supposed to obey those standing in front); the quantity of goods allotted per person (this was also decided collectively), etc."[1]

The details may vary (the seller, for instance, may have set the amount of goods allotted), but Sorokin's description of resource allocation expressed as a set of rules perfectly describes the migration of software imperatives into everyday life and does so in a context in which systems of management have already preempted, made advances on, and prepared such integration. Indeed, as a written book, Sorokin's text relies on a linear organization of letters and words into orthogonally organized space, in itself a form of attention queue, which it manipulates to produce its own kind of multivalence. The waiting line triggers stories, couplings, dodges, and free association, all traced in the dialogue between, which loops, backtracks, jumps ahead, takes long detours, slopes off, goes back to bed, never quite climaxes, while the line of text continues on its way.

Running through several of the stratagems collected in this book is an idea that is derived from the computational theory of mind—and expanded from its seat in the "central processor" of the brain, into the realm of expanded cognition into objects, the social, and systems—that you can "arrange your syntax and the semantics comes for free."[2] In computationalism, this is the idea that if a device that is sufficiently structurally analogous to a mind is assembled, then it will inevitably and unavoidably start to interact with the world: it will begin to cogitate. In political thinking, this is equivalent to the idea that if the appropriate decision-making structure is established, all the decisions it arrives at will, for reasons depending on the type of structure sought, be correct, just, or, at worst, the least bad. Whether the chosen structure is a workers' council, a representative democracy, the "benevolent dictator" beloved of software development narratives, or some other form, the emphasis is on the rule of law as that of process. Here a differentiation between ends and means is rendered superfluous, because the means are considered to be transcendent.

One virtue of this approach is that it foregrounds the formalism as generative, as yielding something other than itself. This should be contrasted with the sleights of hand that attempt to frame a hidden structuration as a freedom from ordering (as is characteristic of standard neoliberal accounts). Making the formalism visible suggests the possibility that it may be evaluated or learned from and indeed changed. Where we need to pay attention is in those cases where what lies outside the model and what ought to be subject to it have difficulty in conforming to it.

In certain territories, queuing has been raised to the level of a surrogate for culture. In such places, the ability to interiorize and repeat a respect for proper participation in queue formation, such as the principle of first come, first served, or that of ladies first, of no pushing in, of either standing in an ordered line or appearing to memorize the order of arrival of fellow queuers to the point of queue formation, guarantees—to a certain degree of probability—that such a person satisfies the qualities required for the award of citizenship. Such rules of formation are often characterized as modes of discipline that may apply in different queue contexts.[3] Conversely, some models of behavior emphasize the usefulness, in certain contexts, of relative deregulation in queue discipline. Jockeying activity among car drivers at a junction, or in the capriciousness of "chess players" moving for advantage across lanes, is inherently pleasurable, and a display of skill, as well as action that speeds up overall traffic flow. Cultural assumptions of this sort about queuing being indicative of good moral character may, however, reveal a limited appreciation of the rich variety and subtle textures of queuing or waiting-line models.

Contributing to such a history, the development of supermarkets is partly a history of queue design. While the back-end work of the structure is that of logistics, the front end is one that couples desire with sequencing and the planning, preparing, ordering, and execution of discrete events. One of the most impressive early architectures was that of Clarence Saunders's Piggly Wiggly stores of the early twentieth century. Manned by a single operative seated at a till by the exit, from the entrance via turnstile, these stores provided a single lane through which people could progress through a winding, one-way maze of attractively packaged, ready-to-purchase goods.[4] Customers were queued and positioned to view the widest range of products as they moved, pushing shopping carts, themselves then a contemporary innovation, toward the checkout. Here, ideally at least, the unilateral nature of the consumption line recapitulates that of production. In other cases, privileging the network as a mode of desire and of organization, different forms of nonlinear queue architecture are appropriate and come to the fore.

As the generic characteristics of waiting-line systems expand to encompass a vast cosmology of types, qualities, and contexts, the ontology of queues is established as a baseline fundament of opportunity. To return to Sorokin and his description of the archetypes of the queue and its articulation of this ontology: the sequential numeration of comrades participating in the Soviet queue equates to the concrete abstractions of arrivals and input processes described by the deep logistical imaginary of operations research; the queue's periodic roll call and strict hierarchy describe a coupled form of queue discipline; and the quantity of goods allotted per person at the shop or stall describes key aspects of a particular service mechanism. Although a disparate range of societies, when coded in ideological terms, exhibit queue formation, one need not argue that the queue amounts to a universal vocabulary of form to recognize its usefulness. It is, rather, in the fine and gentle art of ordering, waiting, and allocation architectures that such forms articulate their value.

Know Your Sorts

Sorting takes a sequence of entities and permutates that sequence to arrive at a result that renders it more useful. As a stratagematic force in its own right, therefore, sorting should be understood both as something that yields results, in the form of a ranking, and as something that generates its own terms of composition, shifting relations between things that are sorted in ways that imply multiple kinds of use and attention.

Among other qualities, permutation, the process of shifting and sifting the order of things, has an aesthetics of its own, which renders it distinct from the conceptual lockdown of nominally Platonic essentialism favored in certain kinds of mathematically grounded accounts of software. Such an aesthetics establishes a vivid dynamic of interplay between algorithms, the machinic context of hardware and software resources, and the data that are being handled, all of which make demands on the others and combine to render each permutational process individual. Further iterations and enfoldings of sorting in other media—such as social processes—make sorting particularly interesting. In such a context, knowing your sorts, gaining a sense of the aesthetic dimensions of ordering, is crucial. But aside from the way in which it engages the sensorial aspect of being, sorting has a profound and intricate relationship to systems of ordering. Among these, sorting is distinct from categorization, to which it is naturally affiliated. Categorization may be the result of a sort, and categories may also be sorted, but we are concerned here with the permutational moment and the kinds of power it produces and invokes.

As a distinct field of thought, computer science usefully maintains intellectual and technical reserve in relation to its application, its wider place in the world. As such it maintains relations of pretended universality, in that everything finds its place in computation but also equally establishes its separateness. In such a context of technical neutrality, sorts are evaluated in terms of the optimal use of resources both for processing code and for handling data during runtime, and in terms of the speed of execution in relation to different sorting problems. In the field, questions of optimality or optimization of this kind may be complicated by those of the efficiencies of management, but since most sorting algorithms are readily available within standard libraries, such forms of interference tend not to coincide.

Within the computational articulation of sorts, material is typically handled via an alphanumeric key, a pointer, that maintains a relation to the records, numbers, or other single or clustered entities that the key in turn is able to treat as satellites. What is sorted, then, is not at first the "primary" data, such as a record or file, or what it may refer to, such as an event or a person. What sorting first acts on are the numeric values by which those events or persons are handled. Once the values are organized, sorting can concatenate out. As such, a general literacy of sorting is to be recommended.

Arguments against instrumental reason,[5] averring that it is one more form of knowledge that subordinates means to ends, are usefully transformed by other forms of sorting in which not the numeric handler but rather the data themselves are understood to have an intrinsic and indexical relation to things in the world. "Social sorting," as it is termed by scholars in critical surveillance studies,[6] adopts a mode of sorting in which mechanisms for managing entitlement, control, and protection are deployed to maximize efficiency, convenience, and speed. Opponents of sorting tend to concern themselves not with the underlying logic of such rules but with the moments at which they become inefficient, inconvenient, and slow. They may also attend to the way in which vague social classifiers such as race are mobilized to provide surety and the opportunity for the randomized, unjust, or unaccountable exercise of power. The likelihood of racial category providing insight into someone's level of criminality is roughly equivalent to such analysis being made on the basis of shared name. That this is so does not preclude either association being made.

Imagine the quandary of an eight-year-old boy who has the same name as a person who is for some reason on a terror watch list, and is therefore subject to body searches before boarding any plane.[7] The boy's problem arises because he is being sorted on the basis of a referencing system that specifies an alphanumeric identifier—his name—which, due to social convention and a resulting limited name space, is most likely held by more than one person. It is perhaps better to name children with strong passwords that are unlikely to be duplicated or easily memorized. Alternately it is possible to identify citizens on the basis of unique identifiers, such as passport numbers and identification cards, which provide an easily exploitable sense of security. These may be triangulated with probabilistically unique identifiers such as biometrics, nominally unchanging and accessible features that can be turned into a record that can in turn be assigned an alphanumeric code.

The primary method of sorting in computing is by comparison. In such cases, data are sorted in relation to other data, for instance, whether a datum has a lesser or greater numeric value.[8] Sorting by comparison implies that the range of data to be sorted is generally not known in advance or does not need to be. In cases where the range is known, algorithms such as bucket sort, radix sort, and pigeonhole sort, among others, work with effective addressing schemas to allocate results. Differences between these can be accounted for at the level of speed, for instance, when using a search engine to query for a common search term whose results are preranked, compared to those that are rarer or unprecedented and thus need to be generated on the fly.

Comparison essentially involves allocating a position on the basis of a greater-than or less-than calculation. While it is tempting to assume that simply because something is sorted by comparison, it is reduced to a place within a schema of greater or lesser rank, this assumption would overestimate its effects and possibly misrecognize the importance of the process of being sorted as significant in itself before a place in such an array is determined. Ranking can be an extremely useful effect in combination with a queuing system or resource allocation process as a way of entraining what is ranked. Ranking regimes that are active through the differential ordering of interacting entities of different scales are inherently interesting. As an example, the ranking of academics by numerous interacting rank-based mechanisms (such as those of scholars, departments, institutions, articles, citations, journals) confirms the benefit of such approaches in terms of simplifying the evaluation of research into a quantifiable metric. The ease with which such a system can be interpreted and summarized allows for all positions within it to adapt to and canalize the required behavior. The fine tuning of results can be achieved by more obscure means of handling, such as those evinced by social networks.

All forms of sorting require the use of resources. In resource-constrained environments, when choosing which sort may be adopted, testing which sort may be applied or to which one is subject, or estimating the employment of a sort of any kind as useful, it is advisable to evaluate its implications in terms of calculation and processing. Because sorts imply such costs, they are often identified as implying a deliberate sacrifice of resources, especially time, on the altar of rather obscure gods. As an important dimension of the experience of sorting, this sacrifice is something itself to take into account. Here the deployment of sorts can act usefully as a form of immobilization, an occlusion of the identification of the beneficiaries of the sorting process, or for the generation of support for new resource requirements. While in some cases, the least number of comparisons should be aimed at for the sake of efficiency, each opportunity for ordering is one that should also be taken as a test of the worth of ordering in itself and should therefore be evaluated carefully.

An example of the unpredictable results of the introduction of sorting practices is to be found in the work of postal delivery. By its very nature, the work requires numerous stages of sorting. The number and range of address to be delivered to are generally known and fixed into the "frame" used to position the run of things to be delivered during their preparation in the sorting office. One exemplary factor that complicates the work is often the uneven physical distribution of the addresses. A street may be laid out in a higgledy-piggledy fashion, various plots of land having perhaps been developed at different times, being of different sizes, or arrayed nonuniformly owing to natural features. Working out the optimal route may further be complicated by many factors (such as the slope of the ground or the presence of parcels in the delivery load). Thus every person delivering post experiences their own daily version of the Traveling Salesman's Problem.[9] This problem is usually understood to be resolvable only in exponentially calculable time but is solved here by the tacit knowledge and the labor of the postal worker who knows and sorts the route. Attempts to automate the process of sorting and route planning in ways that marginalize or contradict this local and habitual knowledge—on the undisclosed assumption that such knowledge lacks the quantifiable virtue of the explicit and so can easily be confused with stupidity—raise a number of problems that are exploitable as stratagems but mitigate against an optimal postal service.[10] The case of the trickiness of the postal sort reminds us that the virtue of a stratagem must not be mistaken for an illusory efficiency. It also makes evident, however, that certain problems of sorting can be offloaded by such means. The efficient circulation of an illusion is something to be appreciated.

Invoke Recursion

Recursion is one of the special pleasures of programmers, the use of a procedure that involves a series of discrete steps, one of which is the relaunch of the procedure. This relaunching, which aids both concision and economy, does not have to be simply stacked one inside the other. Recursion may involve the launch of another procedure that in turn launches the first one—such as a piece of software working its way through Web sites by following one link, then another, at each point splitting into a copy of itself that carries out the same behavior, deleting itself once an end point in the chain of links has been reached.

As a technique, recursion is typically handled by a loop, a sequence of instructions in which a program performs a set of operations, looping back to repeat them again until a specific condition is satisfied. But recursion may also be something far more systematic and pleasing—a characteristic feature of some entity or other, definable in terms of the kind of recursive mathematical function that programmers are taught to exploit. First of all, recursion is not inevitably a reinstantiation of the same.[11] It may consist of a derivable pattern of activity, of self-similarity, but in a condition in which each recursive event is different, in terms of its scale, location in time, the complications it may entail, and its place in relation to its nesting within other recursions or to those in which it is in turn nested. As such, recursion may be used to organize heterogeneous material into a singular pattern.

Control requires recursion, and this is its innovative answer to the ancient question put to Socrates in Plato's *The Republic* (and then repeated by Juvenal): Quis custodiet ipsos custodes? Who watches the watchmen? To which the answer was: their own deluded sense of duty—checks and balances. The recursiveness of control mechanisms in evil media creates a situation in which no upper layer exists that would be required to use its merely moral strength to fight the seductions of corruption, since it is always topped out by another cycle of recursion. That recursion has this quality means that it requires meticulous handling for it not to spill out in unrecuperable ways, generating patterns in excess of the tacit norms of its exercise. As formalizations increasingly spread out from programmable systems into those that exhibit greater degrees of unpredictability, the usefulness of implementing recursive forms increases. One notable recent example is the use of eye-tracking devices to monitor, control, and derive information from the eye movements of those watching CCTV feeds.[12]

But control as such also invites simple forms of deviation, falling out of the conditions of one loop, as a means of resistance. Recursions need to be correctly stacked for the multilevel "business ontology"[13] that structures the innards and horizons of contemporary life to be fully encompassing with appropriate inevitability. It is an ontology of (predictable) unpredictability and modularity, structured by a hungrily flexible grammar generating cohesion and instability out of potential future profit or a perpetual state of getting by until the moment of opportunity arises to take on one's rightful mantle of star, celebrity, entrepreneur, or gambler.

The answer to the question of who controls control is, then, that when control controls controlling, control is formally dexterous enough to conjugate itself, endlessly. Control becomes an automatism that has acquired such solid entrenchment in the perceptual, affective, and conceptual habits of experience that it acquires an agency all its own. This creates a situation in which control is cyclically deferred, with no identifiable center, and at the same time is able to enact itself at multiscalar levels with absolute specificity and requisite variety. At this point, resistance to control becomes not something of interest simply to underlings or those who are used to acting as the appendages of their devices but to anyone who needs to take the initiative of using disturbance or carving out a little creative autonomy. Needless to say, the anonymous algorithmic perfection of such an admirably constructed world does not yet exist, except in tendency. But as a concrete abstraction unfolding with hands-free autonomy into the various locales of the real, it offers much to desire.

Such organization, however, does not arise from a revolutionary rationalism, an imperative to establish media systems as a "clean slate,"[14] to ground all future operations on a foundational scission with the past and start anew under perfect conditions. Rather, the imperative is to work with the messiness, intractability, and chaos that pertain. What needs to be established is the framework that enables all this activity to take place—such is the strategy of cloud computing and social network facilitation, for instance. It is a strategy that works well to supplement or triangulate the perils of audit, in which quantitatively fixed terms of required achievement simply become fixtures to be worked around. Here the work-around is already anticipated, tracked, and installed as the next target, and the recursion plays out in the cybernetic dance of target finding and avoidance.

If topology involves a means of recognizing the invariance of forms in space, recursion is a means of establishing invariance over time. The characteristic problems of topology, homotopy, and continuous functions become manifest here in relational terms that are articulated through the arrangement of staging sequences and processes. Recursion as a stratagem is thus immediately distinguishable from one that aims at all too simple domination, but it is a stratagem that also compels its use in a moderate manner. Calculus—originally invented to track "the motions of the planets, the comets, the moon and the sea"[15]—is a tool for tracing recursions across time, but it thus also provides a means for describing the cyclical movements of a world, one that it is wise to be able to step out from, as well as being able to bend oneself and others toward.

The efficacy of recursion as a stratagematic technique derives from the way in which it draws on particular kinds of patterning that already exist in things, people, processes, and organizations themselves. Yet the risks that recursion poses derive from the inevitably incomplete characterization that a recursive function provides: extending a process through recursion can generate arbitrary forms of continuity that rapidly diverge and loop off in directions initially unforeseen. The formal and the empirical do not mesh: poorly implemented recursion may even have the propensity to rapidly generate extreme phenomena.

Abstract Captures

Designing a piece of software or a programmable digital artifact of any kind entails a process of abstraction: capturing the logic of what an application, a gadget, a system, or a device is supposed to do within a set of algorithms, and understanding how those algorithms will behave, is a preeminent technical skill of software engineers. Appropriately precise technical knowledge amounts here to a detailed understanding of the states of the algorithm, program, or system. A programmer will want to know that an algorithm will terminate and not just loop forever, reach a position of catatonic stasis, or collapse as the result of incremental leaks in memory.

The ability to abstract is not, however, to be understood as primarily a matter of individual psychology, as if in the world of the computer programmer there came first a concrete world, then the process of cognition, and finally the algorithm as the abstracted result. Abstraction is a real, transindividual process,[16] present in social practices, languages, and technologies, as much as in the design discussions and mod-eling diagrams of the development team. We are infected and birthed by abstractions and have become immune to, and unaware of, some of their effects, sometimes inten-tionally so (as with abstraction layers). Equally layers of abstraction are embedded in flowcharts, naming conventions (the "end user"), design tools, programming libraries, assembly languages, and so on, which mean that a programmer doesn't have to be able to talk directly to a machine in terms of the minutiae of processes of bit shifting. And lengthy, more or less routinized, chains of translation also give tractable, program-mable shape to the design requirements for an application.

Abstraction operating on abstraction, this complex set of processes involved in specifying, segmenting, structuring, and parsing quantities considered as data or instruction underlines the strangely material qualities of the communicative poten-tials modeled in computational formalism. While such processes can be captured more or less readily in the notational formatting of algorithms and data structures, the realities on which those algorithms and data structures operate must themselves be organized so that they interface smoothly with them. Simulating real-world processes is made considerably easier if the real world already operates like a machine, with a precisely specifiable set of degrees of freedom accorded to the processes in question. A user interface is a carefully and restrictively controlled entity that allows a variable, albeit fairly minimal, latitude of enunciative freedom to the user on the basis of a precise set of parameters. Design techniques can be and are used to ensure that a machine is addressed in a way that the machine will understand, rather than any other.

With its frequent propensity for figuring cognitive operations in computational terms, psychology is a discipline apt to promote the kind of algorithmic subjectivity that interfaces most appropriately with machines. Consider, for example, the stepwise operation of the finite-state machine as it works in a regular-expression engine. (When a regex engine parses a string of characters as a regular expression, it compares input characters with regular-expression characters on a sequential, one-at-a-time basis. If the regular expression to be matched is *aa* but the input string is *ba*, the engine returns a "no match" result after the first comparison. If the input string is *ac*, the "no match" result is returned after the second comparison, and so on.)[17] This highly pernickety, stepwise operation is characteristic of the logic of the finite-state machine, but it equally infiltrates everyday practices: the short-listing meeting for selecting candidates for a job interview, for example, or the border guards profiling visitors to the West from anywhere it has recently bought democracy to. You do it yourself when you check your eligibility for personal finance (unless you visit a pawnshop, where a different chain of negotiations is adopted). Some psychologists call this process of pattern matching *intuition*. It is what organizational decision makers are praised for; it is an automatism of great virtue,[18] one that exemplifies the pervasive quality of the real abstractions operative in social life.

But if we can think of computational media forms as expressing such abstractions, they can in turn represent a means for further extending the zones within which to realize them and give them effective purchase. In some ways, this possibility is inherent in the epistemic claims made on behalf of the Turing machine, Turing's proof that any computable function could be simulated by an appropriately configured machine, with its laborious, step-by-step movements of a notional tape (itself a variant of the logic of the finite-state machine).[19] As a device endowed with the universal ability to simulate, the Turing machine acts as an article of faith, yielding the conviction that any computable machine process can—whatever the problem—be translated into and modeled in Turing terms.[20] Some argue that this establishes a new way of exploring processes of value extraction in the economy. At the least, it gives a suggestive set of theoretical resonances to the practical operations of the knowledge economy—"Can it be modeled as a Turing machine?" coming to mean "Can knowledge of how to do this be extracted from the workers who know how to do it?"[21]

But Turing machines are characterized by a certain inflexibility for practical purposes, for the technical reason that their operations are characterized in terms of the minute operations of shifting of bits. How to specify, and hence discern and extract, the appropriately algorithmic qualities of a regular, semiregular, or regulated process is not something one would do directly in terms of a Turing machine per se—in just the same way that one would not measure a coastline with a meter ruler. Hence we see the pragmatic virtues of abstraction layers, which obviate the need to think computationally in terms of machine addressable processes. But the flip side of this issue is that a great many computational processes rapidly become incredibly opaque, because ignorance, a selective forgetting, is a crucial element of abstraction. Consequently, as real-world tasks get translated into finite algorithmic operations, the possibility that a program will generate ballooningly complex sets of machine states, as is the case with the pattern matching of regular-expression engines, for example, becomes a significant likelihood, because of the multifaceted, many-layered ignorance that abstraction produces.

Trying to match an extremely complicated expression, requiring all sorts of backtracking through previously matched sets of data, will flood computational memory with possible matches, the programmatic equivalent of the neurotic indecision produced by excess memories. Technically this is a problem of computational complexity (the very problem that the finite-state machine was originally used to analyze), but it is not just a technical matter: *algorithmic complexity attacks*, which, to provoke the breakdown of a system, exploit the resource-intensive nature of multiplication of state that some computational processes entail, show that management of state is a real-world problem with significant implications. Such attacks derive not from the break-down of a formalism but from its excess, from a deliberately engineered overproduction of what the formalism allows, so as to generate processing problems in excess of the material resources that can be allocated for their solution. Control begets control as abstraction begets abstraction.

In this respect, the concept of the *abstract*-state machine and the "specification languages" to which it gives rise is of particular, and not solely technical, interest. The abstract-state machine offers a formal notation that purports to have a capacity to *capture and model logics* in motion. Along with the associated technique of evolution-ary algebra, the abstract-state machine represents an important attempt at introducing dynamism into logic, where mathematics might still often be tempted to consider static entities. As Yuri Gurevich points out, "Mathematical structures (graphs, groups, topological spaces, etc.) do not change in time whereas computer science objects (databases, machines) often do."[22] The strictures of computer science and mathematics here point toward the possibilities of developing engineering practices that are able to *capture* ever more complex, changeable real-life processes, the kinds of processes that, where simulated in machines, generate precisely the ballooning state and the difficulty of its control so effectively exploited in complexity attacks.

The theory of abstract-state machines offers a bridge into the process whereby cultural practices, machine apparatuses, flows of work, and processes of communica-tion are—or can be—translated into programmatically tractable finite-state machines. To put it slightly differently, the abstract-state machine offers a more tractable means for putting the generalized desire to simulate and automate into practice: "Can one generalize Turing machines so that any algorithm, never mind how abstract, can be modeled by a generalized machine very closely and faithfully?" Unlike the Turing model, the theory of abstract-state machines is, as one commentator put it, a "wide spectrum method" to "bridge the gap between the two ends of system development: the human understanding and formulation of real-world problems; [and] the deploy-ment of their algorithmic solutions by code-executing machines on changing plat-forms."[23] Capturing a set of material operations inevitably requires these two ends of the spectrum, but doing so is a lengthy and costly process: imagine specifying the steps involved in making a phone call in terms of bit-shift operations, in the Boolean logic of binary code. Making that process easier obviously extends the range of operations that can be encompassed in a programmable technology.

The success of a corporate operation of capture (will this device be adopted, will it provide a seamless user experience, or will the user's fingers bridle at the operations they must accomplish?) is in part a question of intrusiveness. Clunky mediators are simply too visible. A device or application that captures the attention, the energy, the *time*, of a user most successfully is in all likelihood the device or application that obtrudes least in the practices of which it is a part (note that where the obtrusiveness cannot be mitigated, it is best to recode this obtrusiveness as display, decoration, or ornamentation). Getting work to flow smoothly is a media design imperative for lifestyle strategies, and a political option to boot, particularly when it comes to remediating work.[24] The flexibilization and osmotic dispersion of work processes throughout life (a strong tendency in ubiquitous computing) is accompanied by a transformation of the logics of computational architectures in the direction of greater and greater mobility: mainframe, terminal, desktop, client–server, thin client, mobile, wireless, distributed, virtualized, cloud . . . But with this proliferation and dispersion, devices and applications are called on to present more, and more certain, configurational flexibility, as well as the capacity to handle greater degrees of complexity. The mission-critical role of software in the operation of machines, a car, a plane, or a drone, for example, in a risk- and litigation-averse society entails the minute and mathematically accurate specification of the behavior of a device or application, as well as exhaustive testing.

Producing an accurate specification of the desirably flexible operation of devices or applications is itself a highly ramified process. The chain of translation that connects the whims of an executive dreaming up a killer app to the outsourced coding of low-level assembly language optimizations of its first version is long, and while many of the links in this chain are made explicitly, much depends on shared, but tacit, knowledge. Naturally this offers plenty of scope for ignorance and plausible deniability, and the latitude for deviation along the chain is considerable, a fact that goes some way to explaining why—like the development of drugs by pharmaceutical companies—processes of media design operate by the introduction of incremental, infinitesimal quantities of difference, margins of variation in the imitative capacities of computational code.

It is prudent here to accept the simple fact of the matter: a certain degree of obfuscation characterizes the process whereby mediators, at different layers of abstraction, chain or agglomerate together in the production of a connection (which then typically appears transparent). The obvious tendency is to focus on what remains invariant, at the cost of a failure to see what happens in the middle (see, for example, the "refinements" that a middle manager brings to the directives of senior management in a large organization), especially when the result is in your favor. Equally, as a device for managing abstraction, for controlling the smooth transition from the wishful thinking of vaporware, the hawking of dreams and fantasies of total digital mastery to the drudgery of optimizing the machine address of assembly language, the abstract-state machine indicates the eminently practical role that an attentive reworking of fundamental concepts of computer science can have for regulating even the most microscopic of transitions of a digital media system.

Structures

Structure Data

The concept of the algorithm has been pressed into service in recent years for thinking through processes that would not at first blush be considered to have any of the features that computer scientists normally associate with their core area of expertise: the dynamics of particular kinds of cultural forms, social networking, or brand behavior, for example. Extended in this way, the algorithm, as an idea, thus becomes an "analyzer" of social relations, particularly for processes that do not appear to have any obvious, explicit implementation in computational systems as such.

The algorithmic qualities of particular kinds of social relation, gray media objects and the interfaces they have with the everyday world, are readily evident in a number of fields. The filtering of social-housing hopefuls, nightclub bouncers operating a door policy, putting together a burger, or sorting a mate all attest to the algorithmicity of social life, as do the routine work-arounds used to deal with poor software. And the algorithm has a particularly seductive quality: the effectiveness of a finite set of steps for solving problems, along with the tacit assumption that the specification of an algorithm can change, points to a certain desired formal level of control.

Sociologists, media and cultural theorists, and the like have paid considerably less attention to the near-indispensable correlate of the algorithm, that without which—actual, explicit, and formal or virtual, implicit, and informal—an algorithm would have little to work with: the data structure, or, more simply put, a way of storing and arranging data. Part of the interest of considering things algorithmically has to do with their imitability, their replicability (in the sense that an algorithm extracts an identical, often apparently optimized set of steps from a process), and the inexorability of their finite progress toward a termination point. Imitate. Replicate. Terminate. Optimally. An algorithm is sometimes considered the sum of logic and control. But equally, a program may be considered the sum of algorithms and data structures. If a controllable universe is a sum of programs, a *summa programmae*, then data structures are essential to the effective operation of processes of control and as such represent an equivalently important stratagematic analyzer of social relations, perhaps even more so.

Other stratagems in this book have drawn on the complex interplay of the formal and the empirical evident with the diffusion of programmable mediation throughout culture, and have attended in particular to the tacitly prescriptive nature of specific media forms (e.g., the process of regularizing expression, which forms a way of ensuring the existence of parseable, structured pattern). The requirement that data be structured extends this interplay into the more general abstract architecture of social and cultural practices organized by, for, and as information. If algorithms work most efficiently with well-designed data structures, then the organization of people and things in a manner commensurate with these structural forms will facilitate the smooth flow and control of data.

Consider the most basic operation of an algorithm, one for sorting, say, as discussed in the previous essay, in the stratagem "Know Your Sorts." Sorting algorithms are typically used to arrange lists of data such as numbers, names, credit codes, or other intimacies. Many programming languages natively provide the *array* data structure, which allows you to store collections of elements in one contiguous set of spaces in memory (so you might declare an array of type *integer* or *float*, for example). If your sorting algorithm was for sorting whole numbers, you might pass it an array of integers to work with. However, the array might not be the best data structure to use in a specific case. Arrays allocate memory in advance, so you need to be able to say how big your list will be. What if you don't know how big the list is going to be, or if its size will change? It would be like renting a warehouse for a business without any clear idea of the amount of stock you need to hold. Too big, and you have excessive overheads. Too small, and your stock has no home. Instead you might choose to use a *linked list*, which is a bit like an array except that it can grow or shrink as needs require, and does not require the advance allocation of contiguous blocks of memory.

The point is that data structures help optimize the operations of algorithms by providing a way of organizing memory—computational, living, or material memory—so as to extract the data located in them as rapidly and effectively as possible (arrays are quicker than linked lists, for example). Different kinds of data structure provide different ways of organizing that memory, ways that are more or less appropriate to the task in question. This is as true of a task performed by humans as by machines.

The legendarily astonishing levels of productivity achieved by Alexei Stakhanov, for example, depended on the organization of the working environment in a manner optimal for the hero and his collective. Conversely, restructuring an environment without consideration for the underlying implementation of data extraction processes thwarts productivity: virtualize an office into a paperless universe without due consideration for the operations that depend on visually easy-to-identify stacks of papers and files or face-to-face conversations (now distributed across an intranet, say), and the speed of data retrieval will plummet. As quasi-cybernetic computational entities, formally and informally specified data structures and the operations that can be performed on them become critical mediators, and the space of lived experience is riddled with a complex mix of virtual and actual affordances and opportunities (which are less well-known or evident to generations habituated to working on earlier forms of materiality).

A data structure forms a sort of intermediate level, an abstraction mechanism, in the process of addressing machine memory.[1] An operating system will ultimately take responsibility for how memory is allocated, but a data structure offers a way of abstracting from things to organize them for processing most effectively, without the programmer needing to know the specific details of how a particular type of machine organizes memory allocation. This process of abstraction from the specifics of machine addressable memory is extended by the notion of the abstract data type (ADT), which defines purely theoretical kinds of data structures and the operations that can specifically be performed on them: containers, double-ended queues, multimaps, priority lists, heaps, and trees are represent forms of abstract data type. The implementation of an ADT entails a form of black boxing, in the sense that nested within the ADT, a range of different data structures may be operating, the details of which will be hidden. Equally, different implementations of the same abstract type could entail different data structures. I use a diary; you use a personal organizer. I pile my papers on the desk. You put yours in a filing cabinet. I use memory sticks, you use a networked drive, but we are both working on and retrieving data.

The development of thinking about data and data structures, about abstraction and abstraction mechanisms in computing science, offers precious indicators for the well-crafted development of control.[2] The creation of ever newer layers of abstraction, greater degrees of distance from concrete machine addressable memory,[3] and hence creative of forms of mediation is the general direction of movement. These layers of abstraction have their own operatives and experts to be nurtured: management consultants, facilitators, and knowledge engineers who have a particular interest in shaping new abstract data types.

Because abstraction might be understood as a kind of selective forgetting, however, data structuring can produce difficulties, a particular kind of ignorance about implementation details, which lead humans to a kind of infernal alternative: either refashion yourself to meet the imperious demands of more and different types of data, or consign yourself to data oblivion. Alternately, life may be enhanced as a set of more or less well-linked data structures that, with each synchronizing beat of the ever-more-rapid CPU clock, can undergo process and sort, filter, and queue problems at ever-improved rates. The effectiveness of the popular self-help book *Getting Things Done*, for example, derives from the way that its techniques enable individuals to deal with—or rather process—much more data, provided that they treat them as *data*, with lists (just like Lisp) and memory pointers (just like C++).[4] The algorithm it puts into play, not unlike a Petri net,[5] with these associated data structures can cope with unpredictable eventuality, provided that it can be assimilated into the abstract constraining structure required to ensure the continued throughput, the continued, continual, never-ending *flow* of data. Part of the attraction of such schemas is that they allow one to navigate contemporary life in its raw format.

It is not difficult to realize how important it is to insinuate oneself into the virtual abstract data type of the person: try to work with the glut of e-mail that is a characteristic feature of many lives, without appropriate configuration (file hierarchies, etc.), and life quickly sinks under a welter of unread and unknown obligations. Here hell is not—as Sartre thought—other people but an unstructured inbox. The ongoing exteriorization of memory, initiative, structure, and spontaneity in gadgets, applications, devices, and networks requires and induces this structuring of data, both in the explicit computational sense and in the implicit architectures of everyday life.[6]

Subjectively, an ineffective response to the data structure requirements of data processing can manifest itself as burnout, the desire to downsize, bucolic fantasies about the countryside, a nostalgia for work the way it used to be. More generally it has been proposed as having an affinity with the rise of stress-related illnesses and mental health problems—although there are plenty of layers useful to obfuscate such direct cause.[7] The quasi-imperative need to *abstract oneself*, to become commensurate with sophisticated algorithmic operations on data offers an effectively blameless, perfectly deniable means for upgrading populations toward the production and over-production of information. Implementation details can be, and are, ignored, and the intelligent media operative can only accede to such a foreknowledge of the importance of data structure and the complex set of relations between the different layers of abstraction that these kinds of mediators introduce with prudence.

Work Abstraction Layers

A number of stratagems emphasize the benefits and uses of noise, confusion, and the generative powers of mistakes. The key role of time in establishing any process of veridiction in computation and the generation of possibilities for delay, attenuation, and exhaustion, as well as impossible speed, has also been noted. Other stratagems tend toward the use of facilitation and empowerment, or the encouragement of creativity and the provision of an escape hatch giving access to the ineffable. Entropy, exuberance, and chance are crucial, but the switch between clarity and chaos and back is also essential as a means of articulating the full range of dynamic forms in organization, personality, and process. As such, the stratagematic use of clear demarcations and boundaries is not to be neglected in evil media.

The specificity of a boundary should be understood as both mobilizing and stabilizing behaviors, as both an affordance and an obstacle, and as taking on the role of impassive and objective fact. In either mode, the tendency of a boundary is to draw processes of gaming toward it: the boundary is inviting as something to mobilize in additional layers of derivation, operations that may in turn act as handlers, prompts, and blockages or fuel minor fritterings of energy of no consequence. Such boundaries may be operative in security, in permissions structures, in the activity of a specific molecule in instructing and calming the nervous system, or in establishing the sequence of events and operands at various scales within a program. Boundaries in turn work, like blinkers, to decrease the cognitive load of operations.

A specifically interesting kind of boundary is one known as an abstraction layer. These are boundaries of conception and transmission in the layers of a program that are staged as a means of filtering the quantity or complexity of information required for a particular decision to be made or state to be reached. Historically they derive from differentiating the logical or functional description of a system from its physical form.[8] This process of differentiation continues through the development of operating systems, languages, interfaces, applications, class libraries, and so on, all of which in some way reduce the need to engage with the processes and means by which they are implemented, or provide an appropriate degree of detail for the specific task.

An example, in some operating systems, would be the relation between an icon and the file that it represents. At the layer of the GUI, the file is clicked on to be opened before it can be entered at another layer, that of execution or editing. Such a file may also be operated on by means of algorithms, themselves operating via another layer—articulation in code—which allow them to be parsed or processed without being opened by a user, an apparition that in turn exists at another layer of abstraction.

An abstraction layer might call for a task to be completed, a square to be drawn, or a statement to be composed, without specifying the means required. As such, this kind of abstraction layer suggests a universalizable managerial imperative, in that it does not necessarily matter which process, register, object, instance, or person carries out the work so long as it is done. Abstraction thus implies a measure of operation that is "hands-off."

Abstraction in this sense allows an effective joining of the formal and empirical dimensions of media operation, developing suggestible techniques for the use of high-level formalizations both with and against the grain of other forms of composition. As such, it is easy to see that abstraction layers are themselves inherently medial. They are worked when answering the voice on the other end of the phone (it's a voice rather than the entity it may provide interface to) or become clear through the agency of the microphone that remains clipped to the lapel of the muttering politician when he retreats from an encounter with a specimen of the public into his car to reveal the thoughts he deposits in the ear of an assistant. Abstraction layers imply a relation to other entities, moves of presence or nonpresence, and the interplay of performances of openness, closure, and answerability.

Abstraction layers also perform in ways that integrate well into flexible hierarchies that may be collapsed and expanded as necessary, and in this they rearticulate the technics of contemporary power in a way that again demonstrates the exemplary value of software as an object for understanding its operations. The ostensive art of liberal governance is threefold. First, freedom of interpretation, maneuver, and operation within a bounded set of conditions forms a crucial part of the technics of politics. This can be exemplified in the idea that a bank account is a device that may be used to perform an abstraction on a building: so long as the rent comes in from tenants, or the mortgage is paid, the place is still working regardless of the specific implementation details. Second, the provision of conditions for free development of certain layers involves a dependency on the complex and possibly disturbing activity of other layers and as such, relations between layers requires filtering in order to avoid leakage.[9] Third, in consequence, it is important to register how abstraction layers arise naturally, based on need, such as may occur when an aspect of a system or assemblage migrates across implementations. The more that different functions of a process, society, or software can be integrated by one layer or implementation, the wider it circulates and coalesces. The more generality an abstraction is capable of, the greater its degree of usefulness; and the greater its tenacity in self-stabilization, the more activity is arrayed around it.

Abstraction layers can be inadequately implemented. And here we see the possibility of inverting the condition of the boundary that draws activity to it, repulsing use. The abstraction layer that is more complicated than what it handles, for instance, a telephone answering system that acts as a lengthy, multilayer denial-of-service attack on "clients," is among the class of such systems. Rather more sophisticated and pragmatic is the recognition that abstractions often require extensions and work-arounds. Clean, powerful abstractions that hide their implementation to the point where they achieve what passes for transparency invite such supplements. More regularly, an abstraction layer may leak, bringing aspects of lower layers up the chain of abstractions, defeating its generality. At this point, skill in the stratagematic coupling of formalisms with empirical work becomes readily apparent, and such work-arounds may require the development of bespoke, domain-specific responses.

Multiply Interfaces

To secure their freedoms, members of advanced societies maintain relations with multiple kinds of agencies and entities. By the same token, it is important to encourage, filter, or maintain such dependencies, and to regulate one's own freedom from them. Thus the interface to such systems becomes a matter of crucial importance, one that invites consideration of multiple kinds of handler.

Every life event—such as a change of address, citizenship, residence permit, death, change of job or legal partner—is a moment when people tend to yield large amounts of fresh data for several systems simultaneously. Many will imply negotiating access to a decision-making mechanism or to a resource. All will require handling, sorting, evaluating, and processing. Each triggers the possibility for procedures of inertia, transparent function, delay, or the risk of loss of contact or of records, but they can be used more convincingly and usefully.

The bureaucratic world described by Kafka, in its scenes of slow, abiding menace and confusion, is composed at the speed of paper. The rolling of an eyeball over text, the scratch and glide of an underling's fountain pen as documents are copied in triplicate, clacking typewriters measured in words per minute, the footfall of a courier moving documents from one office to another or that of a messenger delivering a summons, the time to arrive at a decision: the duration is that of waiting, of slow inscription by hand, of the invisibility of a decision-making process as it occurs through inscrutable ritual and the minds of the participants. Contemporary management systems that still involve the human in decision-making processes essentially operate at this speed. Paper-speed management, whether it has been made electronic or not, subsists on systems of forms in which requests and reports are made and reviewed in more or less standardized ways and approved or denied at a speed that at best resembles that of an organization's internal postal system or the time it takes to assemble the interorganizational thought on a decision. In many cases, it matters little that much of this communication is carried out through electronic means; the bottleneck in decision making is the human component.

In *The Social Life of Information*,[10] John Seely Brown and Paul Duguid commend the humane nature of this arrangement, the way that it allows for the filtering of decisions, a slowing down of computational processes that might otherwise be mismatched to their tasks, and its production of an intermediate space in which knowledge may be developed and recouped. This speed is slow enough to remain inhabitable by Bartleby the Scrivener,[11] a clerk who, in Melville's story, sagely withdraws from work through the utter diminution of his needs. Those who are not capable of such frugality will require other ways of working. Among humans, numerous techniques have arisen for this purpose. The activity known as speed-reading, for instance, largely consists of overriding the subliminal vocalizations involved in reading, so as to bypass the throat in favor of direct connections between the eyes and the brain. Many such forms of training involve the production of intuition through the automation of behaviors— whether they are physical responses, as in dance or sport, or calculative, as in trading. Rather than engaging with such forms of training for every kind of decision, it is important to develop standardized, readily intuitive materials and systems for working with ideas, objects, properties, and behaviors. These can usefully be grouped under the term "interface."

The relation between an interface and the ideas, information, and processes it makes available and transforms is a crucial one. People work with arrangements of information, categories, tools, equipment, document systems, as well as other media, and since "an idea or something that has been learned can also be considered as having material-objective force in its consequences and mediations,"[12] the understanding of the material nature of ideas, and their relation to medial activity such as reading, navigation, and calculating, has become commonplace. It may even be possible to achieve useful effects by circulating the idea that ideas have different kinds of objecthood at metaphysical, social, operational, and neurological levels, with characteristics that can be articulated and modified at each of these scales with concomitant degrees of variety or invariance.

The speed of interaction required by a paper-based bureaucracy accords ideas an important scale to work on. This is something to be recognized especially in their circulation as a form of speculative property and in their direct correlation with the status of the object as something alienable, describable, and ownable (with the additional possible qualities of being reproducible and improvable). We have attained only a rudimentary stage in this development, lacking philosophical rigor in fitting all the noumenal forms of ideality into clear relation to the four or five (depending on location) basic states of intellectual property, trademark, patent, copyright, moral right, and trade secret. Considerable questions remain about the ways in which every form of intellection can fully be incorporated into existing IP frameworks to leverage their full capacity for innovation, or whether further forms of property require invention. How states of doubt, curiosity, desire, or melancholy might be rendered compliant with the requirements of the World Intellectual Property Organization or other agencies remains an open field for regulatory invention. The recent enthusiasm for a philosophy of affect, constructing an articulable bridge between affect, sensation, emotion, and other forms of ideas such as reason or linguistic tractability and description, may be a useful early move in this direction.

Before such a system—a model that would at least allow transactions in ideas to gain all the benefits of the market—becomes available, it is important to consider those systems that either do not require an obligatory point of passage through a human bottleneck or tend to reduce their number and variability in favor of a computational assay of the situation. In this case, numerous advantages present themselves, including those of the grounds for a great variety of choice, absolute certitude of decision, and great speed.

In terms of knowledge management, a good example of an interface is the user-generated encyclopedia Wikipedia. This site provides many things, among them a means for ideas to combine. Such combination occurs as aggregation, testing, and propagation. Ideas aggregate because they are gathered in one state and location. They test each other because the site's users subject ideas and their expressions to the norms of the project, and they propagate ideas, since the explanation of one topic naturally requires the explanation of many others. The Wikipedia interface is produced by a range of partially transformable rules, resources, tools, behaviors, and its status as a resource that motivates and facilitates contributions. In the same way that boundaries to medieval cities, the city gates—usually managed by trade guilds—became the foci of the greatest business, of trading, sneaking, adulterating, and rumormongering, the interface, like an abstraction layer, is a point that gathers activity to it. Wikipedia, however, is an interface to itself, its process and its contents. When these relations and the way they are governed by interface are opened to the outside, a joint project can be developed. Users come to the site to feed it as well as to read it, to proliferate disputes and interests. The site operates, like many other things, as a system of relations, of relations between relations, and the means to work with and operate on those relations. As such it requires new forms of sophistry.

To keep the kinds of relations it works with simple, Wikipedia operates by using a small set of rhetorical rules, conventions such as the observation of an imagined and codified neutral point of view, the prohibition of interpretation and original research, and a number of procedural conventions known mainly to committed volunteers.[13] For many organizations, quality and service can be highly problematic "externalities."[14] The advantage of peer production methods such as those developed by Wikipedia is that they specifically work to internalize such externalities by expanding the question of quality and service out to users. The quality of the material available through the site remains at a roughly consistent level because of the thousands of acts of addition and normalization carried out on it every day. This approach, primarily effective at the level of small-scale incremental improvements or other changes, is characterized by Eric Raymond's declaration that in open-source software, "Many eyeballs make all bugs shallow."[15] Irrespective of the acuity of this law, these thousands of acts of daily normalization can effectively be compared to those carried out by entering data into databases, with the exception that the norms of Wikipedia are, as well as consisting of data, themselves also relational: they make references, definitions, descriptions, inclusions, exclusions, quantifications, and so on.

We can compare this approach to that of a standard utility company, the provider of water, network, banking, pensions, or electricity. The interface here is designed to operate at the lowest functional level of quality, with staff operating to scripts presented to them on-screen by "wizards" and according to strict levels of permission to minimize the time demands on more highly paid decision makers or advisers.[16] Once the marginal benefit of outsourcing transaction costs in coordination and stress to users via the use of human-mediated telephone interfaces becomes vanishingly small, what we are left with is the opportunity for some novel forms of manipulation. Such forms are not those of the market, with its often overly simple means of apportioning attention via monetary value, or those of the degradation of interaction via interfaces that de-skill and disempower the operatives of human voice interfaces to transaction systems. These potentially highly fruitful operations work precisely on the more abstract, but utterly concrete, level of relations.

One move in this direction has been to remove layers of intermediation between users and services that they can be encouraged to collaborate on to deliver, as a way of sharing the costs of change, such as when an operating system is shipped without adequate functionality, for example.[17] The relations between digital objects, users, networks, and processes are inhibited by such systems and motivate forms of figuring out and working round when they occur.

Another move that emphasizes the shift to relations but concentrates them in one domain is the proliferation of the relational database. Here every entity is, in part, its own interface as well as its own "thing" and is mobilized and made useful by its composition within systems of relations. The relational database, in its original incarnation in the work of Edgar Codd, was also a way of shifting power in the handling of data from the program, or the writer of programs, to the user of data.[18]

It is worth noting in this account of relationality, and its gauging, filtering, and production through interfaces, that in his discussion of fortune or luck, Machiavelli advises that no single approach can be adopted at all times. A particular stratagem may "flourish one day and come to grief the next."[19] The prosperity of stratagems is ephemeral, dependent on local, timely, conditions. Insofar as is possible, these must be made, and the path to doing so is through the creation, development, and manipulation of relations.

As with fortune's effect on operators, so too with relations. Thousands of software projects and Web sites remain as only the husks of imagined participation: some because they are useless, others because their users have yet to be invented, still others because of the capricious operations of fortune. Simply creating a toolbox is not enough.

Let Datasets Advance

In the "bureaucracy of statistics," few objects are grayer than the dataset. Soliciting punctiliousness through the technical prerequisites of the precise specification of rules, definitions, and data types and formats, the humble dataset is an unlikely candidate for consideration as a critical component in the shifting constellations of power relations in modern society. However, the standardized specification of elements of information considered pertinent for describing anything from an insurance claim to the treatment of a metastasized tumor, the internal state of a human body in locomotion to the behavioral traits of potentially criminal activity, packaged in a recognized, machine-readable format ("dataset" was once an IBM term for a file),[20] can become an important strategic agent in its own right, playing a role that more often than not goes unnoticed in the many gray components of institutions, knowledges, and technologies.

Datasets are in widespread use as the raw material of statistical analysis, wherein a range of standard techniques used in statistics to describe patterns of distribution of data, and the considerably more sophisticated techniques of data mining, are applied to the values that make up such datasets. For its nominal addressee (the statistician, the data miner, the computer scientist), the dataset is but a representation (before analysis, a somewhat opaque one) of some state of affairs or other, cast in the language of discrete, continuous, and binary attributes (alive = 1, dead = 0). As such, the dataset provides a technical extension and refinement of the bureaucracy that plays such an important part in exercising surveillance and control over populations. Ian Hacking has suggested that as a historically significant element in the development of contemporary forms of governance, the bureaucracy of statistics provides a way of "determining classifications in which people must think of themselves and of the actions that are open to them."[21]

It is not so much the possibilities of statistical analysis to adduce a representation of the self that interests us here (even if doubts regarding the purchase that such analysis offers for gaining scientific knowledge are not irrelevant). Of greater interest is the way that possibilities for control and manipulation shift when one starts to consider the role that the dataset might have as an active medium in its own right, and more specifically in the way that it determines the classifications by which *machines must think humans* and determine the actions that are open to them. As long as data move at similar speeds to discourse as conveyed through paper-based message systems (an archive, in Foucauldian terms), we are correct to explore the efficacy of the kind of statistical knowledge enveloped in datasets as a component part of discursive strategies. But with the growth of forms of machine readability, under which data in various forms become a significant parameter in programmable operations, something of a shift occurs.[22] Under such circumstances, machine classification—in conjunction with the bureaucratic labor of more humanly devised taxonomies—starts to operate in quite decisive forms of "action on action."

From the quantitative viewpoint of media hardware, as with other aspects of the devices available for use in strategies of contemporary governance, the significant cheapening of computer memory and the increasing processor speeds and bandwidth of Internet traffic conjoin with database systems and powerfully flexible forms of markup language (the various dialects of XML in particular) to make the collecting and processing of information, in forms readily amenable to statistical analysis and computational processing, a viable option for a great many kinds of activity. However, from a qualitative point of view, the incremental, continuous nature of these shifts in processing power, bandwidth, and speed can obscure the new layers of connection and configuration that become possible.

Consider, for example, the difference between a routine checkup at your local doctor's office and the continuous monitoring of the same physiological data using biosensors. In the case of the office visit, every six months the doctor measures your heart rate, blood pressure, and so on. The doctor asks if are you getting much exercise, how well you are sleeping, and other general questions about your state of health. In the second case, connected to a device to collect signals from sensors attached to your body, a transmitter (perhaps your phone) aggregates and packages those data, serializes the information and sends it to a centralized repository. No doctor, but the possibility of real-time data processing that evaluates your state of well-being—possibly making some judgments on your behalf, particularly if the kinds of activities you engage in are monitored, too—and then makes the data available to insurers, your employer, your partner, perhaps commercial sponsors of the system who provide it in return for certain services or levels of access.

When data gathering and processing in the absence of human mediators are accomplished in this way (without the possibility that humans offer for unforeseen "follow-up" questions) and clinical judgment can be made by machine as part of a decision support mechanism (invalidate that insurance policy) or directly implemented as machinic decision (immobilize the car), when the bureaucracy of statistics migrates into practices, machines, and devices across the social, the dataset is susceptible to becoming an agency that no longer merely molds citizens but rather spins not their words but their activities continuously by changing the shape of the environment in which they act, innocuously, felicitously, abruptly. Such is the discretion of machines.

A stratagematic reading of the Internet of things and the growth of ubiquitous computing with which it is associated thus links the humble dataset directly to the parametric control of machines: in this context, the refrigerator that stores a list of regular foodstuffs, their cost, shelf life, nutritional information, and so on. It will possibly provide helpful advice about when to go to the supermarket (better still, when to place an order, or perhaps streaming loyalty rewards to its manufacturer when presets are used) and exemplifies the great virtues of a precise appreciation of the relevant variables of everyday action and the preemptive possibilities that well-crafted processing of datasets provide. Of course, the seamless, fluid integration of data-driven machinery into everyday life is something of a fable. It has, for its flip side, unanswered questions about the devising of appropriate kinds of formal ontologies (the term adopted to characterize the markup languages that will allow machines to communicate with each other and with users in this new world), the coordination of standards and agreements over protocols.

More specifically, as an object itself, which must be defined, shaped, and deployed, as an actor with the capacity to mediate in an ensemble of human and nonhuman processes, the dataset raises the possibility of new dissymmetries, new divergences, new gaps and fault lines of which it is itself an agent: just defining a dataset is a collective task in its own right, knowledge by committee. The technocratic dream of seamless flow, in which objects are exhaustively specified by the ends to which they are devoted, ignores the new opportunities for experimentation, deviance, and improvisation such objects provide. We have no need to go as far as futuristic extrapolations to appreciate the room for maneuver that too coarse a specification of relevant variables provides, for example. At the scale of the organization, "key performance indicators" offer the crafty management team, or canny individuals happy to play with a new system of appearances, plenty of scope to shape themselves as successful, high performing, or simply honest and dutiful, and here the dataset combines usefully with the opportunities of audit. At the more labile scale of the smart device or intelligent machine, the slips and cracks that emerge when a gadget shapes or restricts one's scope for action in unexpected ways call for an attentiveness to configuration and a perception attuned to the glitches and idiosyncrasies of machine-coded action. Operating transversally across different scales of reality, the generative activity of the dataset is never completely assured in its outcomes, producing new forms of uncertainty and indeterminacy even as it accomplishes its allotted tasks of automation and control.

Mine Data for Probabilities

The loose ensemble of techniques and technologies concerned with processes of knowledge engineering and management has received a huge adrenalin shot in recent years with the development of increasingly sophisticated practices of the analysis of statistical information or unstructured data usually considered under the rubric of *data mining*. The ease with which information can be collected under conditions of digital communication, and the decrease in cost of storing or warehousing it in large quantities, makes it possible to amass large datasets on which sophisticated forms of statistical inference can be performed, making a range of forms of multivariate statistical methods (such as k-means clustering, artificial neural networks, principal components analysis), as well as other techniques for processing and analyzing more than one data variable at a time, into a potentially invaluable set of tools in developing refined forms of manipulation and influence.

What is one to do with all the apparently meaningless information that years of sales into the high street and mall offer? How can you better turn terabytes of data about the online browsing habits of your customers to your advantage? And what about the masses of information about the locations, durations, and destinations of a population's mobile telephone calls or their journeys around a capital city's public transport network? Notwithstanding the civilian concern with snooping, electronic eavesdropping, and personal privacy, the search for and machine recognition of *patterns* in large ensembles of data or the extrapolative prediction of trends allow for a more informed shaping of the relationship between production (of decisions, information, commands, goods) and consumption (or reception, execution, or comprehension) in ways that were difficult to imagine even a decade ago or could perhaps only have been imagined as variants of the uncanny predictive capacities of missile guidance systems.

If the dataset offers a prescriptive model of the relevant data variables to collect to produce a representation of a particular state of affairs (presuming to a large extent that one knows, in advance, what the pertinent variables are for developing a viable representation), this is not necessarily the case in a data warehouse where vast quantities of information may have been amassed as a by-product of the routine accounting of business operations. Does a correlation exist between the kind of cheese somebody purchases at the supermarket and a preference for oven cleaner or political news? Am I more likely to go to the meat counter if I shop late on a Thursday night or first thing on a Saturday morning, and what, at either time, can be linked to such a purchase? The seduction of data mining is that of finding exploitable patterns in vast quantities of data, modeling probabilities, predicting trends, anticipating next moves, extracting "truth from trash."[23]

Civil libertarians only get half the story right in their well-meant concern with the vast extension in scope of data gathering and mining. From some points of view, the growing volume of personal data available does indeed look likely to threaten a totalitarian encroachment on basic human rights. But it should also be considered as an important element in optimizing the functioning of market processes. In this respect, consideration of data mining would lead to an exploration of the rather less well-understood use of patterns and pattern recognition as an element in the process of the modeling and production of subjectivity, as a component in the selection and extraction of new forms of the supply of subjectivity for the demand of markets.[24] It is far easier to facilitate, rather than directly control, people if they can be modeled in acceptable ways. By examining patterns of behavior, purchasing decisions, affiliation networks, and so on (or so the theory goes), it becomes possible to create a better fit between what consumers want (consumers of goods and services, law and order, policy decisions, political creeds) and what producers can and will supply. In part this represents what some political economists think of as the "linguistic" or "communicational" turn in the economy today, the hyper-rapid production of goods and services on a just-in-time basis.[25] From this point of view, being able to accurately predict future customer preferences from past preferences allows vendors to avoid problems such as the ruinous buildup of stocks of things that people won't want. Information produced as a by-product of everyday activities, or solicited through the development of low-budget, lo-fi apps for social media addicts, presents a shift in the rationalization of market activity—watching an advertisement on television is a bit hit and miss for the targeted leisure-time work of the consumer,[26] since one can always turn off or turn over if one isn't turned on. Yielding up information as grist to the mill of the correlation machine, by contrast, works all the better when it doesn't require any additional extra effort or special attentiveness.

The use of myriad forms of data in this way for data-mining purposes represents, among other things, a vast process of the *semioticization* of behavior, a recasting of jittery point-and-click navigation during a work break or the idle messing around with half-baked applications on a social media site as the expression of a set of consumer preferences. For the data miner, that target is always already a consumer, always already being mapped as if sharing a belief in the legitimacy of a political system, and so on. Recast in this way, extracted or abstracted from the particular sets of relations that perhaps made them an act of spite (the teenage daughter buying songs with the father's credit card), revenge or deception (logging on under your partner's name to surf some particularly nefarious porn sites), boredom (browsing on a phone under the table during a sales presentation), or other kinds, correlations can then be established with a more or less sophisticated set of basic demographic information to provide a picture of the user's interests. This set of correlations—the residue of desires, hopes, fears, and the mundane tasks and activities of everyday life—can then be used to optimize decision making.

As a statistical process, the aim here is not so much to find causes as to make correlations, statistical correspondences, to model probabilities the better to shape purchasing decisions, opinions, beliefs, and so on, to ensure that what people want coincides with what is on offer.[27]

Data mining for probabilities obviously benefits from the cultural prestige attached in the West to matters hi-tech and from the fuzzy boundaries between science and the technology it draws on. But there are subtle differences in the way that algorithms from computing and cognitive science are used when they shift out of the research laboratories of universities and into the back rooms of corporations, banks, insurance companies, and agencies of the state. The obscurity of such differences and the equivocations they make possible can be turned to one's favor, giving a nuance of scientific value to otherwise remarkably conservative practices.

The difference between using specific kinds of pattern recognition algorithms for scientific purposes (as in, say, the use of neural networks to try to understand how evolutionarily simple forms of intelligence emerge) and the use of the same to predict the consumption preferences of people in specific demographic groupings, or stock market prices, might appear slight. But when one experiments with a neural network, genetic algorithm, or a random Boolean network to understand the possibilities of the convergence on a solution, the "optimization" that the algorithms demonstrate in finding solutions to a problem is an optimization within a notional model of a biological system whose relation to reality is not necessarily evident. For example, the use of such models to explore the operations of the immune system generates interesting avenues for further research, not definitive answers to questions. But when modeling with such algorithms to find mathematically optimized solutions to problems forms part of a model that guides economic or strategic decisions, the ground has shifted. The solution functions not to generate *more* questions but to stop questions being asked, to close the deal, to provide a form of objective evidence for a decision to take. The way in which the rhetoric and technics of scientific objectivity operate here is valuable, giving stability to markets that operate in fragile conditions, foreclosing any probing that might shake the confidence such markets are generally presumed to require. Scientific merits aside, the take-up of David Li's "Gaussian copula" to assess collateralized debt obligations was a marvelous tool to help to discredit the mere common sense that says what goes up must come down.[28]

Considered from a stratagematic point of view, the key to the functioning of data mining is revealed in the delicate repurposing of algorithms as they move out of the laboratory and into the real world. Everything is already understood, predefined; one is always already a consumer; what one wants is only a function, a combinatorial variant of what is already on offer, the corporation deciding in advance the reality within which the consumer will then exercise his or her sovereignty. Subjects here are not produced through the process known as "interpellation" or other more or less crude representations; instead the ideological messages contained in interactive media are a smoke screen for the indirect shaping of the self through production decisions, investment shifts, campaign funding allocations, repurposing of Web sites, the generation of new business models: operative environmental constraints that run through subjective forms.

The idea that today's economy is a knowledge economy gets a lot of play, but one could just as easily argue that economically speaking, ignorance is really the most important value to trade on. Only going as far as you are enabled by the assumptions that you want to confirm—or as far as the demand for stability plausibly allows—is a way to ensure that giving the public what it wants correlates, more or less, with what you want to give it. Finding out more about your subjects than what you need to base your decisions on is a risky, potentially distracting affair, the likely source of niggling ethical anxieties. So employing methods that demonstrate that you actually need to ask new, more complicated questions about the forces you want to capture is likely to be problematic—and a poor sales pitch to boot.

Leak Early, Leak Often

We have countless models of the kinds of narratives available to us when telling tales, templates such as the unlikely hero, unrequitable love, the averted disaster. While narratives have been studied and cataloged for millennia, the means by which stories become known have not benefited from quite as much attention. We have no general taxonomy of the leak. It is, however, one of the crucial means for the dissemination of every kind of narrative, and from straightforward falsehood to near truth, the style with which it is delivered requires meticulous thought. But we are concerned here not with the right moment to use such a maneuver but with the kinds of ways in which leaks arise and render themselves amenable.

If the interpretation of ambiguity in the sifting of documents, behaviors, and clues provides a mode for operations that occur within a world of shifting, clotting, and liquefying films of chiaroscuro, the shuffling of translucent layers that prompt the opportunity for a reskilled literary workforce to go to town on the operations of real-politik, obversely a certain bluntness inheres in the dumping of things to be interpreted from one domain into another. The leak is the emission liberated from its proper place by an act of omission, or neglect of right containment. As such, it tells something of the truth and in doing so provides a certain kind of reliability.

The following is offered not as an exhaustive set of all leaks but more as a rough diagram to those that may be encountered in an average day in the office. Needless to say, one kind may effectively be used to mask another, or a concatenation of leaks may be profitably effected.

One form of leak often used in government and other areas such as game design or film production occurs in advance to be able to be denied as a draft. A specimen such as a document describing a potential policy is made available so as to be quickly briefed against. Just as a technical prototype may surface to mobilize advance user feedback, the alpha version of anything is always a form of decoy.

Such a leak can usefully be understood to mobilize and disable the power of networked critical reception, in that what emerges as the actual of the document has already been filtered and managed in the leak stage, that of preappearance or tactical virtuality. Thus rather than preemption being a means by which the present captures the future, the future, that of a splendid product, mobilizes the present for its purposes.

Related forms that deal with the revealing and handling of materials before they can actually said to have occurred include the offer of exclusive, off-the-record information briefed in advance to manipulate, dampen, or heighten its reception and to entrain its recipients. Obversely, one may encounter the nonembargoed publication, or information released in a form that flattens its content or buries itself in a larger document set or system of encoding.

Accident is often the most propitious form of leak. A slip of the tongue, a drunken gambit, or an unwitting cc are the reliable tools of the practitioner with time, but such a leak may also take the form of a lost briefcase, document, or memory device. Such a leak can be intentional or accidental, and in many cases it hardly matters which, since the condition of the possibility of a leak must be understood to be designed into a system. The doctrine of network-centric warfare, for instance, in its assumption that all members of the services are fully incorporated into a secure mind-set, pushes information out to the minions at the periphery of the organization, ensuring permeability. Over time we may see that an intentional leak is rather more than likely to contain information at variance with the understanding of leaked material to be naturally transparent and truthful. Agents may be turned, documents may become labyrinths, accidents may be had by another source.

But a related kind of leak is not the accident but the elimination, the trash that takes itself out: insufficiently harsh deletions; waste dumps; secondhand trades in magnetic memory; tingles running through discarded hard drives; papers, due to be shredded or burned that make it as far as the dump and the freedom formed by decay or by a pair of sharp eyes forming a gateway to the black market.

A particularly risky (but often judicious) form of leak is generated by a whistle-blower motivated by the possibility of exposing an injustice. The degree of automation that may be brought to bear on such an operation is disputable, but as long as a steady, albeit attenuated, number of people remain enthused with ideas about a better world or correct modes of operation, certain aspects of the use of this kind of leak can be guaranteed.

It is not possible to assume that by the time people reach a point where they are able to safely handle difficult material, they are inured to its implications. A voluntary leak by a principled operative committed to transparency may also require certain kinds of theater to find itself adequately obscured. Equally, ensuring that normal operations may—when useful—be leaked means that the interplay between what appears as an injustice, and what does not, may usefully be manipulated. It is always useful to be accidentally exposed as doing what is right, but in a modest, accomplished manner. In this way, the sheer humbleness of pious behavior can be released to the surface; one thinks here of princesses whose secret visits to tend to the needy are preceded by discreet phone calls to the vultures with large lenses.

The nonleak of staged exclusivity is the stock in trade of celebrity gossip, its lower-budget versions being standard journalism or the nods and winks of the workplace. In this case still, the leak finds its form: mumbles from a trusted informant; remarks traded for favors; transfers back to the paid insider; breaches of a walled garden, not through the masonry, but in the plants. Here leaks have a relation to differentials of pressure or to suction, to alimentation, rubbings, or slipperiness. The greasing of palms, the mobilization of suckers, zones of asymmetric titillation, righteousness and fear, coupling furiously with leak anxiety, an anxiety always rendering itself immobile through the imaginary of perfect security. This phantasm, of security as a state of perfection moves across to a further variant: unlawfully obtained data laundered through a third party. The unlawful here means simply the unrighteous rather than the illegal, direct trespass, the induction of leaks by milking machines, tapping phones, accessing directories, recording keystrokes, watching for patterns, locations, transgressions, some breach of hygiene, haunting the voicemail of the dead.

All these kinds of leaks are doubled by the widespread practice of ostensive leaking. A document reannounces something that has already been decided but may have lost momentum or needs reviving to show that some kind of initiative, any kind of initiative, is occurring. Such material stands in a close relation to the economy of the production of policies in some organizations in which management exudes documents, just as thought is secreted by its appropriate organ. Like the dismal leak in its doldrums, a press release from no one to nothing, it is ignored, buried, layered into other statements to the point where it is not simply superfluous but never happened.

The leak operates by means of establishing relations between different registers of the inside and the outside, between those who already know, those who might possibly know if they had the time, those who should have been told, the scandalized, doomed, or grateful recipient of truth, and those who do not need to know or would rather not, among others. Thus the particular style of the leak establishes resonances between all these figures, each of whom may adopt one or more of the available positions according to the nature of the leak and their possible operations on and through it. Naturally the position of the knower is one also held by various forms of storage device, such as archives, which hold the leak until a moment when it may become historically appropriate to activate it in certain conjunctions. The existence of the leak as a mode of storage brings it into relation with the measure of time. That a leak is initiated does not mean that it actually happens, or that it has been received by an apparatus capable of distinguishing it from any other noise. The leak can be understood as a speech act with an unwilling speaker, but it can also remain simply as a gray anticipation, a document waiting nowhere for the eyes of no one, held in abeyance by a forensic disinterest. Such a leak is like every other document, an anonymous squirt into the ocean, but one that dreams of becoming the center of a whirlpool.

The leak, then, is an attempt to capture and mobilize the dynamics of unintended consequences, to enter into the domain of the accident, the double agent, confusion, and to render it fruitful. The leak, however, is never simply bivalent. For some, everything cries out for it, trying, if only by dint of time, to edge its way past the demon of the chamber of equivalence in which it is trapped, hungry for a connection, the accident of knowledge, for that or the chance to turn to dust, unnoticed and indifferent.

Technicalities

Workflow

One of the many different "systemic" ways of addressing the shape of practices in the world of production, workflow recommends itself to a study of evil media because of the peculiar place that the ensemble of tools, techniques, and technologies that make it up occupy in the creation of the abstract spaces of the contemporary economy.

Defined as the "automation of a business process, in whole or part, during which documents, information or tasks are passed from one participant to another for action, according to a set of procedural rules,"[1] workflow has the requisite aura of scientificity about it. However, once this aura is put aside and its status as a set of techniques is restored, workflow appears as a means of extracting control from the coordination and cooperation required to undertake particular forms of work, to distribute the information needed to perform particular acts of work, to make decisions about the allocation of resources, and so on. Disjoining work in this way from the irritating initiatives that people take when trying to execute complex tasks or the misplaced ideas that they might form if they came across the wrong piece of information in the workplace is what, precisely, allows work to "flow."

Commenting on the benefits of globalization, Thomas L. Friedman has argued that workflow software is one of the ten causes of what he calls the flattening of the world. A "quiet revolution that no-one knew was happening,"[2] in Friedman's account, workflow effectively permits the extension of production into a global, and hence twenty-four-hours-a-day, seven-days-a-week, set of processes. In the virtual factory, everything from making animated movies to booking a dentist's appointment to applying for a mortgage becomes fluid, malleable, and geographically nonspecific work, directable or divertible at will. In the global imaginary, workflow is endowed with a magical capacity with far-reaching effects, an enchanting power that any strategist should want to understand in its own right.

As with many of the other forms of media technics we are cataloging here, workflow is often understood in terms of a strictly formal nomenclature, and more specifically—following the contemporary imperative to *design* the social relations into which people are inserted—as a set of *patterns*. Experts in the workflow community typically categorize general and recurring patterns of work activity in terms of how these patterns bear on *control* over the work process, the distribution and availability of *data*, the specification and allocation of human and nonhuman *resources* and the handling of *exceptions*. We will examine some concrete examples of these patterns in due course. For the moment, it should be noted that as much as workflow forms a set of techniques for modeling work, it also forms an unparalleled tool for understanding the implementation of structures of domination and control within the workplace, a quasi-scientific notation for the distribution and redistribution of cognition and agency.

While general and recurring patterns of working activity may well be annotated using a variety of formalisms, workflow appears strangely refractory to unequivocal definition. Indeed, the seemingly uncontrollable extension of the term in contemporary accounts might suggest that as a result of the rapid diffusion of new media technologies throughout the pores of society, work has managed to seep into almost everything we do. When Friedman discusses it, workflow is incarnated in everything from the personal computer, the protocols used to define the exchange of information in e-mail (SMTP), or the operations of browsers (HTTP requests) through to more expansive notational standards such as XML, SOAP (Simple Object Access Protocol, used to exchange "structured" information over the Internet), and even the AJAX coding that Web designers use to make interactions with Web pages less bureaucratic. And this is before one even begins to consider dedicated workware (Lotus Notes for example) or the proprietary packages that the large corporations of NASDAQ offer to help the intelligent consultant fluidify all too solid forms of working practice. There are also dedicated modeling tools (UML activity diagrams, for example) and even languages for workflow—the Web Services Business Process Execution Language (expressing an unusual level of agreement and cooperation between normally competitive tech corporations),[3] and YAWL (Yet Another Workflow Language, the open-source alternative).

While this displacement away from the mundane activity of producing "digital content" (which, in Friedman's libidinally inflected turn of phrase, we now "shoot" around the office)[4] occludes the relations of force that workflow expresses, as well as the more material forms of working activity, giving the impression that work has become a sort of spontaneous emission of an indeterminate flow,[5] it highlights a significant point: the routinization of work within a formalized set of digital patterns depends on a whole weft of technologies, techniques, protocols, sets of know-how, and practices. For work activity to be redistributed as a global set of flows, myriad other media forms are also necessary: simple sketches in a notebook; the more complex charts of process mapping; the formalized codifications of modeling tools and languages already noted; the computer science abstractions of Petri nets or event-driven process chains. If workflow is really abstract, that is, an abstraction that has a material effectiveness and is embodied in actual practices,[6] its abstraction results from the coordinated activities of a new set of agents, allies in the ongoing sanitization and routinization of production. However, as will become apparent, it is best not to make too obvious the dependence of command-and-control structures on these other agents, as it tends to spoil the illusion of work as an eternal flow of life itself.

The image of a flow—from Newton's method of fluxions, to the chemist's evaluation of rates of change in catalytic processes, to Molly Bloom's mental blurt, to Wilhelm Reich's streaming libido—provides the shield of a warm feeling, somatic memories of amniotic fluid, nocturnal emissions, and peaceful states of creativity. But no flow happens without breaks producing the intervals between which a flow is engendered: far from a flat surface, the world must be possessed of more and more differences in gradients for anything to flow at all. A flat surface produces stagnation.

Real flow-producing differences in gradient are helpfully absent from the formalized patterns of activity modeled by workflow software. Understood as both a real process (modeling a workflow is itself a coordinated, cooperative activity) and a real product (a modeled workflow is incarnated in actual working situations), a workflow is nevertheless a formalized idealization and abstraction from real activity. From the point of view of the exercise of command and control, this dual quality is both a workflow's greatest strength and its greatest weakness. It is its strength because figuring work as formal sequences of activity allows many aspects of rationalized, routinized work to be safely ignored, moved off the books, rendered irrelevant as a datum. For instance, in a world where corporations rely heavily on brand, anything that prevents the communicator or visionary in your operation from staying "on message" is a potentially disadvantageous distraction. It is not helpful (the technicians themselves would admit this) to know about alienation in the workplace,[7] whether that be due to scripted communication from call centers in India, hived-off, mass-produced computer code in Russia, burger flipping in a fast-food joint, or frothing the milk in a coffee shop. It is likely that in the process of patiently fabricating spontaneous workflows, sensitive souls may have qualms about outsourcing and de-skilling: it is better to be able to model a purely formal work design pattern than to have to draw attention to the informal details that might permit a practice to be designated in its concrete specifics.

Examples of the benefits of this formal nomenclature are not difficult to find. In the streamlined activities of paramedics, for example, the simultaneous activities of "checking for pulse" and "checking for insurance" on an emergency call form a *parallel split*. Repeated calls from a team leader to come back from lunch early become a *persistent trigger*. A process that depends on several workers to accomplish effectively because a whole series of checks is required before the process can kick off again becomes a *blocking discriminator*. A *structured synchronizing merge* occurs in the benefits office when a clerical officer calls the police and cancels a benefit at the same time.[8]

Coordinating different aspects of workflow can often become difficult with a semantically neutral terminology of this sort. Control-flow operations and data-flow operations often have to be combined, for example. Consider the difficulties that arise when a control-flow sequence "turn down loan application" is combined with an incorrect data-flow data visibility distribution, resulting in a loan applicant learning that ethnicity *is* a factor in the decision-making process.

The remediation of work in these abstract terms has other advantages. Refigured as abstractable business processes, work is more readily tractable to configuration and control within digitally enhanced forms of "supply chain management." Standardized, decontextualized, ideally simplified, and divested of any of the specificities that would tie it to a geographic locale, work that flows requires less skill to accomplish and becomes highly mobile. An extensive body of research on the sociology of work permits us to understand some of what is entailed in these processes that are sometimes discussed in terms of the notion of de-skilling,[9] and they allow us to understand better why Friedman was correct to consider workflow in the broader, less technically precise sense, not as formalism but as ensemble of technologies: these technologies are themselves the coded stock of knowledge of a range of clerical and communicational activities.[10] We are not saying that the personal computer or hypertext transfer protocol is the product of the knowledge transduced from clerks to machines. We are suggesting that without the processes of what might be called "knowledge transfer," as analyzed by Harry Braverman, much of what now counts in the production and configuration of workflow would be unthinkable. However, these are issues to be considered elsewhere.

In addition to the strategically advantageous uses of workflow, it is important also to look at some of its disadvantages. In the global imaginary, workflow presents the fantastic image of work as a kind of "seamless" communication.[11] What precisely is meant by this term is not always clear, although the dictionary definition of "seamless" as lacking any obvious or apparent joins suggests that it has something of the conjurer's trick about it. The perceptibility of a seam, an edge, or a join might risk making apparent something that should not be. At the least, an asperity, a snag, a fault in the smooth surfaces along which globalized work is designed, risks causing an eddy, a momentary hesitation, a thought, in the automated flow of activity.

The fantastic virtue of workflow formalism as an ensemble of patterns for generic and recurrent activity, as we have seen already, is that it is precisely that: generic, perfectly ignorant of the specificities of any activity. In a sense, then, workflow formalism communicates directly with the economic conception of labor as abstract quantity cashed out in specific roles designating a position in the production process (rather than specific qualities inhering in individuals). To this abstract quantity corresponds a purely formal proposition in an axiomatic system, a formal proposition that may or may not in turn correspond to the strategic allocation of resources within one or many workflow patterns.

The problem is that any (conceptually) global process or putatively universal concept can only be actualized locally, in a specific situation, and doing so means having to negotiate "implementation details." And the negotiation of implementation details means learning how to handle flows that are not so readily or obviously finalized as productive work and hence can leak from or cause blockages: counterflows, hemorrhages, coagulations, subterranean streams, stickiness. Generically, work is designed to flow with as little thought for execution of the task as possible: if a worker *thinks* about the script she follows in the call center, she won't be able to read her lines. In a sense, a set of processes that has been formalized in terms of a series of generally recurrent activities is incapable of understanding how antagonism toward it might arise.

Alienation, we can imagine, is reasonably well understood: dehumanizing work leads to a higher turnover of staff, but that can be strategically functional and can safely be ignored, because as long as workers feel alienated, you can be sure that they still have a real investment in the work process as such (historically, alienation is figured as the alienation of a subject from his or her essence). Antagonism, by contrast, creeps up from inside, accumulates invisibly, never quite localizable because each locus and each activity in the system is generic, perfectly ignorant of singularity.

Of particular interest, then, are the ways in which workflow seeks to handle *exceptions*. An exception might loosely be defined as an "undesirable event" that occurs during the execution of the workflow process. The precise real status of an exception is rarely of interest in the modeling of generic processes; they are, after all, undesirable. The intrinsic nature of an event (why did this triple-A-rated subprime mortgage pool fail) is not considered on its own terms; indeed, it cannot be (such singular occurrences are too fine grained to be considered in their specifics). As with the process of exception handling in more obviously computational processes (such as software design), the point is to allow the primary process to continue running and to minimize recovery cost. Modelers typically have to classify exceptions in one way or another to make them tractable to handling in a generic system. One set of researchers distinguishes five types of exception: *work item failure* (the computer crashed, the night goggles failed), *deadline expiry* (the date this processed meat should not be used after), *resource unavailability* (before the process starts: I couldn't make it to work today; during process execution: my flu symptoms made working impossible), *external trigger* (the legal freezing of someone's assets puts account payments on hold), *constraint violation* (a subcontractor turns out not to meet the terms of employment required by the contracting corporation, e.g., the subcontractor was undisguisedly employing child labor).

However, the literature indicates clearly that exception handling is poorly understood, more often than not requiring a modeler's intuitions about how a process might go wrong, rather than a more solid grounding in "scientific" fact. Workflow is, as commentators have pointed out, an *idealization* of real-world activity, of work.[12] In practice, when something goes wrong at work, which the system cannot anticipate, forms of coordination and cooperation that were deemed irrelevant to the execution of work come into play. However, with the globalizing extension of workflow to *everything*, so that it has no outside, the fatal flaw is that undesirable events will provoke rather more extensive kinds of collapse.

Express Regularly, But Not Too Regularly

A regular expression is a formal notation for a pattern of symbols combined in a string.[13] The term often arises in linguistics, but restated in terms of finite-state machines, the regular expression becomes a device for parsing strings of symbols (as input) and determining a match—or not (as output, or terminal state.)[14] Regular expressions are modeled in a range of programming languages and technologies and are an important component of software engineering for digital media, where their use in pattern matching is of enormous value for the processing of language. Developed from tools designed to expedite the practice of working with a command-line interface, the practical use of regular-expression technologies is now associated with the logistical issue of dealing with large amounts of *unstructured* text: that of searching for and replacing words in documents, for example, or searching for and performing operations on large numbers of files within a directory. Regular-expression technology forms a significant, although usually discrete, element of core Internet technologies: browsers, document readers, packet sniffers, and so on. The presence of regular-expression notation in the RFC documents by which Internet computing standards are generated and disseminated also demonstrates the structuring and coordinating role the regular expression has beyond its implementation in specific technologies.[15]

The *regularization* of expression, by contrast, is a broader tendency evident in practices of the organization of people and things *as* and *for* data in computational culture, following the general principle that structured data are more tractable to processing than unstructured data.[16] Numerous more or less formal means for the regularization of expression, for producing the *incipience* of tractable and abstractable, reproducible structure, are available: the formal, tabular principles organizing the layout of Web sites in HTML, the displacement of linguistic commonplaces in the production of communication by the use of forms,[17] or more broadly the structured, sequenced scripting of communication (call centers, NLP, "clean language," etc.).[18] In this sense, regularizing expression, which might be considered an aspect of the disciplinary operations of formalism,[19] offers a way of translating preexisting social relations and actions, such as "thumbs up," "like," "friend," "select," into the syntax of machines and inventing new ones bearing the force of that syntax, presenting the possibility of managing communication through uniform, finite, and preferably automatic steps. In turn, the image of free forms of cognition such as intuition are also brought into combination with such measures, suggesting the plausibility of redescribing intuition as a kind of pattern matching by psychologists who rely on the predominance of regularized expression in organized communication practices.[20]

While a regular expression is a precisely specifiable pattern, regularizing expression is the specification that there *be* pattern, that there be an ongoing production of redundancy.[21] The two are inseparable, in the prosaic sense that there can be no patterns to *match* without there being *patterns* to match. It is a standard dictum for programmers and sophists alike to know who you are addressing: for the programmer, the more one knows about the "data" to be given to a machine, the better. The obvious next step is to ensure that machines get data in exactly the form that they want. So, less prosaically, regularized expression points to the fact that for machines to address humans and things in *their* languages, humans and things must address machines in *their* languages. This need not always result simply in the lock-in of formalisms discussed earlier. One possible and often fortuitous result of this ambiguous situation is that a zone of indiscernibility (and hence undecidability) is created, where one doesn't quite know who is speaking whose language. One is transformed into the other in a kind of double-crossing of language. Obscure though it may be, this uncertain zone creates possibilities of interference—in both the technical and folk senses of the word—wherein the transactions between formal and natural are negotiated, allowing for the diverting and looting of sense.

As ordering devices of a more or less formal nature, regular expressions belong to a broader strategy for the regulated transformation of signs and symbols. Regularizing expression concerns the treatment of people and things ("prehensible" events, as discussed by Warren McCulloch and Walter Pitts)[22] so as to extract syntactically well-formed strings of symbols, to a greater or lesser degree of machine compatibility. From things to strings, this forms part of a kind of sociotechnical governance that bears on the logistical reorganization of situations of enunciation, a rescripting of enunciation wherein speech or writing can be translated into scrolling, pointing, clicking, and data entry. Through the invention of programming languages, compilers, the mundane panoply of list boxes, tick boxes, data fields, radio buttons, or the more emotively named button-vocabulary of social networking, as well as through specified ortho-graphic rules (your password must be at least eight characters long) and regulated transformations (strip out white space, remove commas), what you can machinically enunciate must correspond with the arrangements of the data structure. The event of communication—the fact *that one speaks*, that signs are emitted—is traduced and remains hidden behind what the software parses of what is said.[23] In point of fact, the user need not really say much, since it is the form of expression, not its content, that satisfices.

The computer is a medium, and software is an entity that occurs, in part, at a lin-guistic scale. For this reason, observers are more perceptive than they might think in their view that work involving symbol manipulation is an important characteristic of the contemporary economy. But this category does useful work only if such manipula-tion is taken in its most capaciously sophisticated sense. Shifting numbers around on a spreadsheet, making trades, cutting and pasting doctoral research into government documents: all these things count as symbol manipulation—and some of them may be more economically productive than others. But manipulating people, processes, and things as symbols and ciphers opens up questions about the production of infor-mation (the extraction and abstraction of signs) and about the injection of sophistic politicking into the economy of communication. A certain relief can be gained from the fact that one never quite has clean hands when one manipulates symbols, but a special kind of cunning is needed to make the obdurate insistence—in truth, the sociotechnical *prescription*—of expressing regularly actually work.[24]

Treating people and things as bearers of incipiently regular expressions creates the possibility of extracting strings (usually ASCII or Unicode) from them that can be processed according to the rules of a relatively simple syntax, one that is traversable by finite automatons. By this virtual reordering of communication into regular, well-formed, machine-parseable chunks, natural language statements can be manipulated into something susceptible to algorithmic treatment, something that a machine can understand—even if you cannot—which contributes to the emergence of a new regime of signs,[25] the translation of deictic operators (here I am, there you are), and the pragmatic ability of language to do things with words translated into preformatted computational structures. When one thinks programmatically, something everyone does once in negotiation with the opaque materiality of machines, natural language is not much help. But the existence or otherwise of a regime of signs specific to this shift per se is not what is of sole importance here: what *is* of interest is what happens in the process of translation itself.

By translating and transforming natural language into a form more commensurate with algorithmic treatment, the regularization of expression entails discarding crucial elements of the pragmatics of language, those aspects of language use that, although completely conventional, meant that one could do things with words. The commands that a computer allows to be issued to it do not have quite the same latitude of negotiation or the possibility of infelicity: failure to respond correctly to the signals issued by the machine, its array of insistent messages, conveyed in bleeps, status changes, screen updates, color or icon modulations, will yield a refusal to cooperate. So as one completes data fields, ticks checkboxes, and makes a selection from a dropdown list, or mouses around a visual field laid out in terms of precisely rastered coordinates, or when one breaks a search string down into separate lexical items and chooses to capitalize or not, to look only for items that match the exact string or not, to allow plurals or not (and so on), a process of subjection to the machine takes place. The latitude one had for a little virtuoso play within one's interactions, the opportunity for the humor or irony that allows one to ask for something without it being issued as a command, is transformed by the computational recoding of the commonplaces of language.

Such subjection is not inherently a bad thing. In some circumstances, it saves the tiresome bother of thinking.[26] In any case, the conceit that one necessarily speaks more freely to humans than machines is something that doesn't bear up to close scrutiny, given that discourse is just as likely to speak us as the other way around; but regularizing expression does facilitate a certain kind of highly structured forgetting. It is not just that the implicatures of interaction, and the kinds of games they allow you to play, can be, and are, discarded.[27] It is that when the disciplinary regularizing of expression occurs, a critical shift in attention takes place. In a conversation, a dialogue, perhaps even an interrogation, a constant process of repair, or its staging, is going on, facilitated in part by the anticipations and expectations of role. In situations of regularized expression, one of the participants will never really admit to being wrong: the logic of user error dictates that only one side repairs the holes, gaps, or non sequiturs in the flow of machinic discourse, although the autocompletion of data fields or the use of predictive texting algorithms is increasingly called on to help out.[28] Of course, should one place too great an insistence on user repair, generate too many errors, or insist on too rigidly formal or prolix a process of machine enunciation, the interaction will have to be redesigned: under such circumstances, tricks like personalization, variegated security permissions and user profiling can be adopted to facilitate a more constrained production of regularized statements, thus making less formal processes of communication more amenable to treatment in formal informational terms.[29]

Look After Your Relations

A propitious but underdocumented feature of relational databases, or databases of any sort, is that they tend to be received as fundamentally boring. Such a view is not without its merits—inciting failures of attention is also a crucial means of veiling things of most interest—but let us propose another possibility here, that of drawing participants into a system. While not exactly making databases immediately gratifying, such a result can often be achieved via the popular approach of facilitation at the front end, data mining at the rear, as well as other opportunities. Relational databases have become such a crucial part of the conceptual and material infrastructure of the present that it is difficult to imagine many contemporary media systems without their existence as a foundation.

In a short series of key papers in which he established the basis for the relational database management system, Edgar Codd developed a sophisticated understanding of all entities in a tabular system as dynamic, in states of possible or actual combination.[30] Such combination was rendered possible either through the analytical fragmentation of entities into predicates or qualities articulable as data or, without undergoing any preliminary fragmentation, by creating the conditions for "born digital" materials to be generated in such conditions. Such work establishes the conditions for data not simply to be stored but also to be structured, and Codd's work went on to establish such states of combination as fundamental, but finite, entities to be handled in themselves. The development of a field of reality, the material stuff of which is to one degree or another interpretable and manipulable as elements in a table, allows for the amassing of relations between the entities in that table. Importantly, guided by a keen insight into the importance of bringing data handling out of the hands of specialists, Codd also shifted database design toward the realm of natural rather than procedural formal languages. Data banks were to be useful to people other than stock controllers or technicians. Gradually, as data entry, deletion, modification, sorting, and query grew (perhaps by one or more remove) into the habits of daily life, such entities also began to populate the everyday. Because of their high degree of abstraction as structure-building structures, relational databases are immensely useful as stratagematic breeding grounds and as such work as part of what we can understand as the abstract infrastructure of flexibilization and of the increasing interpretability of processes and resources. Such interpretability should never be mistaken for transparency, however, and all kinds of users would be wise to recognize and to work with this.

Relations managed and induced by such systems have, in different jurisdictions, become subject to various kinds of interest, being seen as property in legal terms, as often distinct from the raw data that they manage.[31] Rent is to be derived from relations rather than the terms or objects of such relations. As such, the management of relations between relations is a means of capturing and mobilizing permutational force. The value of relational databases for such purposes can be understood by their basic qualities.

Within databases, the tractability of data and relations depends in no small part on the degree of normalization of data and the structures it is entered into. Normalization means the treatment of each piece of data and each relation as a separate entity. It involves stripping away unnecessary hierarchies or other structures within data. This means that as data are updated, deleted, or inserted, they do not carry any dependencies on other data or structures (such as nesting within a set of parent–child nodes). Normalization implies a neutrality as to the relative importance of one datum as compared to another. What it thus allows is for a query to be formulated through any point in the network of relations mapped by the table. Nonnormalized data offer one kind of resistance, in that they require nested sets of dependencies. A red round thing may be a cricket ball or an apple, and neither may exactly be round, but once they are normalized and interpretable as simply exemplars of bearers of one or more of the categorizations *red*, *round*, and *thing*, they lose their specificity. The quality of irreducibility is transferred from the entity described to the categories into which its qualities are organized.

Relational databases have, in principle, infinite capacities of scalability and, due to their capacity of abstraction, of requisite variety, although to affirm such a capacity is to test luck as much as logic. Built on the ability of a Turing machine to make possible the computation of any formalizable statement, databases make possible the organization of populations of normalized statements. That data are normalized has no bearing on whether what they handle is in turn formalized. This is why databases are so crucial in establishing links between rules structures and the outside world. This capacity for logical ordering enables the induction of combinatoriality and sorting for things outside the database, as well as within it; the introduction of new kinds of entities that are natively "artificial"[32]; the production of new rules for relations; and the harvesting of relations generated by the population of databases by live data-generating processes.

The now traditional use of databases has had a substantial impact on organization. This can primarily be understood in two ways. First, they allow for fast assessment of the states of entities in an organization (for instance, in the logistical needs of an airline: an assessment of numbers, location, states and timings of planes, crew, passengers, with factors such as states of repair or crew flying hours made tractable but discrete). A related capacity is, given a database already populated with entities and factors, the affordance of the simulation or prognosis of future events: to use sets of relations to model, given a relatively stable set or entities and factors, what is likely to occur given their recombination under different conditions.

As more and more data flow through and into databases, something other than the logistical imagination is able to grow. Data mining allows for the identification of unforeseen relations and factors. Concentrations of data establish new centers of gravity as they couple with sorting systems, giving shape to an understanding and a politics based on probabilities. This may give rise to multiple kinds of masking of hidden factors beneath a shimmer of data abstracted from their relation to other scales of reality. On the other hand, relational databases make tractable, sortable, and usable relations that are not otherwise apparent. On the face of it, most databases are best understood as describing sets, operating through the working methods of predicate logic in that they allow the selection, differentiation, union, analysis, and possible projection of the attributes of a relation,[33] but we can also recognize that a relational database is a topological machine. Any table of related data, a nomograph or even a bus timetable, establishing links between a finite number of stable, discrete, and interconnected entities, constitutes a topological machine. They establish networks of relations, the points of intersection between data and what those data link to and trigger. Where they differ is that in many cases, topology tends to describe a network from a position outside that network (it would require a higher-dimensional topology to incorporate the topological generation of topologies). Relational databases, on the other hand, work through systems of relations to establish, confirm, or discover relations.

A database understood through such a network model can usually be entered at any point, via predicates (or attributes), by relation, or by entity, and sorted on that basis. In this way, every element can be sorted by its actual relations, consisting of its categorical, relationally derived relation or nonrelation to all others. As databases increasingly face toward users configured as consumers, the tailoring of access to such ways of working often represents a key feature. For instance, try to find a way of searching for all books of a certain price (rather than another term, such as the author's name) on an online bookseller. While sellers offer a parade of desire from one title to the next, to sort titles by other means remains unavailable. Ways into the network of relations are constrained. A hierarchy is simply another way of using a network, arranging the links in a manner in which they only flow one way. Access to the knowledge of a topology is thus a tricky matter. While topological machines should only allow the privileged gaze of the overview to those with the correct access setting, this is only to read them as conforming to traditional models of power.

One way in which they encourage us to develop an understanding of other formations of power is through a capability inherent to such databases themselves: the production of relations and of disassociations. The aggregation of vast "banks" of data, to work with a term that described databases at their birth, sees all the kinds of experimentation, consolidation, and the power to convince that characterize banks that specialize in money. Whereas a taxonomy of the modes of aggregation, circulation, speculation, and dissipation of capital is constantly under way, it is at present left solely to the stratagematic imagination to work this out in practice in the case of data. A means by which this imagination stimulates itself is in the ability to cross-reference data from different sources,[34] and to aggregate databases using common standards, effectively consolidating them into one body. Such strategies are relevant across all sectors, but there is yet little rigorous work on their effective yields in control and prediction, and hence little advance restraint on them or their consequences. With such encouragement, work must be carried out empirically in the laboratory of the world.

The Justifiable Ignorance of the Exception

In the fraught and largely uncharted interplay between the empirical and the formal, it is difficult, if not impossible, to produce a definitive list of exceptions to algorithmic rule. Exceptions occupy a potentially troubling zone of nonknowledge and represent a significant threat to the smooth operations of friction-free, fluid, and transparent formal-material media processes. In the technical sense, exceptions arise when a piece of code—perhaps a class in an object-oriented programming language—encounters an abnormal condition that it cannot handle, when an event occurs that lies outside the expected range of possibilities that code is expected to cope with. But we also have a broader sense of what an exception is, touching on philosophical, political, and poetic reflection,[35] which might usefully be factored in to the technics, because almost by definition, the zone that exceptions occupy is not well understood. As such, trafficking with this zone remains fruitfully—although riskily—obscure.

The German political theorist Carl Schmitt encapsulates the more speculative brand of thinking about exceptions when he says: "The exception is more interesting than the rule. The rule proves nothing; the exception proves everything: It confirms not only the rule but also its existence, which derives only from the exception."[36] Now, if Schmitt's observation gives this set of sociotechnical considerations a speculative twist, then all the better: one should never imagine that technology doesn't release some form of cogitation.[37] Alfred Jarry speaks even more directly to the need for considerations of this nature in his characterization of 'pataphysics as the science of the particular: "Despite the common opinion that the only science is that of the general ['pataphysics] will examine the laws which govern exceptions."[38] An exception in this broader framework might be considered something that infringes the deductive, the nomothetic or the formal-logical principles of knowledge, a point at which language falters and stumbles in its ability to pick things out.[39]

For as long as it remains covered by a general (and perhaps even *principled*) ignorance—for reasons that Jarry helps us understand—the domain of exceptions allows operations to be pursued unhindered, implicitly, despite (or perhaps because of) the fact that in the technical domain, techniques have been developed for the *handling* of exceptions, which ward off the systemic collapse that infractions to the law of code threaten.[40] In this way, in its technical sense as something that must be handled programmatically, the exception offers a neat way of deranging the scanners interested in the limits of code, or exceptions in the second sense.

When designing a software system, a general and widely accepted principle is that one should always code *defensively*. In the assumptions that the designer or developer will make about the environment in which an application will operate, prudence dictates that one always design and develop as if the worst might happen. The designer of digitally mediated communications conceives of the world as an unremittingly hostile place; believes users, at baseline, to be irredeemably moronic (always validate user input, in case they don't know how to talk to computers); and considers other software to be unreliable and unstable at best (one doesn't *assume* that the database a Web site connects to is *necessarily* available). While numerous principles govern the imperative of writing "secure" code, the authors of one popular guide suggest that one should consider the maxim "all input is evil."[41] In this regard, the invention of exception handling—particularly important in, but not originating with, object-oriented programming—offers one way to deal with the nefarious contingencies of an incompletely predictable environment, an environment in which the jurisdiction of code is incomplete, because knowledge is incomplete.

Coders often distinguish between bugs, errors, and exceptions. A bug is a mistake of some sort made when writing code. An error is typically thought of as something resulting from the actions of a user—and requires that one have, in anticipation, a low opinion of that user's abilities. Exceptions, by contrast, represent a sort of principle of predictable unpredictability, the generic shape of the way that the unforeseen or the contingent makes an incursion into the algorithmic flow of control between segments of code. When something happens that lies outside the normal expectations of a piece of code—a Web site makes a request to a database, for example, or a client computer requests a URL—an exception handler might be used to "throw" an exception, meaning that the flow of control in the execution of the program is directed somewhere else so that the software can continue running without crashing (often with a message to the user to state what has happened: "404, server not found"). The distinction between errors and exceptions is a fuzzy one, not least because a user error might give rise to an exception. Typical advice, though, is to handle the idiocy of a user within other coding structures (warn the user not to input anything evil into the software).

As an initial approximation, exceptions are what a developer remains happy to be relatively ignorant about. The *outside* of a piece of software is by definition the bearer of infinitely many events about which the software can know nothing. Only a minuscule fraction of these possibilities will matter to the programmer, who knows that a particular software application may only ever know of an attack on an information infrastructure if a database is unavailable or a server fails to respond to a query. What exception handling does, though, is *delegate* responsibility for dealing with the problem, by passing it from one section of code—one object, often—to another, and ultimately to a block of code dedicated to exception handling.

The point about doing this is that it offers a way of preserving the general architecture of the software and of maintaining the "need-to-know" principle, and division of labor, that application development requires. For perhaps the dominant form of software development today, as too for some kinds of philosophy, the world is made up of a potentially infinite series of relatively self-contained, sealed objects, objects whose commerce with what is exterior to them takes place under highly specified conditions. Object-oriented programming is organized in terms of a regulated inter-play of concealment and exposure, interactions at the surface and a need-to-know principle: to programmatically use an object designed by someone else, I don't need to know anything about what goes on inside it (a principle sometimes referred to as *encapsulation*); I just need to know about the "public" methods that allow me access to what it can do. Encapsulation—or information hiding—allows a public face of certainty to coexist with a privately uncertain implementation of the workings of an object, or what are known as "difficult design decisions." To put it more technically: encapsulation separates the "contractual interface of an abstraction and its implemen-tation."[42] The boss who, using the correct abstraction layer, says, "I don't care how you get the job done, just get it done," thinks of his or her organization in object-oriented terms, benefiting from a strict insistence on the formal, abstract specification of roles and responsibilities to justify ignorance of the day-to-day.

Oddly enough, in this world, exceptions are no exception: like everything else, they are objects, entities that can be passed around (one *throws* an exception in this way, rather than throwing a fit) without infringing the black-boxing encapsulation rule of the segmentation or division of object labor: I don't care how you get the job done. One might think of this process as one of delegation, a little like the way in which complaints might be dealt with in an organization: they can occur anywhere, but an obedient object will say, "I don't know anything about that, you'd better talk to the boss," or "I'll have to ask my supervisor," or "Go to our Web site," as work to rule is played out as a form of obedience. Exception handling is designed to ensure that objects retain the stable and (more or less) precisely defined role they are given to play, which should not be upset by anything from the outside, anything that their role has not supplied the methods to handle. The point is to keep control of the flow. In this respect, exception handling is a form of pacification or stabilization, the art of which lies not so much in how the problem is eventually dealt with but in the signals that the exception handler generates about what has happened (the point about encapsulation is to ensure that only the right people get to rummage around in the secret insides of objects: messaging is a way to do this).

This highly effective abstraction of the exception from the complex, heterogeneous diversity of the empirical and the basic principles of how exceptions are then handled demonstrate the crucial lesson that formal-material mediation offers for a stratagem for the effective handling of the unknown *as* unknown. Translating the anomalous conditions of the empirical into the rule-governed algorithms of the formal, the abstractive virtue of exception handling lies in its ability to keep the unknown bracketed off through a sociotechnical principle of ignorance: well-programmed routines, a well-defined division of labor, and a formal protocol for exchanging messages between objects or defining their interaction keep the outside world at bay. By turning an exception into an object, one can apply the same principles to it as other objects (the exception inherits from other classes, one can extend it by adding methods, and so on).[43]

A full discussion of the technicalities of exception handling falls outside the scope of this stratagem. Sociotechnicalities, however, are a different matter. If—following the principle that artifacts, machines, things themselves, have a cognitive life of sorts—we imagine a digital system to embody an intelligence all its own, the sociotechnicality to be exploited here derives from the highly restricted, intransigent filtering out of all but the barest formal-material essentials of the outside world. Given that programmable objects are objects that operate on the principle of a highly regulated, rigidly defined contractual interface with other objects, then exception handling demonstrates that the outside world becomes one gigantic object, whose inner workings become not just strangely but also desirably secret. Let us call this the justifiable ignorance of the exception.

Encourage Error

It is a mistake to believe that computation simply introduces a new, finer, more demanding form of control. This is undoubtedly part of its catalog of features, but like the justifiable ignorance of the exception, there is much also to admire in its capacity for recklessness and indifference. It is generally understood that an error is something that falls outside logic. This is not to claim that it is impossible to make errors of logic, but that the aim of logic is to reduce errors internal to it. The proposition that this stratagem exploits rests on the idea that a more profound interrelation conjoins the two.

One of the advantages of error when it enters the domain of computational gray media is that it no longer represents simply interpretation, miscomprehension, inaccuracy, or at best an intuitive fuzziness, but becomes productive. This happens only in part because computation has now fundamentally leaked beyond the first ranks of technicians who nurtured the mainframes, then out of the boxes on the desktop, then into billions of embedded gadgets and sensors, and thus into the world. At another scale, error occurs at the level of logic, which—although it is abundant in its capacity for internal rigor and intolerance of incorrectness—no longer imagines itself a totality.[44] Computation has begun to recognize its tangledness with other aspects of culture, recognizing them as providing a means for "a new and improved physis."[45] The nature, the idiosyncratic patterns of growth and conjugation, of computing changes in these mixings.

Error is not simply productive in terms of simple mistakes or misconstruals of a matter of fact, such as those that might, under a regimen of exuberant charitability, be understood to be of a kind liable to lead to the launch of a war. Neither is it something entirely congruent with the ideal of chance, though they might at moments intertwine. What we also need to account for here in stratagematic terms is the intertangling of rule sets, error produced by an appropriate dose of reason. These may occur within a program as the inability to finish a cycle, but they can perhaps most classically be exemplified by the establishment of a priority inversion.

A priority inversion is a type of problem in which the ordering of resource allocations between the tasks in a program creates interferences.[46] Within any piece of software, certain tasks are more important than others. They may be relied on to keep a computer running or to provide fast interaction to a user. Each task is dynamically ranked in order of priority. A priority inversion can occur when a lower-priority task "hijacks" a resource needed for a higher one. In the time that the priority takes to be reordered, a third task may take over the resource, leaving the first task incomplete, risking a crash, delaying critical processes, or generating a novel condition. Related problems occur when two or more updates are made concurrently to a date in a database, operating system, or other software. Unless a means exists for adjudicating priority, the system deadlocks. With many multiples of users carrying out different processes on the same or linked pieces of data in an environment of multithreaded, multicore processors, the degree of complication of the mechanisms that govern locking and unlocking data and apportioning priority of access can be profound.

An example of such an event in the generation of another form of medial physis can be found in the following story. A man is convicted of repeated violence against another, against whom he may still hold a grudge. Upon his release from prison, he is prohibited from going near the other's home or place of work. He is tagged with a GPS-based device that alerts the target and the police each time he enters the specified area, or if the system is tampered with in a way that results in his disappearing from view of the satellite. The geology of the area is characterized by steep valleys, and because of the cold climate, the buildings are traditionally constructed with thick walls. These conditions create substantial GPS "shadows." Each time the man enters such a shadow, the other is alerted that he may be attacked, and the police are impelled to respond by attending to the place where the signal was last registered. In such a situation, nonevents that may occur several times a day generate an emergency response. The problem is generated neither by the intentions of the man, nor the precautions taken, nor necessarily the technology per se, but by its interactions with its location. Intending to free the victim from the fear of attack, the system instead results in his constant susceptibility to inordinate crisis.

Regardless of the specificities of this particular case, we should ask how this kind of function can be understood, and what kinds of affordances it establishes. It is possible to imagine proposed solutions to this general problem coming from law, engineering, policing, the introduction of weapons, psychiatry, vigilantism or popular justice, architecture and other areas of expertise. This is an argument for collaboration between disciplines or agencies. But in stratagematic terms, it is also useful to explore the direct conditions such mixtures of forces, capacities, and materials produce. Each new form of structuration and mediation of the world generates its own kind of collateral damage. Here it is useful to turn to work in situated cognition, best exemplified in robotics, to think through the quality of error as productive rather than solely as an impediment to good function.

The "subsumption architecture" robotics characteristic of the work of Rodney Brooks and his collaborators, such as Luc Steels and Pattie Maes, builds up effective and useful behavior in robots by linking a series of finite-state machines to govern specific states.[47] These simple circuits decide whether or not it is appropriate to move forward, to turn, to locate and lift and object, to stop, or to carry out some other function. As Brooks and Lynn Andrea Stein state, "There is no end to a computation or final result; all is continuously being computed and recomputed, and actions in the world are the 'outputs' of the system."[48] They avoid the problem characteristic of earlier waves of artificial intelligence, which emphasized signal processing by basing decisions and behaviors on the results of such behaviors in interactions with the world. This leads to a robust architecture in which useful results are achieved directly by "using the world as its own best model,"[49] rather than being modeled in advance. A robot can thus be judged on the basis of its actual behaviors rather than on any more complex model of its intentions or the range and quality of the abstractions it employs. Aggregations of simple behaviors allow robots to operate in noisily complicated domains, to operate via trial and error.

It is here that a stratagematic intelligence again differs from a strategic one. While the strategic point of view would understand error as only a delay on the way to a trial yielding the correct result, the stratagematic is also able to recognize the productive yield of error, not as the lack of expected result but as the proof of a capacity of displacement (as of water volume), interaction, and generativity in the world.

Another way in which such phenomena occur is in the playback of recorded music. As the population of CD players gradually ages and falls apart after the decline of their short supremacy, they wear out in ways that generate an idiosyncratic sound. In the last years of their dominance, their mechanisms, the motor to rotate the disc, the drive to move the read-head, begin to gently accompany the music that they deliver with their own modest trills, sussurations, and whirs. Error accompanies proper function not as its opposite but as its exploratory double, probing for ways of being in the world after straightforward function has passed on. It is in the sensing, mobilization, and use of this excessive capacity that media exceed their functionalist bounds, through their own excessive functionality.

Technical error here allies with the tyranny and arbitrariness, the stern and grandiose stupidity, of European thought that is venerated by Nietzsche as a means of generating strength, inciting curiosity, and breeding "subtle agility."[50] Where such error differs, however, is that we do not need to look for something—such as the human subject—that is kept beyond an abstraction boundary as the recipient of derogations and futile tasks in the understanding that such cruelty generates an ascetic gain, reciprocal rage, or thick spine of desire as a form of training or asymmetric response. To understand or to validate error, we do not automatically need this additional layer of interpretation, whether of symbols or of disciplined beings. Error has its own kind of craftiness. A means of alternation between knowing and inhabiting its physis, recognizing the inevitability of its occurrence, its coextensivity with and generation by reason, and its escape from mere rationality: in all of these qualities error establishes the arts of stratagematic media.

Productivity

Keep It Personal

A basic scenario sketched out across the range of stratagems we have explored here is one in which some technique, technology, tool, device, practice, chemical, concept, or other such thing operates to shape and configure the possibilities of a situation, influencing the way in which it can change, the dynamics operative within it. Such mediators are not necessarily transparent and are often far from stable, and this gives them some latitude for experimentation and a considerable coefficient of ambiguity that opens them up to the wandering of fortune.

The concept of tacit knowledge, as it has been deployed within the theory and practice of management, seems to play an exemplary role in facilitating the kinds of cunning that we have been exploring here, and provides a crucial indicator of the tensions that systems or networks of mediators are subject to.[1] Developed by the scientist-turned-philosopher Michael Polanyi in his book *Personal Knowledge*, the characterization of a type of knowing as tacit—that is, difficult, even impossible, to verbalize—gives scope to its recasting in terms of a sort of inarticulable "connoisseurship" that offers an exceptional resource for flattery, especially when brought into contrast with the abstract and impersonal structures of the kind of critical philosophy that Polanyi opposed. While flattery of the powerful was not Polanyi's goal (his undertaking was to explore crucial aspects of the development of scientific knowledge that critical philosophy could not), such ideas become more malleable when (mis)applied in the expediently instrumental realm of the corporate.[2]

Indeed, from this point of view, one distinct advantage that Polanyi's conception of the tacit can offer is a satisfying sense that the ineffable nous of leaders is the source of their expertise (and elevated position), that a rounded personality whose appreciation of the bouquet of a fine wine harmonizes richly with an intuition that the market will appreciate a move to downsize or restructure, and that a hefty bonus is a legitimate reward for all this inarticulable personal capital. A concept of knowing as tacit or personal cashed out as a refined connoisseurship or down-to-earth geek insight (the specific qualities are irrelevant) harmonizes here with a rhetoric of intellectual capital and market overbidding for "excellence." Recent work on the brain, a substance rich in genetically endowed connections, might yet provide a color-coded scan to prove the point.[3]

Further, by appealing to the necessary inarticulacy of a process of imitation in which an apprentice follows the gestures of the master, picking up along the way a range of gestures that even the master didn't know he was making, Polanyi's conception of the tacit also captures a sense of the embedding of knowledge in practices, where knowing *how* is as important as, if not more important than, knowing *that*.

Likewise, in these mute processes of imitation, it points to something of the dynamic of authority and hierarchy in an organizational practice. Doing what someone tells you to do because they are presumed to know better, even if they are unable to explain why, finds a flattering explanation through the notion of tacit knowledge. At the least, an alibi is provided for a leader who, unable to argue the toss, bullies his inferiors into submission and is hailed for "being a forceful personality." In the refractoriness of making doing amenable to propositional articulation, even the slightest gesture can be imagined as crucial to the cognitive capital of an organization, the generic qualities of work processes ornamented through the ineffable uniqueness of the personal touch. As managers increasingly become leaders, their every gesture is invested in and mused over for the secret of success it might contain.

The historical links of the tacit with attempts to explain how science works also suggest a continuity between scientific endeavor and the more dubitably objective practices of the world of commerce: the quantimetrics of scientific management find a positive reason for their limitations in the mute shapings of gesture.

But as a device for shaping knowledge management strategies, the tacit acts as a vector for drawing human factors together, for promoting the intimacy and warmth of communication and cooperation among elements of an organization. If knowledge is personal, it can only be mediated through personal input. And when knowledge has been acquired through the subconscious processes of the tacit, as with the apprentice learning by imitative doing, work gains a feeling of continuity, a feeling that, helpfully, directs attention away from deeper ruptures, gaps, and breaks with the past.

However, a thin and highly uncertain line separates the ineffable from the inadmissible and the inarticulable from the nonexistent, and some management theorists have not been slow to realize that the concept of tacit knowledge can easily play into the hands of hucksters, charlatans, and con men: bullshitters of all stripes.[4] After all, if your most prized possession—your knowledge—cannot be articulated explicitly or, more practically, turned into a formalism, who's to say whether or not you really know what you claim to know? How might one separate craft from the crafty? The popular rejoinder "It's too complicated to explain" might not be an exemplar of personal knowledge per se, but the speed with which it is proffered as a threat to the overly inquisitive is indicative of the curious affordances that even the mildly ineffable provides for diversionary tactics and sleight of hand. The fragile rewards of status are also easily threatened if employees lower in the pecking order are thought of as connoisseurs. Artisans, yes, at a pinch, but connoisseurship has to be a much rarer talent.[5] Naturally the ready application of knowledge-engineering practices that can ignore the more valuable skills some workers might possess, because they don't know how to explain them, also has its value. And more obviously, in a situation in which organizations are delocalized, production is networked, and work made to flow, strategies based on the explicit and the codifiable are more desirable than those that might promote solidarity and bodily cooperation among the workforce. Indeed, when an organization's effective domination and control of a situation depend on disseminating and sharing knowledge for its continued viability, the ineffability of the tacit offers a somewhat more equivocal set of prospects.

This much becomes obvious when one considers that the aim of processes of knowledge management is to extract knowledge from a workforce so as to congeal that knowledge into replicable commodity form (as in outsourcing practices, for example). From this point of view, knowledge management requires the extraction and algorithmic codification of patterns of knowledge and activity. Whether it is the knowledge of the weavers encoded in the Jacquard loom, the outsourcing of legal and accounting services, or the marketizing of consumer preferences, a process of making the implicit explicit forms a crucial element in the economic construction of work per se (and perhaps a more general cultural condition). At this point, the tacit becomes something of a hindrance, calling for expensive processes of knowledge extraction and codification, a more detailed understanding (or, alternately, a willing ignorance) about the way in which work is accomplished.[6]

There are other directions in which an understanding of tacit knowledge might be advanced in the interests of the more effective management of knowledge within an organization. A crucial element of the personal, according to Polanyi, lies in what the "intellectual domination" of a situation bestows on an individual. In the field of scientific knowledge, granted, this unarticulated capacity to appreciate what is at stake in an experiment, a controversy, seems indispensable. But in the less certain realm of activities such as work, where an incontrovertible scientific outcome is less important than maintaining market profile, deflating dissent, or simply suppressing disorder, "intellectual domination of a situation" points toward a different kind of know-how. Here a concept such as the habitus, proposed by Pierre Bourdieu, might offer us a slightly more lucid appreciation of the equivocal limits of the ineffable: like tacit knowledges, the knowing that is encoded in the habitus is inseparably corporeal and, at least when Bourdieu investigates the socially differentiated field of "distinction," can correspond to a refined, connoisseurial flair, a nose for something, a kind of intuition on the limits of the explicit and the codifiable. It is a "matrix of perceptions, appreciations, and actions."[7] But unlike tacit knowledge, the knowing that is embodied in the habitus is most definitely codified and articulable. It is through the habitus that strategies of domination and control are accomplished: the imitation of the gestures of the master in a process of learning is equally about learning to inhabit a corporeal scheme that maintains a structure of domination. If this knowing is not articulated, though, it is because it can only be so at the cost of calling into question the social structures that it supports.

A great future might just lie ahead for the concept of the tacit and the clouds of dust that it manages to kick up. But if the current propensity for transparency, efficiency, and all-in stakeholder participation holds (exemplified in the enthusiasm for 360-degree appraisal), and knowledge managers take a more inquisitive stance toward the polymorphous functioning of the personal, practices of knowledge engineering might confer a less flattering allure on many instances of the unspoken.

All the World's an Audition

To breed an animal with the right to make promises is one of the transition points Nietzsche establishes as tending toward the contemporary human.[8] To breed an animal with the ability to sign contracts and conform to a meshwork of audit trails is the program of much of today's software as it shapes and gives form to the contemporary imaginary of control. When speaking about such systems, to use the word "control" as such is a misnomer. It smacks too much of despotism and neurosis; what is wanted instead is to make sure people have a feeling of belonging. The universal aim is to perform a cleansing detox on social relations, to take part in a fitness-enhancing "dressage of the brain."[9] One of the means of doing so is to displace any relationships that might give rise to tension into automated systems, thus allowing humans to concentrate on what really gives them pleasure and fulfillment—relying on media and other actuation systems to get the job done. If promises are a mnemonic that sustains the self as reliable, regular, and automatic, audit is a means of sustaining the systemic context in which the self unfolds.

While virtue inheres in the common hypocrisy of proclaiming the benefits of openness while practicing the creation of boundaries, to restrain our creative palette to such overly contrasting tones is to deny the possibilities of subtlety and ambiguity. Equally, to focus solely on the means of systematization of relations, relying on distributed formatting of events by empowering people with your tools and protocols, to displace the conduct of effectiveness from a concentrated source into a system of circulation, vocabularies, and devices, is to miss some of the simpler pleasures of singular acts of creation or destruction available to a canonical authority. Such an approach may be right for contexts that are stable enough not to be disrupted by hunger, invasion, or other crises and can rely on the possibility of consensus. Not only are these contexts rare, but in that homogeneity incites the alien, they are often in turn most open for use. To develop systems of audit, distributed management, and self-evaluation is a third and complementary tendency.

In the 1940s, it was possible to imagine the emergence of a new class, that of the managers who had come to dominate planned and wartime economies and found in various forms of fascism, Marxism-Leninism, and the New Deal particular ideological inflections or flavors to suit their purposes.[10] Today the world is far more interesting, and what we find instead is the growth of managerialism as a set of techniques that sets itself up not simply as the domain of a specific class but as a common treasury for all: with many subfields proliferating from traffic management to anger management, all of which recommend themselves as distinct schools but equally allow a trade in metaphor from one managerial domain to another. The circulation and development of these techniques starts with the desire for efficiency, new levels of synergy between the atoms of the organization or project. They have no ends but outcomes and the infinitesimally fine-grained milling of relations between people, quality, process, and product.

Making explicit the means by which people are checked or may check themselves allows the generator of the system of checks to withdraw from direct interaction but still receive benefits from the visible hand of organization.[11] Such techniques allow the honesty and aspirations of others to become a most valuable tool for evil media. Through fields, tick boxes, appraisals, targets, reports, rankings, personal development plans, all are given the chance to experience what they really are in transparent terms. Audit mechanisms such as these are a neutral means by which people are empowered to connect their life narratives to wider social forces such as markets and pseudo-markets, strategic objectives, research assessment, customer satisfaction, good practice, and the success of the firm or society.[12] The synergy achieved by such means allows citizens to apprise themselves of their own achievements, but also—and this is important—to use their own cunning in cleaving more closely to targets and objectives.[13] In this way, audit favors as virtuous those who assimilate themselves to its requirements. Whether they are adventurous or timid, profligate or frugal, full of conspiracy or yearning for obedience, all can find this virtuousness echoed in themselves and so make themselves available for evaluation, encouragement, and trimming.

Bear in mind, however, that the virtue of the audit finds its own true believers. Not being accustomed to coming close to power, and judging too readily on the basis of appearances and presentations, the true believer is scandalized by a few small stones tumbled along in the running river of power. As Machiavelli reminds us, "Everyone is in a position to watch, few are in a position to come into close touch."[14] Proof of what comes into intimacy with power is as highly prized by idle speculators as planetary trivia is to astrologers. For this reason, it is important to recognize that the power of audit leaks out and begins to organize all walks of life. Every organization will require records to be kept according to certain formulas, but in a society where power is distributed in a proper manner, even the minutiae of leaked expenses claims seem a closer guide to the soul than whether a man launches the invasion of another country. As such, once unleashed, the audit becomes a new domain for the establishment of truth.

And there lies a crucial problem. In Louis Althusser's reading of *The Prince*, the ruler may choose to operate by means of law and by the more bestial power of coercive force.[15] If a ruler relies solely on either, he will be short lived, but operating above and between them is the cunning of deception. In the time of Machiavelli, courting and encountering the emergence of the idea of the modern from one of the few unadorned rooms in the Palazzo Vecchio in Florence, it was possible to state that deception was recognizable as the opposite of law. The grotesque aesthetic of cunning or fraud, however, was necessary as a second-order operation of evaluation, of strategy as a force of thought in itself, and as a pragmatics of conjuncture necessary at the least for the recognition of the operations of others. Later, game theory arises as a vast manifold of truth tables drawn up by the multilayered coiterations of force, law, and deception. Both of these cases, the new prince and the wilderness-of-mirrors realism of game theory, rely on another layer of interpretation, that of the project: founding, maintaining, or expanding a state or extrapolating the conditions of an existing one into every possible future. To navigate the interpretive proliferation of this layer, the wily operator uses a hierarchy of evaluating events: against the project, the ends or outcomes;

at the level of cunning, the selection of whether to adopt means that are "good" or "bad"; and at the level of active implementation, the choice of tactics and techniques; all of these in relation to the relations between other actors, forces, conditions, and resources. And here we can see that the software management of audit is useful, because it natively consists of the management of relations and, as such, naturalizes their invention and effects.

Whether for governor or governed, the audit promises a perfectly discrete form of micromanagement, a taking in hand and measuring of the most minute of gestures against statistically established or externally required norms. The very ease with which one can implement an audit trail within a database—and, with minimal technological extension, in the mundane software-based tools of everyday life, in social networks, for example—fuels the proliferation of audit and establishes the conditions for its extension to more and more kinds of social relation.

Tracking interaction with a database (a technological form that is prerequisite to the vast majority of corporate gray media) may be accomplished at extremely fine levels of granularity: which user, during which session, on which day, from which location, modified this record or that? Using simple SQL statements, wrapped up in some appropriate form of "middleware" technology, one can both trigger and monitor specific audit "events." What is more, one can do so without even the need for any specific kind of form filling or box ticking, despite the salutatory effects of the pointless time consumption of this form of labor and the liberating chances of mistakes and defaults it sets in play.

Gray media, such as that embodied in software, is often referred to as a form of law, in that, crudely speaking, it codifies behaviors between itself and other entities, with its effects proliferating outward into standardized behaviors.[16] In this context, the three layers of project, strategy, and implementation often find themselves flattened. And here the risk of that training or domestication implied by the ability to make promises becomes perceptible. If part of the project of statistics was to establish a means for the state to trace the contours and speculate on the inner workings of the beast that it governs,[17] and thus to remain separate from it while knowing it, the proliferation of audit risks bringing the idealizations of normativity, of quality, of standardization and the vengeful banal morality of the normed, into immanent relation not only with what audit handles but with its handlers, too. Here we see the necessity of the difference between theorematic and stratagematic thinking. A theorematic approach to evil media means unwavering compliance to laws and axioms laid out in advance, something that may end up biting the brush of the most cunning fox. A stratagematic approach, however, allows cunning to detach itself a little more from the flattening effect of universal audit, the salutatory effect of which is a certain freedom to maintain operations.

Mythologize Decision Making

Historically considered, the archetypal decision support system is probably not the spreadsheet or the database, the coin or the cards, but the book. The Bible, for Christians. Machiavelli's *The Prince* for the more worldly and godless. The Qur'an and the *Book of Ruses* for those profiled for and targeted in ancient and modern crusades, and so on. But not all decisions are made in the frame of monotheistic religion or political absolutism, and one should guard against thinking that the book can ever itself be an infallibly certain object, as if decision support was, in an echo of the Cartesian cogito, about the provision of a rock-solid point of departure.[18] Geomancy and tarot, for example, offer less word-based advice, semiformal interpretative systems for the same, although they perhaps lack the social and cultural credibility accruing to the expert or to the statistic. Support for decisions, indicators for alternative courses of action, the weighing of consequences, can also be mediated through much less obvious, informal means. The relative size of piles of paper on a desk might indicate how to organize a working day; the shifting body language of colleagues might influence your decision on how to conduct a meeting.

   In its standard form, a decision support system (DSS) is a structured way of integrating data about a problem, modeling interventions, visualizing results, and shaping decisions with reference to business models, strategies, and operational policies. DSS are used in business, complex resource management—such as that governing ecological or military operations—and medicine. We might be stretching the meaning of the notion of a decision support system here a little, but if a team of knowledge engineers from Mars landed on Earth tomorrow, wanting to discover how decision making works, they would face a complicated, and not entirely coherent, set of situations, practices, techniques, concepts, and attitudes, a state of affairs that justifies the liberties we are taking here. If we assume that the Martians would want to learn something from us,[19] would they take as their starting point Beau Brummell, a man so practiced in the art of delegating decisions that, although he could select a fine jacket himself, he would ask his valet to tell him (or so the story goes) which of the Cumbrian lakes he most admired? Or perhaps, if our Martians were readers of Herbert Simon (who felt decision making to be synonymous with management), might they take a random sample of middle managers and observe them in their by turns bumbling, obfuscatory, dogmatic, and exasperated day-to-day practices? What a contrast they would find if, as recent philosophers might recommend, they then sought to talk with Carl Schmitt, seeking clarifications of his adventurous thinking about authority, sovereignty, and so on. In short, the picture is more than a little fuzzy, and as ever, equivocation provides ample opportunity for ruseful cunning.

The knowledge engineers would perhaps also be confounded by the relative absence of mediating artifacts from theoretical considerations of the decision-making process (neither the experiential critics of AI or its enthusiastic mechanical advocates address the role of things or the idea that a composite apparatus may be central in decision making, for example), and their difficulties would doubtless also be compounded by the considerable scope for subterfuge that characterizes decision-making processes. Such subterfuge is legion: the executive who hires a management consulting company to turn the prior decision to sack 30 percent of the workforce into a rational response to a report on streamlining and efficiency savings; the politician whose resignation dissimulates his or her being fired; or the bogus telephone vote giving the seal of approval to a carve-up between artist management companies; all are not infrequent occurrences. The knowledge engineers might be perplexed, too, by the well-established practice of claiming to have taken the initiative when it is not yours to take, or of pretending to be taking it when you have in fact taken it already. Such are ploys with which most people will be familiar, but they are ploys that make it difficult to get a clear idea about how decision making occurs and what exactly it is. Are we dealing with decision making or role-playing here?

It seems that one is unlikely to obtain a consistent or reliable set of answers from humans about decision making per se, so it would not be unreasonable to turn to software, to the less ticklish stability of computational systems, to gain a cleaner understanding. Despite the mise-en-scène of a certain guile in the founding specula-tions about artificial intelligence,[20] the only deception that intelligent machines have managed to perpetrate with any degree of success is the idea that the decisions of a machine are somehow infallible, a hoax that crafty users sometimes manage to turn to their own ends, with practiced insincerity; "I'm very sorry, but the computer has rejected your application for a bank account . . ."

A plethora of technologies, from newsfeeds and recommendation systems, through the indexing and weighting algorithms used in ordering preferences automatically, to decision support systems proper, do at least have the merit of operating on a replicable, reproducible, and mathematically quantifiable basis—which is perhaps why certain psychologists take such inspiration from the computer when making assertions about human cognitive processes. But were one to commence an understanding of decision making beginning with the machine, one might end up with a rather different picture of the process.

Despite the mythology that surrounds the decision and the decision maker (as seen in both Schmitt and Simon), decision support systems are fairly widespread. While the specific notion of decision support first entered vocabularies in the 1960s,[21] that history places Caesar in consultation with his auguries, Abraham Lincoln with his medium, or the Godfather with his consigliere (to say nothing of the modern politician with his assortment of focus groups and opinion polls) suggests that the power and authority that accrue to the decision maker represent only one element of a process that is distributed in a much more diffuse and problematic manner than our mythologies imagine.

Decision support systems in the strict sense offer a good starting point for exploring the deceptive ways in which decision making operates, and the value to be gained from introducing artifacts into this process. The decision support system seeks not to substitute for the presumed fallible expert in systems of the same name but to facilitate and expedite the process of problem solving by providing timely and accurate information and what-if models and scenarios—alternative courses of action and their consequences. In this restricted, technical sense, a decision support system could be something as simple as a spreadsheet, but it might be something considerably more complicated—a database with some sort of OLAP facility,[22] for example, used to provide suites of reports on appropriate issues. Contrasted with the expert system, a spreadsheet does not take the place of a person (it might replace certain of their perceptions, but that is a slightly different matter), nor does it directly replace the power of judgment of an individual (although it does present him or her with a range of options for consideration). The decision support system does, however, tend to presuppose and then reinforce a certain organizational and psychological model of thinking that may intersect opportunely with what can be figured as the realities of practice.

So the interest of the decision support system lies less in the quality of advice it provides than in its redistributive function, in the way that it can help displace and redefine expertise, valid knowledge, the landscape of choice and the rationalizations one makes of it. It effectuates a subtle kind of remodeling, which tends to operate on the forms of material about which decisions can be made, and promotes certain kinds of decisions as inherently more tractable, more likely to be resolved, and hence more important than others. To put it crudely, the point is that if you can quantify it, and your database gathers information about it, the decision support system might be able to help you make a decision about it. The importance of the decision support system, beyond the simple manner in which it gathers and centralizes information, thus has more to do with the way that it bolsters hierarchies and refocuses organizing and organizational energies. Once the spreadsheet or the database report becomes a mediator in the review meeting, critical efforts will focus on getting a "fairer," more accurate representation of the problem in question, rather than contesting the nature of the problem.

Herbert Simon's well-known four-stage model of decision making, in part at least, attempted to shift thinking away from the tendency to emphasize the heroic moment of decision, in favor of deeper consideration of a process that he saw as consisting of intelligence, design, choice, and review.[23] But although this model has a capacious latitude for feedback loops at every step of the way, thus factoring in uncertainty and the room for optimizability, it does little to mitigate the fundamentally linear assumptions on which the model is built, a linearity that is built into and shapes organizational processes.[24] More significantly, when such a model is used to design a system—as opposed to formalizing a phenomenological description—it entails defining in advance what kinds of problems one will have to deal with, so that the system will be constructed in such a way as to collect the necessary intelligence to feed into the modeling of solutions. Thus it effectively presupposes or requires an environment that is reasonably stable (failing which, the problems your system is set up to deal with cease to be appropriate). Naturally there may be many processes about which decisions can be supported in this way, but this seems tendentially unlikely.

However, there are other reasons to use a decision support system than to get support for a decision. The preservation of an organizational hierarchy may be one. From a practical point of view, it is rare for everyone to have access to such systems. Even if the decisions that it makes are unnecessary, the executive reports, what-if scenarios, business projections, and so on, that they provide are of incomparable benefit in producing subjects who take themselves to be decisive. In this respect, one might consider the decision support system to be an important element in the production of particular kinds of subjectivity. Furthermore, the semiotics, or even aesthetics, of the business report have a certain differential value that reinforces a hierarchy of reliability and accuracy: a proposed course of action that can be modeled with financial projections three years into the future (regardless of whether the input data are fact or fiction) has a certain well-formed quality that may inspire more confidence than figures inscribed on the back of a cigarette packet or on a paper napkin. Strategy documents with the predictive accuracy of a fortune-teller's ruminations can acquire a certain power of conviction when produced in this way. Further, there is the sense that a decision that is mediated through a series of obviously disinterested data-crunching algorithms has greater trustworthiness than decisions mediated through the representations of greedy, lazy, whining employees. One can rely here on a certain forgetfulness of the initial remit of system designers and a culturally entrenched sense that technical issues are not politically framed, that they arise from the self-evidence of the necessities of the day.

In its physical implementation, the decision support system effects the kind of concrete closure that Simon argued was necessary to allow humans to effectively decide something: the possibility of rational decision modeled on explicit, formally deductible lines could only be preserved on this basis. From within the world modeled by the decision support system, arguments that revolve around alternative lines of questioning and different ways of problematizing an issue will thus inevitably appear to be irrational, even inconceivable. Slipping into the psychology of prestige, saving face, and the myriad masks that stupidity can assume, such arguments will be further reinforced by the issue of capital outlay: there will always be a certain reluctance to decommission a system that is not fit for purpose, that asks the wrong questions about false problems, particularly if the demands for its acquisition were high or if it has a nice user interface.

The Occult Virtue of the Project Plan

From its background in operations research, and its historically determinable connections to the military-industrial complex more generally, few things break the promise of rational, ordered planning and decision making with such monotonous regularity than the project, which seems destined to live up to its promise only through a judicious mixing of juggling, conjuring, and myriad other magic tricks and illusions. To intone the word "project" is to awaken the baleful anticipation of life lived as geek cliché: budgets overspent, sleepless nights, relationship failure, and substance abuse. The activities of the project manager, whose "personal qualities" and more particularly "authority" are so often the focus of the technical literature, occupy a space of calculation that magically encourages the hellish descent into what some have called the "death march project," the sort of endeavor that is so gloomily weighed down with the leaden emotions of failure that it recalls the enforced destructions of sociopolitical dramas run aground on their own denial of reality.[25] A death march project is one that, on the basis of "an unbiased, objective risk assessment,"[26] would be given a less than 50 percent chance of success and would never be undertaken (unless, perhaps, the risks of failure were tied to some form of appropriately unpleasant physical punishment for those in charge). Of course, "objective risk assessment" here means both "objective assessment of risks" and "assessment of risks to objects," and in this sense, it is precisely because of this selective focus of objective risk assessment that the *projective* qualities of the project are forgotten.

As well as an outcome to be avoided, a limit state of organized activity, death march projects themselves are symptomatic of the subjective negligence of bureaucratic reason. Yet despite the ever-present threat of failure, and the conscious awareness that *maybe* the concept of the project is not all it is cracked up to be, there is a compulsion to repeat such projects, a drive to tie productive activity into a doom-laden spiral, to burn and squander, to organize, rationalize, and then extinguish energies mobilized in a wildly optimistic estimate of goals, a cascading chain of overshot targets, emergency budget extensions, and visions become missions. Viewed with the squinting eye of the strategist, this willingness to contemplate failure in the specifics from the outset, so as to save project management as a form, is one of its secret, occulted strengths, a strength that we must learn to read in the subjective effects of its idioms, methods, user groups, and bulletin boards, even in the generic qualities of its publications.[27] To lead your troops to certain doom is to act for the heroic perpetuation of an ideal. The field of project management might thus usefully be considered one wherein strategic value derives from the malicious effects of the channeling or semioticization of activity that it accomplishes. Extract resources from the mundane rhythms of the habitual self-definitions of routine work, mobilize in a separate space and time, and watch as libidinal energies spiral.[28]

Projects are never started: they are always *initiated*.[29] The occult virtue of the project should thus be located not so much in the material impact of its logistical management of resources as in the binding force of emotive adhesion that its tools and techniques produce. Considered stratagematically, project management is best viewed, then, as a technique for the production of particular types of subjectivity, a delicate process of fabrication negotiating the psychic hinterlands between neurosis, paranoia, and psychosis along with enthusiasm and a can-do spirit.[30] The matter of the promotion or production of subjectivity is not explicitly the central concern of theoretical research on project management (although the first paper on project management in the *Harvard Business Review* focused on "the project manager")[31] but is palpably evident to the many people who participate *in* projects, swept away as they are in the peculiar mixture of delirium and tedium that the form foments. The status of subjectivity itself, as what might be called a conceptual *externality* to project thinking, has some efficacy insofar as one should always consider it a strategic misjudgment to draw attention to or "topicalize" such vital resources.[32] A good magician is a master of attention management: focus on the task in hand so that you can't see what is happening elsewhere.

So aside from anything else that it might do, project management should be considered as a way to order and reorder emotional force, offering an abstracted spatio-temporal grid for the investment of personal energy. The project unfolds in a different dimension to that of work, and by yoking human resources into the hierarchical linearity of unfolding tasks, it also provides a way to marshal or channel affect, condensing and displacing the anxiety of time-strapped resources onto acceptable goals. The prerogative of the project manager to underestimate the time required to do things and the underling's tendency to do the converse (while frequently sharing the overall aims and goals of the project as a whole) can in this sense be followed as an outcome of the peculiar forms of semiotic intermediation that the project produces, fomenting subjective states and active tendencies.[33] Borderline states that would be recognized for such when manifest in other areas of life (maintaining lists of kitchen utensils on a drawer-by-drawer basis, screaming at the trash collector for a late pickup) are not only tolerated but exacerbated and intensified through the relentless refiguring of activity within a semiotically neutralized abstract space-time.[34]

Project management avails itself of numerous techniques in its bid for fine logistical ordering. The critical-path method, Project Evaluation Review Techniques, PRINCE2, and so on, are well-known, highly brochured and implemented examples. At a lower scale, but mission-critical in the productive, mediating function of project management is the ubiquitous project plan. Distributed to the team as a photocopied handout, displayed prominently in an office as a wall chart, the project plan acts discreetly, at a safe distance, a crucial but unacknowledged member of the collective. More often than not, it is maintained online in one of many proprietary software packages that offer the security of automated management of the mundane scheduling tasks and myriad other calculations of management activity. In so doing, some aspects of the agency of the project plan as *semiotechnical machine* become more visible, factored into the machinic constraints of logistically purposed algorithms. With an allure of measure and cascading hierarchies of dependency, the project plan channels process into geometry, mapping activity in a gridded, linear matrix, generating signals to be processed by humans and machines alike.

Considered as a representation, the project plan—typically, although by no means always, mapped out using the Gantt chart format[35]—offers a synoptic overview of the distribution of resources, relative time scales of tasks, deadlines, milestones, and dependencies. It poses questions of accuracy—will the duration of a task and its cascading chain of dependencies (foundations must be completed before floor can be laid)—provide an accurate overview of what has to be done and when? And it poses questions of responsibility (who has not met their deadline?). In the recurrent review meeting that punctuates the project, the project plan serves a unifying function, a disciplinary tool to channel and hierarchize cooperation and coordination by focusing on the logical form of the relationships of work activity, and it gives the manager the industrial equivalent of a chess set to play with, resources to be moved around, shuffled and rejiggered, as problems emerge or priorities change, a gray media weapon fighting the invisible enemy, time, made manageable in semiotic space.

By abstracting from the messy relationships and heterogeneous durations that activity entails, the semiotic grid of the project plan, with its sometimes harmonious play of Cartesian proportion, accomplishes a similar task to that of perspective space in the Renaissance, valuing the symbolic mastery of space(s), allowing the project manager to think metrologically, to focus on abstract quantities of work, unbundled from sensory-motor vehicles, to move from the material through the logical to the logistical.

From the point of view of representation, the project plan poses a problem of information design, a variant of the more generic problem of the visual display of quantitative information:[36] how can we represent these activities in such a way as to make their relationships easier to understand? From a stratagematic point of view, by contrast, we need to be able to read the project plan "symptomatically" if we wish to better understand how it functions as a technique.

As a project increases in complexity, as more resources and more tasks are brought in to the process, or as activities fall out of step with each other, the clean two-dimensional "prison grid" that charted relationships, deadlines, milestones, and so on, loses its synoptic quality. Spreading over pages or on screen after screen of a high-resolution pixelated matrix, the representation twists as dependencies multiply and timelines for task completion proliferate. Logically the relationships between tasks remain, but conveyed within such a convoluted topology that one senses the presence of other forces at play, the ugly dissonance and anxiogenic must of signs gone bad.

The distortions and opacities of synoptic vision in the plan here give away its peculiar role as a repressing representation,[37] the two-dimensional geometry of wish fulfillment, twisting and creaking under the impact of forces of another nature. The logical space of representation aims to transform the "unknowns" of problems into simple obstacles to be overcome, refiguring activity and the relationships it requires.[38] This process of mobilizing productive energy and forcing it into a geometrically rationalized space-time is a form of semiotechnical delegation.[39] By interceding between workers and work, the plan shears off the mess and variable libidinal attachment of individuals to their activity at the same time as it shifts responsibility for cooperation and communication onto the manager.[40] Links between activities, the problems they may raise, the possibility for divergent directions to emerge—all of this is abstracted, delegated, and hence transformed, at the same time as it is warped, mended, and postponed by machines, workers, replete with their own tacit modes of knowledge.

Planned logistically, executed atomically, ordered hierarchically, the project offers an excellent means both of reorganizing the communicative space in which working activity occurs and of shaping the subjective dispositions of workers. In this punctual, segmented, linear space, work can be assimilated to a series of theorematic propositions. But problems cannot be so easily transformed into simple obstacles to be overcome, unless, over time, there is a change in the nature of the problems addressed and the intelligence required to solve them. The project might not, a priori, assume anything about where on the continuum of mental and material an activity might lie; after all, what does the manager care about *how* the work gets done, so long as it *gets done*? However, a segmented, well-ordered conceptual space within which activities relate to each other via an intermediary that takes the initiative for coordination, cooperation, and control is always at risk of confusing map and territory. The troops are muttering; the leader fails to see the disaster to come.

Middle Management

Gunrunners, organizers of coups, keepers of safe houses, deal makers and breakers, the gray eminence, the ethnographer's informant: while one hesitates in the presence of such a diverse band of middlemen, mediators, and intercessors, no compendium of evil media stratagems would be complete without some discussion of middle management. In the context of the divergently resonant question of "knowing what the organization knows" (Nietzschean ears hear the deafening silences implied here), mildly twitchy or overcaffeinated antennae will detect the matter of body counts, skeletons in cupboards, white-collar crime (or sharp practice, at least), and *mani pulite*: the delicate matter of the unspoken. It isn't a matter of accusation here, merely of drawing attention to the risk that the dedicated company man runs of committing what might be called "unthought crimes," crimes that are committed in the labyrinthine and troubled precincts of nonknowledge. Without playing on words too much, it is a question of the spiritualist calling of *mediumnity* and the construction of corporate states of trance or possession—of knowledge transfer and knowledge transference, the occult operations of authority conveyed through the trafficking of metaphor.

Wherever we are in the chain of command, we should put our critical scruples to one side for a moment and try a little harder to appreciate the nature of the work of the middle, the medium. For although the middle manager is often reviled, not just at work but in culture and society more generally, a strangely active and more or less surreptitious transformational aspect inheres to being in the middle. Naturally, when posing as an emissary or acting as a representative, and for different reasons, it is better to appear as a transparent intermediary rather than an active, shape-shifting manipulator or incompetent—because otherwise the accusations of betrayal will not be slow in coming. But great power is involved in the middle, with being a medium, especially if that means becoming an obligatory point of passage.[41] The strategic role of middle management is encapsulated by Herbert Simon in his *Administrative Behavior*: "Even though as far as physical cause and effect are concerned, it is the machine gunner and not the major who fights the battles, the major is likely to have a greater influence upon the outcome of a battle than any single machine gunner."[42]

Early thinking about middle management, with its cyberlogistical black boxing of the organization into input–output systems, tended to envisage the role of middle management largely in passive, information-processing terms, a view that corresponded both to a strictly dualistic conception of the division between mental and manual labor of the kind justly criticized by the Marxist economist and philosopher Alfred Sohn-Rethel and to the growing impact of cybernetics research and systems theory more generally.[43] But it was clearly a role that placed far too much emphasis on the mental end and far too little on the material end. One should not deny the possibility that becoming a smoothly fitting cog in a well-oiled machine—or, to follow the analogy *in silico*, a bug-free information-processing module in an efficiently implemented piece of software—is a crucial motivation for a middle manager (being a transparent intermediary is one way of avoiding responsibility), and it is certainly one that is conducive to the pervasiveness of dualistic, and hence representational, thinking. But it does not tell us much about what *happens* in the middle, often without any explicit knowledge, and how mediation can be and is exploited. This is perhaps better understood in terms of *interpretative effects*, effects that become all the more important as the shift to the wholesale investment of the soul at work[44] brings about a strategic emphasis on intellectual capital, tacit knowledge (or what the organization doesn't yet know that it knows), and flexibilization. Getting the soul to work requires a greater artfulness in the composition of chains of mediators.

By virtue of his or her position, the middle manager is literally an *inter*preter. Doubly so, because any channel, any conduit, offers the possibility of a two-way flow. Indeed, if, as has been argued, the chaotic circumstances in which "self-interested" frontline workers (those doing the work rather than overseeing it, such as Simon's machine gunner) operate give them a "limited perspective" that makes them unable to generate and articulate knowledge by themselves, and the high-level visions of senior management's preoccupation with what "ought to be" in turn make it difficult for them to provide explicit knowledge,[45] middle managers must have a decidedly *productive* role in their interpretive positioning, a role that evidently places them in an at once strategically crucial and risky situation.

While much maligned in the 1990s, decimated as a function of the world-flattening operations of labor arbitrage and replaced by any variety of computational system that might process information better (it was also the era of fantasies about flat management), the middle man has returned. The newly critical importance of the middle manager in the face of the varying fortunes of the organization was recognized in the theory of middle-up-down management developed by Ikujiro Nonaka and Hirotaka Takeuchi. For them, organizational mediumnity could no longer be understood as simply a quasi-computational,[46] one-way function of the operationalization of the unambiguous directives of leadership. In a world in which innovation, leveraging, and monetization in matters of knowledge are deemed crucial, the middle manager acquired a crucial role in the "knowledge spiral," the ongoing process of the creation and sharing of knowledge throughout an organization. By virtue of his or her position between the visions of senior management, which could now be as equivocal as one liked, and the mute empirical experience of frontline workers, the middle manager could play a crucial role in articulating and rendering explicit tacit knowledges of all kinds.

In this new configuration, the upper echelons of the organization are no longer deemed or even required to be the bearers of explicit, clearly formulated knowledge. It suffices to have a *dream*, a vision, if not a fantasy, because it is now the task of the middle manager to articulate such visions, as a way of directing the attention of the workforce, not just to give their work a sense of direction but also to give a material focus to the organization of their affective investment. Visions that are not embodied in such material reality are hallucinations. In such circumstances, the astute middle manager will not, of course, criticize such visions or dreams for being vacuous, vague, or half formulated. Indeed, in the interests of obeisance, remaining neutral in the face of the oneiric discourse of the executive is not an option. On the contrary, a judicious display of enthusiasm is usually the most appropriate response (if only so as not to raise the suspicion that you think the CEO a moron, which could make any operations difficult).

In the theory of middle-up-down management, the middle manager truly comes into his or her interpretive and suggestive own, because she or he not only becomes responsible for organizing and "facilitating" this process of knowledge "conversion" (extracting knowledge from workers, ensuring internalization of directives from management) but, as Nonaka and Takeuchi point out, must become "proficient at employing metaphors in order to help others generate and articulate imagination."[47] Supplying metaphors to articulate the babble of the tacit (and colored pens to draw the mind map), management becomes a more or less sophisticated art of discursive transformation, a quasi-therapeutic process that is all the more necessary given that, in practice, tacit knowledge admits of no easy organizational distinction between refined, connoisseurial expertise and complete ignorance, between fallible intelligence and unassailable stupidity. In any case, the rebadging of incoherence as "strategic equivocality" and the deliberate destruction of infrastructure and cooperative relations as "creative chaos" suggest that the wise manager should be good not only at employing metaphor but also at interpreting euphemisms and detecting oxymorons.[48]

Every bout of blue-skies thinking is an opportune moment for what the psychologist Thierry Melchior calls *proferential language*: not the language that bears verifiable reference ("your colleagues look exhausted") but the language of verbal entities and vague, fuzzy realities ("we are an investor in people").[49] The relation of preference concerns the capacity of language to fabricate things and is especially prevalent in situations where concrete referents are lacking, in moments of downsizing and redeployment, for example, or whenever targets and other quantitative abstractions are proposed.

In the face of the proliferating discourse networks that traverse the organization, a dialectic of tacit and explicit knowledge, thought to be the motor of knowledge creation in an organization, is too coarse a filter through which to understand the transformational art of middle management. In any case, from the point of view of the effective organization and exercise of power, some kinds of knowledge and associated forms of practice are only effective on condition that they are not elevated into public explicitness: not funny handshakes, perhaps, but signs that follow other codes, that tell us who belongs and who doesn't, when a threshold is crossed or a limit reached. The wrong word in a meeting that prompts a scarcely perceptible elevation of the eyebrow, the comment made from behind the hand. Perhaps this is why anecdotal evidence suggests that over 75 percent of management information systems (replacing crucial aspects of middle management strata) are not fit for purpose.[50] It is not necessarily a matter of poor design, although that is often the case. In fact, the better designed a system is, with proper automated audit trails and security permission systems, the less easy it is to fudge decisions, to cover your tracks, to ensure deniability. Information processing lacks guile, which is why software is only initialized. By contrast, a medium, like a project, has to be initiated.

In truth, the mediumnity of middle management was already recognized by some of the gurus who established their reputations at the height of the managerial revolution of the 1960s and 1970s. Warren Bennis, for example, argued that attention management was a crucial element in shaping an organization's vision.[51] More recent work on the culture of organizations establishes the importance of understanding how influence is transmitted throughout an organization.[52] This is not just a matter of having friends in high places. It means having a better understanding of the *influencing machines* that beep, buzz, whir, and click away within the organization: how brains are furnished with the friendly numerological security of a color-coded spreadsheet, rely on the private e-mail address, come to insist on organizing discussion around the official minutes of a meeting, or are locked into the bullet point hits of a slide show briefing.

From this point of view, organizational mediumnity is increasingly a matter of dealing appropriately with psychic ergonomics. As work is globalized, outsourced, casualized, fractionalized, and so on, computational techniques of supply chain management come into increasingly close proximity with the guiding, soliciting, and shaping of the expectations of subjects. It is common to argue nowadays that even the leisure time of consumption is a kind of work, but considered from the point of view of administration, work is equally a kind of consumption, shaped by similar media practices of attention management. Keep your staff on message.

But the more one insists on the transparent accountability of the explicit, codified into denumerable procedure, current doctrine, and official practice, the more the covert trafficking of the tacit comes into play. This suggests another twist on the knowledge spiral and its binary distinction between tacit and explicit knowledge, and of how the organizational imperative of "knowing what you know" brings an element of calculation, and hence the vertigo of interpretive possibility, into processes of mediation.

The deft handling of this kind of calculus, which is as much about nonknowledge as knowledge, gives a ruseful spin to the gray world of administration and is embodied in document classifications, software permissions systems, access to distribution lists, the physical policing of a building, as well as the faux bonhomie of the conversation in the corridor, the departmental jolly, or the ignorance imparted in the informative and friendly five minutes for questions at the end of a presentation. Proponents of the "media richness" theory argue that media use is crucial for managing equivocality and uncertainty,[53] and different media forms are more or less effective at resolving ambiguity and dissolving uncertainty by virtue of the "richness" of the informational cues they contain. Such an argument would be unexceptionable but for two things.

In the first place, media never exist in isolation: ambiguity is just as easily created through multiplying use of media forms. In the second place, with its simplistic evacuation of power from the analysis, the theory ignores the fact that the careful perpetuation, even fomenting, of ambiguity is half the problem of a medium. When you don't know something or there is something you don't want others to know, ambiguity and evasiveness are crucial. In any case, the proferential induction of collective trances (call it a generalized process of team building) is not something that can be accomplished by means of transparency. The supreme skill of the accomplished professional medium, the adept of the catch-up session or the special committee, is to manage the hazy borderline between knowledge and nonknowledge, to pass off *flatus vocis* as informative briefing and ensure that a liberal scattering of bullet points doesn't expose too many holes.

Excellence

Metamodel, or Formalize, Virtue

In other stratagems, we have noted the existence of a "grammar" for continuous reeducation, a grammar that codifies a set of software technologies, of machine environments, and thus offers the possibility of an algorithmic dynamic to thought and to becoming. Such a grammar points toward the possibility of a more parsimonious route into the operations of subject production, one that can be conducted directly on and through language.[1] If we have a machine grammar—a techno*logy*—for continuous reeducation, embodied across a range of hardware, software, and wetware options, perhaps some more condensed formulations of the multitudinous syntax that such a grammar affords might be possible. In this regard, the set of techniques known as neurolinguistic programming, lately popular among management consultants and psychotherapists alike (the likeness not being entirely accidental) and redolent of the trend toward positive psychology, perhaps offers a suitable candidate for the pressing requirement of engendering new forms of subjectivity. As the experts put it, "These days we need the skills to develop personal flexibility to the extreme."[2] Only individuals able to adapt to, or acquire a closer fit with, the demands of the world in progress will gain the right to call themselves virtuous. In the guise of a practice of modeling—or, rather, *metamodeling*—NLP proposes an approach to reeducation that can, in principle, operate at the micrological level of linguistic form itself, through a disclosure of what its proponents call the "mental syntax" that orders experience. Better still, as a practice for the administration of the self, for minimum outlay (books, toolkit, webinars) NLP can be self-administered, although undoubted financial advantages accrue to becoming expert.

While the notion of the model equivocates delightfully in its use of the armature of science when scaled up beyond the strict confines of the laboratory, in general it condenses and essentializes pertinent variables and significant features in a highly portable, economical manner, even where the associated intellectual technology does not, a priori, require such fixity or closure. To develop a model of a set of events or situations in the real world is to purport to offer an accurate—if abbreviated—representation of those events or that situation. A model thus permits the exploration of scenarios, mapping responses occurring according to variations in the parameters defining the model.[3] For a scientist, the model is a tool designed to capture an aspect of the reality being modeled. From a more strictly mathematical-logical point of view, models have to do with the *interpretation* of formulas in a logical system; that is, they go from being meaningless strings to having a meaningful value: a model-theoretic semantics ensures that syntactically well-formed formulas in a natural language, for example, are susceptible to being considered true or false in a finite, parseable way.[4]

For the neurolinguistic programmer, the model is an underlying mapping, along the lines of a structural grammar (à la Chomsky) of the world, a formal-rhetorical device that, unlike a Chomskyan structure—which is not revisable at will—opens up the possibility of an infinite flexibility, a perpetually revisable relation to the world, the permanent reworking of "mind-body coding" or the structure of subjective experience. These oxymoronic "structures of magic," as the founders of NLP call them, can be placed at the service of the modeling of excellence in all domains, facilitating the techno-therapeutic play of quasi-algebraic rewrite rules—now grasped as critical operators in the process of persuasion engineering—for a sophisticated, and in principle technologically translatable, practice of excellence in communication.[5]

On the assumption of the ultimate existence of some presumed formally adequate syntax, the rewrite rules that metamodelers discern—deletion, distortion, generalization[6]—offer a way of improving communication and, crucially, a form of self-assessment that can be abstracted from the tacit habits of experience, that can be revised and recoded, ideally leading to the unconscious assimilation of patterns of excellence. Self-assessment using such rewrite rules clearly presupposes some abstract communicational machine, a virtual reservoir of well-formed formulas that our intransigence, our lack of excellence, our everyday inflexibilities, prevent us from accessing. The metamodel presides over such processes, in a position of gray eminence, the very existence of which implies, if not ensures, its own requirement to banish the possibility of the evil negativity of malformed language.[7]

The ease with which NLP practitioners flaunt a variable—and not always consistent—jargon, their invocations of Ericksonian "solution-oriented" hypnosis, or their highly pragmatic invocation of science all offer a ready matter for denunciation, one made all the easier by lurid stories about the shadowy lives of the founding fathers of the field. But in fact, in practices where "the truth" is not at stake—except rhetorically, as in the art of always being right—the invocation of science, as elsewhere, can offer useful benefits, the accrual of a certain legitimacy, the stability of a socially well-distributed set of roles to slip into, codifying expectations through the powers of scientific knowledge. Naturally such benefits are open to abuse, as is the promise of measurement more generally. In any case, there are fields of ostensibly scientific endeavor, economics, for example, in which it is apparent that the model has a decisive impact on reality, where the map is not only not the territory (a simple requisite for realism) but productive of the territory that it then claims to map. As such, with this productive role, the broader question of the redundancy or otherwise of affordances that models create, the kind of reeducation of practices they inculcate, is crucial—for both epistemics and technics alike.[8]

But the productive use of models in neurolinguistic programming is more important for the practice of *free indirect action* to which it testifies: in a world where institutions are predicated on the free consent of individuals for their smooth operation, manipulating models, rather than manipulating people, is an exemplary form of indirect action. Models are mediators, of course, and supremely interested ones at that.[9] When target individuals or clients can be encouraged to manipulate such models themselves, in a technology of self-modeling, we enter into the realm of free indirect action,[10] a crucial element for any autonomous practice of reeducation. Acceding to communication free of distortion, generalization, and deletion enables the production of *well-formed outcomes*, objectives that bring the individual into harmony with the culture of audit, the algorithms of workflow, the tasks and deliverables of project management. An "outcome frame" provides a notional setting in which to budget for the allocation of sensory resources: you can make efficiency savings with experience.[11]

With the ethico-aesthetic impulses of an evil media approach firmly in mind, the indirect way in which one inculcates virtuous behavior (excellence being a loose translation of the Aristotelian concept of *arête*) through NLP compels most interest. The artful use of metamodeling questions (a use that admittedly offers some scope for unscrupulous manipulation), situated observation, and an analysis of excellent behavior at a range of neurological levels offers the theoretical possibility of building up models of (domain-specific) excellence. By disclosing the strategies that virtuous exemplars use in fields such as futures trading, project management, strategic thinking, sports, and so on, and codifying these in a formal-rhetorical model of language use, one can not only promise to have extracted the essential features of what generations of scholars have puzzled over, but also to have done so in a format that renders them inherently transmissible. If complete, coherent, and consistent models of excellence in a given domain are not available, a process of divide-and-conquer permits the assimilation of strategies that reorder one's mental syntax bit by bit.

With all the emphasis in the modeling industry on expertise and excellence, and the crossover in the corporate world between New Age and new money,[12] it is not surprising that NLP gurus experience some difficulty in encouraging the unconscious assimilation of excellence in the process by which clients *acquire* excellence. After all, if the specific skill that a guru offers is a technique for remodeling people, almost at will, won't clients take more of an interest in imitating the guru, the modeler, rather than the model role one is learning to play? These circumstances offer perfectly sensible therapeutic and business reasons to encourage those thirsty for success, virtue, or wisdom to self-model: franchise opportunities, online dissemination, a healthy regard for reputation maintenance, among others.

Modeling excellence, which transforms habits of imitation into a process of knowledge engineering for the design of virtue, requires an aptitude for prosopopoeia on the part of the modeler—an ability to speak (on) the part of the model. A model of excellence or exemplar (first party) cannot be transmitted from modeler (second party) to client (third party) if it has not already been assimilated by the second party. Imitation, a chameleonic capacity for mimicry, is here at the service of linguistically inculcated excellence, in which clarity of communication is imperative. You can't *not* communicate, cries the modeler, capturing any claim to ineffable giftedness within patterns of excellence and removing any obstacle or limit to the hopes and dreams one might weave into the magic of neurolinguistic modeling. It would be impossible to reproduce and hence exchange excellence were it not for the redundancies of the pattern that the model captures, an observation that brings neurolinguistic programming into close proximity with the Turing machine.

Modeling as a constructive technique thus raises interesting possibilities. The more speculatively inclined strategist (and from the moment that we aim for, or are subject to, excellence, we are all strategists of one sort or another) might be inclined to further formalize virtue through a direct implementation in software. "Rewrite" rules of the type that the NLP practitioner uses are already present in rudimentary form in interface designs that reformat data input or provide list boxes for appropriate selection of vocabulary; and machines are considerably more flexible in assimilating models of excellence than imperfect, fallible humans, at least for as long as one ignores the faults and cracks in sociotechnical systems. The more skeptical strategist, by contrast, might ask what this incessant bid for excellence discloses—a postponement of the failure of reeducation with mind camps or brain spas fragmenting into franchises, perhaps? From the point of view of this collection of stratagems, both positions are correct; that is to say, their models are operative.

Lifelong Learning

There is nothing as beautiful as education, nothing so intimately wound up with the sense of meaningful life and an openness to the wonders of the universe. Education is both the foundation of independent thought and action and the means for acting in concert, through common understanding and reason. Education is the means by which we anticipate the past and learn from the future. For these reasons, among others, education lies at the core of any systematic implementation of evil media. Education is an affirmative "drawing out of what is there," a transductive aspect of becoming rather than a branding or molding of the individual subject. As such, it is not a tool or a cognitive prosthetic, plugged into an already established and self-sufficient agent (although it may work by providing the chance for the illusion of such); rather, it works as an interweaving, a harmony. Instead of endless revision, it offers open-ended revisability. Withdrawn from the tendentially repressive mechanisms of the pastoral, shepherding order of education, it creates conditions in which people face the need to chart their own path.

Lifelong learning is a commitment of life force to this process, but it is also a means by which a life and its relation to knowledge may be arranged in logistical terms and developed. Whereas many specific stratagems need be used only sparingly, lifelong learning is a permanent commitment. This is not without consequence.

As a problem of becoming, learning is related to the stratagematics of love in the time-space of Bergsonian evolution, in that one can only undergo so many kinds of educational development simultaneously. And this problem of becoming can equally be related to a key question of computation as it negotiates between different kinds of abstraction, theoretical possibility, and the empiricism that rubs up against questions of material resources. A sense of the intractable insistence of infinity through and against finitude is key to stratagematic feeling and incisive thought. In its mediatic, computational form, we can provide instantiations of both. The Turing machine, as a working abstraction, establishes the possibility of infinitely long and complex computations made in finite steps. Beyond this threshold, which might be described as one of intractability, we encounter problems that are effectively incomputable by virtue of their complexity. Compared to the question of the infinite, however, the exigencies of the actual computations that must be made in the world require that we operate within limited timescales: the time it takes to crack a code, work out a profit–cost benefit, project and analyze the consequences of a move, render an object in time to meet a deadline. Such calculations may define the stratagematic and more broadly pragmatic horizon of the computability of a problem, pointing toward the importance of a judicious manipulation of resources when the insistence of infinite possibility opens up.[13]

Integrating lifelong learning into questions of computation and computationalism brings into the picture the shifting nature of the intelligence that learning is supposed to inculcate. It highlights the thorny problem of the extent to which the educational calculus can afford to leave the details of the solutions to complex problems to take care of themselves. The possibilities of automated problem solving that Turing's machine ushered in quickly found their limit when addressed by artificial intelligence programming envisaged as a kind of a priori investigation of the conditions of all possible cognition.[14] Programming every possible state that the automaton would be expected to process from the top down may have corresponded to a pervasive world-historical fantasy of control,[15] but it left machines without the initiative to improvise when the commands from on high were ambiguous. Hence the interest in the schematization of machine learning processes explored by both earlier and more recent forms of electronic brain research (with the caesura between them produced by the switch to symbolic AI). Training a neural network in a form of distributed cognition might or might not yield a solution to a problem that the programmer has no hope of understanding, but it will produce machines that can sometimes take the initiative for themselves. "Dis-organizing" education so that learning is accomplished along the way by a flexibly adaptive brain, rather than programming axioms for all the moves in advance, facilitates an encounter with problems that cannot readily be parsed by a theorematic intelligence.

In network analysis, such difficulties are analogous to the development of "intractable networks" that do not correspond to the clean lines of power laws but stage layer after layer of honeycombed and fissiparous structures that are too irregularly assembled and hence less readily computable. Similar problems are posed by the development of massive, permanently "spammy neighborhoods" on the Internet that exist in the regimes of ordering created by the operations of search engines solely to exploit them by means of automatically generated links. The human brain and the learning processes it takes part in match this disorderly matrix rather well, existing as legacy systems, historical meshes of collapsing and residue structures of interlinkage, produced in real time by vast numbers of actors responding both predictably and unpredictably to stimuli and interaction.

Thus education exists among a class of problems linking complexity, expenditure of resources and capacities, computability, and the activities of humans and computers in operations over time. Education emphasizes the diagram of responsibility that it draws. Rather than being a problem that tends toward equalization of agency across a network, it is one that is located in the learning, self-nurturing subject. But whereas intractability in network analysis leads to problem solving in probabilistic terms, in this type of problem, only one answer is necessary: the responsible citizen.

A need likely exists for a stratagem for the analysis and allocation of agency in relations. Such a stratagem might explore the sophisticated virtues of functionalism. But creating conditions in which citizens achieve responsibility for their choices and educational investments, allowing them better to act in their own interests, voiding in turn the interests of others for such investments entails more than a technical description of human operations; it must also draw on resources such as feeling, the becoming properly speculative of hitherto merely social capital,[16] and the means by which reliable care, and opportunities to reward self-motivating aspiration, can be delivered at point of demand.

Under a classical understanding of the place of education in society, the biography of a citizen might look like this: birth, education, work, species reproduction, work, retirement, death.

Under conditions of lifelong learning, it is likely to look more like this: birth, trauma, therapy, training, internship, recruitment, role-playing, training, deployment, trauma, therapy, retraining, deployment, therapy, death.

These two selections have undergone many kinds of simplification and work here only for purposes of illustration. They may differ in terms of the probable interpolation of gender, occupation, and the extent and quality of service, among other things—trauma, for instance, here being understood to be interchangeable with species reproduction. However, the main difference between the two rows of instructions is not the specific kind of events they include but the greater intensity and variety of knowledge-acquisition events that feature in the latter biography. We can also say that the latter exhibits a greater amount of repetition of the same category or kind of learning event. In the manner of a serial offender, an individual can undergo related processes several times in a lifetime and achieve higher levels of learning incrementally over the course of a biography. But what also changes in these examples is that work itself disappears as a separate, and even notionally separable, term, becoming part of the learning process itself as opportunities for education and reeducation themselves weave in and out of work. Work should be understood to be consonant and coterminous with the now perpetually examined life.

Learning is inherently mediatic, a theater where the self encounters its own becoming and engages in relays of value with the materials, media, organizations, and networks by which it is engaged and evaluated. Equally, therapeutics become core to the conception of learning as part of self-improvement, providing an upgrade in attitude, knowledge, or theoretical orientation. Health loses its simple emphasis on mechanical good function to acknowledge and assimilate a wider, more multidimensional sense of well-being. When work is coterminous with life as an ongoing educational process, the habits that a person acquires in one biographical segment threaten the possibility of adapting flexibly to the next segment. Emphasizing education in relation to health also offers a suitable means of devolving power. Thus lifelong learning operates via a double movement: first, the interiorization, the claiming for the self, of what was previously the work of the state, church, and family; and second, an opening up of possibilities to other kinds of actors and nonstandard learning events.

As a grammar that links events, process management, choice and decision structures, and knowledge, lifelong learning falls within the purview of evil media; but it also gains importance by the way in which it is delivered, by its operation as a media form. Education and training systems, such as virtual learning environments, testing zones, and brain-gym games, not to mention improving music played into the womb, are just some of the ways in which assessment and grading can be brought into a wider range of life experiences and integrated into myriad informatic circuits. Linking learning to testing through more, and more tightly looped, feedback mechanisms, real-time ratings plug-ins, and so on, in this way affords the crucial possibility of introducing distributed competition into the learning process. Algorithms used in processes of machine learning—Teuvo Kohonen's "self-organizing maps," for example—use a form of competitive learning to solve problems, and a formalistic indicator of how this might operate. The problem that the self-organizing map tackles is one of ensuring that a complex set of data inputs can be mapped onto a simpler, more readily calculable two-dimensional network of nodes. Nodes in the network, initially equipped with random weightings, are assessed by their degree of proximity to input data; the node that approximates most closely to the input data is selected as the winner; and other nodes with topological proximity to the winner are updated to respond to input in a similar way. Through round after round of successive comparisons to inputs, one ends up with a plastic, flexibly adaptive network.[17] Arbitrary problems, rewards for the winner, nudging and imitation: the computational formalism points here to an abstract and abstractable logic of autonomous learning. As such, the minuscule inculcations of competition and rivalry and the encouragement to imitate, with a gently nudged weighting to push one way or another, can operate in a distributed fashion. The world is your classroom! As part of a generalized drive to perpetual testing, the logic of the self-organized map introduces a consciousness of a self responsible for one's cognitive states and furnishes a ready explanation for failure that can no longer be blamed on the educational system.

While education can be thought of as an investment, it is never simply that, or, as could be said of many investments, it does not correspond well to such a categorization. Human capital is also a form of consumption, of experience, of the self, and for this reason, lifelong learning is a commitment to a mode of life that never ceases to update itself through inquiry. But it can also be delivered by efficient means: in workplace-based packages or day release schemes; as voluntary or compulsory retraining for the unemployed; or (for those who have been traumatized or disabled) as occupational therapy, work as medicine. A self-directed path of personal growth is equally possible, as is self-directed retribution for criminals. In the context of increasingly responsive and flexible work, the delivery of learning paths grows in importance. Lifelong learning does not require that skills, aptitudes, or ideas become redundant as new ones are added; it merely recognizes their place in a complex adaptive system. While some may die out, the opportunity for learning continues, and the ways in which it can adapt and survive persist.

Be Artistic

At the same time as logic, order, transparency, norms, and regularity have great value, they should never stand in the way of the free flow of tactics. Here it is useful to recount Saul Alinsky's appeal to his fellow community organizers to keep a priori rationalizations of action at arm's length and to follow one's nose when generating a campaign.[18] For Alinsky, this is the seal of power, the ability to drive reality through a freestyle pragmatics while analyzing, attacking, and disrupting prevailing power structures. Driven as much by a lusty curiosity, the feel of an event turning from one state into another, as by the imperatives of justice, this lesson can also be learned in different ways. In the context of media, what is of interest is the way in which such drives couple with formally describable systems. In Alinsky's case, such coupling of drive to system may happen through intermediating mechanisms such as ostensive moralities that can easily resolve into good or bad, or matters of technical or legal compliance. These may be made handleable, in the case of activism on a corporate body, at a further remove through means such as publicity, shareholding, or boycott, but other means link more directly to formal structuration. The question Alinsky poses, however, is important: how do the irrational, the messy, and the unpredictable key into formalizations? And how do these in turn produce new grammars of the unexpected and the wild, rational (rather than irrational) exuberance? Management writers in the muscular style of Tom Peters return to this question as a matter of process, but it can also be treated as a question of a deeper level of formalization.[19]

The generative capacity of interlocking and mutually stimulating formalizations of process can bring its own kind of imagination and creative invention. In the use of both relational structures such as databases and user-facing interfaces, this is something to be remembered. To let the free flow of unanswerable logic concatenate into its ontogenetic state represents something other than the spook's repertoire of ambiguity and shades of interpretation. The clarity of a well-placed formalism leaves the divination of such gray mists for the bluntness of fact, category, and rule, something well exemplified in the following pre-database example from the forced labor camps described in Varlam Shalamov's *Kolyma Tales*: "Transfers from one shift to another were always made to catch the clock's hour hand so that the working day was not lost and the prisoner could not receive a few extra hours of rest."[20] Rectitude has its own rewards, and the invention of this rule meant extracting a grueling double shift every time a change in duties occurred. While this is perhaps an anomalously human-scale example, it does offer a gratifying register for the operations of abstract dynamics made infrastructural and oblivious.

However, imposing a logical reading on reality tends to reduce operations to the mechanistic, losing sensitivity to the individual case or, more systemically, forcing behaviors through a too generally applied grammar. But before we look at this aspect of personalized service, it is worth examining the question of margins established by the story from Kolyma. As cultural theory so readily reminds us, the most interesting activity often occurs in the margin. Imagine the creativity involved in precisely locating the sweet spot between the probability of an event or an illness occurring and the profitable unease that can be mobilized sufficiently to sell an insurance product. Protection against the possibility of unlikely but costly leaks in particular pipes for homeowners, insurance to cover narrowly defined kinds of breast cancer in young women who have credit cards, additional warranty on electrical goods sold at the point of purchase extending to just before the point of failure: the margin between yield and outlay can open up hitherto inaccessible universes of doubt and discomfort and the financial transactions that can be offered up as prayers against their occurrence. But the simple linking of insurance to unease is only one initial domain in which such dynamics may be launched. As the founders of a popular data-mining service note in a paper setting out their problematic in terms of academic information retrieval research, "Usage was important to us because we think some of the most interesting research will involve leveraging the vast amounts of usage data that is available from modern web systems."[21] When this project of leveraging identifiable patterns in data couples with the margins of financial speculation, we are able to witness some of the most powerful abstract imaginings currently synthesizable. There is a race between the fabulations of capital and the ability of technicians to deliver new product, a race that is at the same time mutually stimulating, a structural coupling of phantasmatic numbers and yields that may yet become concrete or do not need to do so because the operative usefulness is in their possibility. Mapping relations between identifiable elements of data, how those data may or may not have directly or probabilistically attachable relations to identities, human bodies, and their actual or future performance, the carbon digestion of forests, user-generated properties, (subprime) housing, the circulations of goods or other data, and recursively to other speculative vehicles and their future values, ownerships, identification, and functions become crucial. Although these proliferating data remain indexically linked to the entities from which they are abstracted, the multidimensional feature space into which they are mapped forms the basis of a new landscape in which such margins may be navigated and enjoyed.

While a user might experience such a system as a "personalized" service, systems of this kind are also treated as data-yielding entities, which to meet the requirements of database normalization are analytically or procedurally disassembled into a sequence of predicates without a subject. As such, their personalization is merely a ruse. What we see, rather, is the technical individuation of another entity generated out of myriad capta, traces, correspondences, likelihoods, and records. Gathered into "buckets"[22] of data of the same category, these may, by a sequence of Boolean expressions, be linked, refined, and queried so as to be reassembled as a different set of qualities and features or, once those that are desirable and those that are undesirable have been assayed, to filter out any entities of the latter category. Just as for artificial intelligence researchers formalization is a means of "freeing their work from the unruliness and imprecision of vernacular language,"[23] so data yielded from more organic or holistically experienced and thus uninterpretable life stories can be a means of bringing meaning to peoples' lives. To be artistic, to work creatively with the generative powers of data fields, means to allow formalizations off the leash, to feel them biting into and shaping reality. Here creativity becomes not simply the domain of traditional intuition but what is traditionally considered its opposite, the meticulous attention to—and gaming of—rules.

Role Play

Prerequisite to the subtle facilitation of life that the smooth, even friction-free operations of the contemporary economy appeal to is a stable distribution of, and accom-
modation to, the playing of roles. While in earlier times knowing your place was a
productive virtue, now a more flexible mode is required. Articles of social and economic governance are still predicated on a stabilization of actors and entities, but they
are more dynamically allocated. Politics depends on an acceptance of roles and a
calculus of the ways in which they can be played against one another (you can be
voter, citizen, employee, employer, parent, child, taxpayer, nationalist, immigrant):
those who belong must have at least one part, and politics has little room for those
who don't. In the formation of the nation, for instance, the expiatory operations of
exclusion heap a heteroclite and never consistent set of determinations on specific
roles in the scripts of national or other kinds of belonging. The political distribution
of roles becomes a more complicated issue when parliament also becomes—in theory,
if not quite in practice—a parliament of things. In recent sociology, roles and actors
multiply, demanding more of a focus on the implication of nonhumans, such as
computers, in the operations and dynamics of power. This in turn increases the importance of crucial but much ignored devices like scripts in the configuration of the
generalized dramaturgy of the social.[24]

As part of such, scripts are vital to any playing of roles. A script is a mediating
device that draws together theatrical, psychological, and machinic roles. Scripts shape
the way in which components in a software system interact with each other, framing
the parameters of behavior *within* a computer toward its outside, or iterating into those
carried out *with* computational media, *in* human–computer symbiosis, to behaviors
that, enabled and entrained, move backward and forward *between* computers, people,
and other agents. Scripts equally afford certain kinds of relations between human
agents, giving the social a dramatic coefficient open to all sorts of stage redirections.

Not all scripts are written, of course, and a sort of circular relationship even exists
between scripts and actors (you need the one for the other, and the other for the one).
Not every role is played with equivalent levels of conscious awareness, good faith, or
algorithmic finality, but each generates a dance of expectant and preemptive behavior
acting on behavior. Roles are defined and played so that tasks are scheduled and
executed. A machine executes its task with less bad faith but with less scope for improvisation, perhaps, than a *garçon de café*, Sartre's exemplary instance of someone playing
at being.[25] This dance of expectation and preemption implies both the opening up of
movements and changes and the engineering of new requirements to smooth the

transition of a script from one component to another. Scripts mediate and are mediated, shaping roles that act on roles: they are prepositional operators that regularize actions by positioning actors in relations of point and counterpoint to each other. Some roles, and they are numerous, require tighter scripting than others: less a sketch for movements than a direct ordering that becomes more prescriptive and constraining as the role is less desirable, less easy. To put all of this in a slightly different way, the heterogeneous world of scripts is a world in which the automation of role play is a central concern.

The importance of the playing of roles in social and cultural life is not a recent discovery, and oratorical virtue sometimes depends on playing a part. Erving Goffman's *The Presentation of Self in Everyday Life* thematized the dramaturgical quality of collective life at the start of the 1960s, and more recently, researchers in the field of artificial intelligence have theorized the scripted quality of cognitive behavior as a prelude to the production of more intelligent machines.[26]

However, in the domain of machines, this thematizing of scripts, roles, and plans presumes but ignores the existence and effectiveness of a more mundane configuration of roles, which makes a technological form a friend of the family, an accepted feature in the office, or a reliable component of everyday life. Intelligent behavior in the wrong context can seem like idiocy. One should not, then, ignore the scripts—batch-processed files of command line instructions, for example—that set machines, or even applications, going as autonomous agents in the first place, that configure them so as not to overly destabilize existing distributions of roles and responsibilities, that configure functions to refine and smooth a purpose. Imagine how tiresome it would be (and how difficult to maintain an appropriately flattering hierarchy of relations) if, with every new application, you had to copy each file and register each setting required to make the software work, by hand. There would be no intelligent medium responsive to "your" needs and whims.[27] The roles of master and slave would be reversed as an entire subdomain so gray it blends into the background would spring to the fore in all its incomprehensible, numerological glory.

It is hardly surprising that such an oversight has developed. Pure and impure: a tacit hierarchy within the world of computer programming and software development, for example, has long differentiated between programming and scripting; scripting is often looked down on because of its involvement with the messiness of pragmatic "real-world" considerations.[28] In the axiology of programmer lore, "script kiddies" with their cut'n'paste code never quite have the elite training or the refined ethics of the genuine hacker. This hierarchy corresponds to a more general sniffiness about the lack of authenticity conveyed by scripting: we suppress our inner actors and pretend not to like scripts, even if the roles they assign us provide comfort, warmth, and familiarity.

What pleasure we can find in taking up and playing a role (in every sense of the verb). Already, given the substitutability that it implies, the notion of role-playing offers the disjoining of parts, a little bit of shadow, the opportunity for hide-and-seek, of not quite being where the explicit role requires. The superposing of multiples roles and the conflict between the different universes of reference they unfold can in turn generate problems of psychosocial dissonance, the chance for a little art or poetry, or the chance to exploit the possibilities for multiple flip-flopping between, or confusion of, the roles an actor is scripted to play.[29] By flouting stable, well-configured expectations—exploited mercilessly by the hacker, slipping deviant commands into the myriad indeterminacies of a machine's operation—an uncertain shift of dynamics can be engineered. Watch closely as the mask slips.

Scripting can entail a machine simulation of a sequence of actions that a user might carry out within an application: the macro written for a spreadsheet encodes the expectations of the application, sometimes without the user making any explicit decision at all. Or a script might be run on the installation of a piece of software, setting the parameters that define the "personalization" of an application (it is *your* amanuensis). The growing importance of scripting languages (Perl, Tcl, JavaScript, Ruby, etc.) in the world of new media indicates a move away from the image of building purposeful applications from a tabula rasa and toward a reconfiguration of specific components, an integration and reuse of parts into a functional whole. This is a pragmatic problematics of intelligence, not a thorematic systematization.

Roles are especially critical in an environment in which one depends on the automation of activity. Script actions to create behavior: this is the requisite formula for the generation of algorithmic subjects, for agents and agency that can be batch processed, shaped and scaled according to a strategic game plan, a set of measurable aims and objectives. You can only customize the operational parameters of a program if its application is certain. But automation, like the endless flexibilization and instability of social life, the move toward precarity, leads to a greater complexity in the distribution and configuration of roles, the growth of contention problems, and the dizzying shift from one position to another. A theory of the transaction costs of subjectivation seems to be required. Scripts provide a ready glue to cross this gap in the meantime.

The play of roles thus requires deftness and cunning. It's not that in themselves they need require anything particular or complicated; indeed, the script itself may be minimal (laugh if a joke is told, vote when an election is called, moan as an orgasm seems due). Indeed, they can make the whole thing more involving, if not more gratifying, but as the universes of reference they suppose multiply, the coordinates that give a performance its consistency can become confused, and sometimes amusingly so. Historical layer piles on historical layer: the call-center employee in India, with the exaggerated English verbal tics of the colonial subaltern, has the scripted phone manner of the helpful servant with the impeccable accent. Sly civility is mobilized as a means and motive for incommunication.[30]

Roles shift with the universe of reference one finds oneself in: a personal computer can be an accountant (you need a pay raise), an informant about the world outside (you are a floating voter), a substitute partner in a failing marriage (onanist), a desired object in child–parent conflict. The plurality of possible roles is large for both human and machine. Comparative analysis suggests that the computer sets the standard. Not only does it not grumble overmuch about being reskilled, but it can also switch settings with greater ease and speed than you—provided you remember to tell it what to do (don't forget to log out). This ability to shift between roles, to recognize the scales at which a role operates, is crucial to avoiding the infelicity of performance failure.[31] The intractable smirk of self-satisfaction is at times a critical parameter for the role of CEO in certain boardrooms, as might also be bonhomie, briskness, the ability to bite throats—though the smirk may not work before a committee of publicity-hungry congressmen under the klieg lights of network television. Some elements of a role may be drastically altered as they scale up and scale out, or not, as the case may be. Project your voice; project your face, emote; feel the depth of my distribution. It is not surprising, then, that techniques such as neurolinguistic programming or role-playing, which are designed to help in the modeling of new roles, appeal to flexibility. When not uniquely about adaptation to the labor market, flexibility might be thought a properly sophisticated virtue, an exemplary form of excellence in communication. The winner is the person who finds it easiest to build up "rapport" with others, with the expectant audience, used to the machine-theater of roles that you, by contrast, might want to shift or modify.[32]

Managing roles and the play to which they give rise becomes more difficult in a distributed environment. Controlling the message when the medium is not just multiplied or dispersed through networks but is an organizing element of the execution of strategy illustrates this clearly. So, following the tightly prescribed rules of military engagement, a U.S. soldier opens fire on Iraqi civilians from a helicopter gunship: scripted perception.[33] As he does so, another script and another role kick in—the conditioned reflex fingers of the late-night gamer playing the role of a marine with his buddies in an online environment. He's a first-person shooter ratcheting up the points before kicking back with pizza or a spliff: confusion of roles, telescoping of distances, blurring of scales. Rules of engagement flicker in and out of memory; roles move up and down the chain of command. "You shoot, I'll talk." The azimuth limits of interpretation from inside a turret script what is seen that was never there; non-combatants grow guns, in turn producing the opportunity for the scripts of the press conference and the acronym-rich jargons of military paperwork.

Conflicts and dissonances generated by the multiplication of roles are not just a matter for the competent authorities. Life being what it is, a full appreciation of what a role consists of must itself be assembled from an extended network of mediators: the narrative possibilities of the script unfold from chat rooms, DVDs, social media groups. "Isn't this what fathers are supposed to do?" the father asks his teenage son as they go to the football match. "No," comes the reply, sifting from the search results for "father + son + bonding." Within the home, a role is organized around a sort of virtual "stub" script, a reduced or minimal piece of code that can be used to initiate a process, for which the bulk of the work is done elsewhere, or as a placeholder for some routine yet to be written. The narrative possibilities for an actor can be severely constrained by the network. The stability of roles thus comes into conflict with their rapid multiplication and overlap. The script is what patches roles together, allowing them to be cut and pasted from one job to the next.

Psychic Ergonomics

The hopes and passions people weave into a gadget, a media system, or a computational assemblage have no essential limit, but equally there is no easy way to know in advance what will work either. This is a crucial factor to acknowledge in a stratagematic approach that, as Terry Winograd says of Google, embraces the capacity to declare, "Here's what we hope will be interesting. Let's find out. Let's try it."[34] This empirical dimension allows Google to remain spontaneous but equipped, able to open up new operations in beta and move on when they don't catch. One of the problems for operating in a stratagematic mode, though, lies in how one might be able to gain a degree of direct manipulation over the conditions in which one operates. To what extent can one couple responsiveness, the ability to try something out, with the operation of positions of mastery? The stratagematic is not exhausted by the tactical mode of thinking on your feet. It also implies the ability to operate across scales, driving things from above.

One of the ways in which such traction can be gained is through psychic ergonomics. That is to say, rather than attempting to engineer users, one works to provide the scaffolding around and through which the user's fears, enthusiasms, and delights may grow and flourish. Psychic ergonomics therefore relates to the stratagems of facilitation but emphasizes the emotional and cognitive aspect of such a gambit. As such it can usefully be understood through an account of media gadgets. In his lucid analysis of the cosmology of objects, Jean Baudrillard describes the functionality of gadgets as being merely subjective, objects that exist primarily for their ability to elicit delighted fascination.[35] While in Baudrillard's account gadgets have a relatively minor role as the creations of eccentrics, such a quality may also serve, at a different moment, to bring them closer to the heart of contemporary matters.

As propositions, gadgets are unlimited in the degree of association that may be yielded as they come into conjuncture with other elements in the world. They do not easily give in to a retentive suck on the pus of experience or a description of the very capacity of perceptibility and naming out of a thing; they are too manifold. Such a willful overinvestment in an object, whether of a jug or an interface, is simply one of a class of approaches that calls for manipulation and not an inherent path to the truth of any essence. Staring at a gadget, feeling it, and testing the means by which it may riddle one's nerves with ideas are means of garnering inspiration, not of harvesting essence or stockpiling reserves of insight or conjugating cloying verbifications.

Among the universe of gadgets, the influencing machines described by Victor Tausk are mechanisms reported by psychiatric patients as able to control their thoughts and senses, consisting of mystical and obscure components known through the popularization of science and technology.[36] In Melanie Klein's terms, these are internal objects, mental concepts, which, as the particular class called influencing machines, are in turn able to steer and dominate others.[37] In D. W. Winnicott's reading of Klein, the internal object is also entangled in its relation to other registers of material objects that are not simply made of thought but can be caressed, licked, held, sucked, pulled at, and bitten.[38] Such objects exist between the child and the world, extending the sensoriality of the child in its transitions to the outside, and are also transitional in the sense that the thickness of engagement with them passes as other developments occur, and if they do not undergo "perversion." Winnicott's work, which has a strong feel for the implications of the partial, the imperfect, and the "good-enough," is a pragmatics—it draws up a means for recognizing growth patterns that interweave the sensorial with materiality of other kinds, operating at other scales.

We find a wider sense of such scaffolding in the thinkers and experimentalists developing the "expanded-mind" arguments in cognitive science, in which a cognitive system is seen to be a combination of agencies and resources that combine to yield thought, whether or not all of them are encased in a single thick coating of skin.[39] Such work contains multiple differentiations along several lines of emphasis (functionalist, phenomenological, information-centric, bio-centric, etc.)[40] and can also be usefully coupled to means by which the generation and circulation of cognitive processes are turned into processes beyond the simple phenomenological scale of the individuated nervous system. A cluster of arguments in the discussion of cognition expanded beyond the brain emphasizes the storage and processing of information as being the key point at which cognition can be registered, information having a quality of sameness that can be registered and measured by familiar means as more or less constant across those that share it. More problematic is the measurement of phenomena that evade figuration as solely informational, such as emotion. Numerous means exist—from "experience design" to torture—that promise the engineering of emotion, and its more or less predictable formation, but they too remain simply means of loading the probabilities toward the achievement of a specific result.

A stratagematic implication of the expanded-mind argument, especially in relation to gadgets, is that it emphasizes not the individual cognitive assemblage—that of one expanded or contracted mind—but multiple minds, inhabiting scaffolds that provide associational frameworks. Minds with waxing and waning boundaries composed by persons, gadgets gorged on services, by apps that lock data into delivery, and by the developing habits of different modes of attentiveness and fidgeting. Here, following the thread of the possibility of emotion as a category in expanded-mind theory, we can turn to literature on the management of software engineering, with its emphasis on aligning desire, expectation, exertion, and communication with a production schedule. The more that emotional assets are incorporated into the management structure, the more such approaches risk yielding substantial multimodal glitches. Such glitches can be as simple as those that occur when an argument comes out of nowhere in a conversation, something that neither person can provide an account of but is engendered by the linguistic difficulty of the retrospectively untraceable misunderstanding, often risking the loss or deletion of significant emotional assets. More substantially, as exemplified by methods that aim to maintain a state of excitement, of "team building," or of morale or esprit, emotion can move from project asset to managerial infrastructure. To truly work, an anatomy of emotion and its technical affordances should avoid a simple functionalism. As if in response to such a need, the gadget provides a technical form that is able to mediate directly between business plan and the tenderness of the soul. As such, returning to the thought we began with, the capacity of a gadget to exemplify human ideals has no essential limit.

Here the question of cognitive scaffold can be of use. As a scaffold, gadgetry is keyed into release schedules, upgrades, features, new models, new visions, the curious charm of obsolescence. But the nature of the gadget is not simply one of users being conned into buying something that is guaranteed to tank a month before their contract runs out or that otherwise exhibits the transience of a lettuce leaf under a heat lamp. This is only a very thinly sliced aspect of the complex pleasures a gadget may find itself sustaining. The question is therefore how to sense the shifting tensions and coagulations that array themselves around the scaffolding of the gadget and the larger structures in which it integrates the user, and how to mobilize them in the right way.

When this happens, even when carried out from a position of relative topsight, the user experiences a certain excitement, a pleasure in the moment at which something exceeds his or her ability to understand how it works, but just feels right. At this distinctive point, the yield of the extended mind couples with the yearnings and passions of underlings, whose human factors synergize, beyond the simple state of user interface, and converge in a phase shift at which cognitive scaffolds give onto proliferating markets and new opportunities. At such a sweet spot, there is no need to follow a particular aesthetic line of the gadget. Indeed, the more that gadgets proliferate and diversify, the more virtualities they are able to mobilize and render into tangible imaginaries, the more able they are to provide metalevels of transitional scaffolding for new opportunities to grow. Such capacities can already be seen in the general tendency of gadgets to go beyond the typology that we sketch in the following paragraph.

Within the domain of consumer-grade computing, users have a primary choice. Either you can choose a coupling of premium levels of specification, customer lock-in, and an interaction grammar of glossy rectitude emphasizing an integrated, neutral, and restrained palette of functions with unprecedented levels of self-consistency, a grandiloquent repertoire of flourishes, and an emphasis on a visual grammar of saturated crispness; or you can opt for a more baroque, chaotic, and unsystematized stack of irreconciled tones, shapes, functions, choice trees, and microdramas of openings and closings, animated sequences of savings, dialing and, recording, held together by wizards and help files. Either of these may in turn be trumped by a rejection of the treatment of files as distinct objects rather than as data, which precludes profound computational behaviors, requiring verbose movements of the hand rather than the expert selection of functions and the promise of total customization and the iron-man rigor of perpetual bug fixing. Here users know that at a certain point they will experience a failure of desire, an unrequited symbiosis with the machine that simply fuels their ardor and dedication to feeding the development cycle. It is the correct choice. Last, for the rare few for whom the world is on its way to amplifying and embroidering their vision of life as a ramified version of existence on the inside of an infinitely expandable Fabergé egg, the luxuriousness of too much detailed information (a pocket sundial that also includes an astrolabe, barometer, tidal predictor, powerful market analytics, and, with a minimum of flips and swooshes of the user interface, the immediate purchase and download of new features in a lasting heirloom of quality craftsmanship with up-to-the-atomically-measured-second features set in a bejeweled yet sober casing) is the only reasonable option.

Each of these modes of the gadget is nuanced by other kinds of triggers and idioms, the rhetoric of the rigor of engineering, which appears to yield to no design imperative but the laws of mathematics and nature, resolved into a kind of robustly milled gunmetal UNIX, or by the figures of users, such as the power user, hacker, or other demographic hallucination and concomitant script position, whose newness yet familiarity keeps marketeers in a state of heightened galvanic skin response. Within such a context, the founding paradigm of direct manipulation that established much of the interface work of personal computing is multiplied by a sense of the exponential scaffolding of new cognitive networks.[41] Here, where "you don't even think about it, you just do,"[42] a stratagematic question in psychic ergonomics simply turns on the art of how to keep the populations of machinic junkies mobilized by the gadgets exacerbating the proliferation of the cognitive scaffold safely within the constraints of their own skin, avoiding their becoming influencing machines of their own.

Optimize Stupidity Flow

Stupidity does not sit on one side and Intelligence on the other. They're like Vice and Virtue—it takes an awfully shrewd mind to tell them apart.
—Gustave Flaubert[43]

A difficult, and somewhat delicate, issue for any group, organization, or institution, particularly in a world that is characterized as a "knowledge economy," is how one tackles stupidity. Stupidity is to be distinguished from a momentary absence of knowledge: with strategic intent, ignorance can be tackled once a representational structure and an epistemology have established how and what it is to know something. Stupidity, by contrast, has to do with the conditions of thinking as such and is not only compatible with knowledge in some of its forms but often indistinguishable from intelligence (as debates over the existence or otherwise of artificial intelligence might suggest).

However, these philosophical issues should not obscure the issue at hand, where the question is one of the risks and opportunities that the existence of stupidity poses to the exercise of power. Research on contemporary bureaucratic practices has brought to light the strategic—or antistrategic —role of a will to ignorance in particular kinds of institutions. Linsey McGoey's work has shown that, in the drug industry in particular, ignorance is mobilized as a means of circumventing regulation, and the shadowy role of nonknowledge in shaping organizational strategies is a widely drawn-on font of innovations.[44] But the functioning of stupidity, by contrast, is a better-kept secret, difficult to bring to light unless one accepts that an image of thought is prevalent in much discussion of organizations and in organizational practice, which assumes that thinking has some sort of a priori affinity with truth and goodwill—the idea that in their natural state, people are oriented toward the truth. It is an image that tends to confuse stupidity and error, implying that removing the errors that people make in their work is enough to guarantee intelligence. Even management theory—which one might imagine would seek to better attune itself to the dimly sensed operations of stupidity—cannot help but assume that the rational structuring of organizations is enough to protect them against the potential for stupidity that the drive to automation promotes, or indeed the fact that stupidity "can bodysnatch intelligence, disguise itself, or, indeed, participate in the formation of certain types of intelligence with which it tends to be confused."[45] One can tolerate the weaknesses of *bureaucratic* rationality for as long one continues to perceive it as bureaucratic *rationality*. And if that is not possible, refiguring the organization as a cybernetic system provides some assurance that if people aren't thinking, at least they aren't thinking *optimally*.

But stupidity is a delicate and difficult issue to tackle, not least because of the immense capital invested in knowledge and the practical imperative that our sophistication places on always being right. Becoming better attuned to stupidity requires a better understanding of how it is generated, what it is associated with, what effects it gives rise to, and what risks it exposes one to. This is a crucial prerequisite to the further problem of tackling, finessing, or leveraging stupidity.

Research in the field of distributed cognition has explored some of the subtle mechanisms by which ensembles of people and devices are organized to accomplish sophisticated cognitive tasks. Navigating a ship, for example, requires successful coordination of, and cooperation between, a complex set of elements—actors, roles, gadgets, competences, and so on.[46] It is not difficult to see the scope for failure built into such ensembles, and how communication failures between the elements of such ensembles might result in erroneous cognition (the ship hits a rock, for example). But the distributed approach has hitherto tended to privilege relatively stable situated actions with well-defined and prescribed goals as its focus and is not as good at casting light on the less frequently acknowledged, and much less formal, operation of myriad objects, techniques, and practices, *assemblages* of variable dimensions, with equally variable connections beyond the explicitly constituted framework of the organization or group.

The tacit, the implicit, the unspoken, and the secret gather on the fringes of the known and acknowledged aspects of organizational life, with its panoply of explicit mental and material structures. The humble document, for example, in its erratic circulation, the fabled water cooler, the gents' toilet before a meeting, the security guard with the spare office key, the regular drink in the pub on a Thursday night, out-of-hours text messaging, scripted kludges to stop a server from collapsing: all of these are just as important as the formal e-mails, policy documents, position papers, minuted meetings, qualifications, and archives. Some of this might be called "articulation work,"[47] but even a concept like articulation work will not tell us much about the occult nature of the group dynamics that informal practices sustain, the entire world of the "subconversation" or the "perceptual politics" of the meeting. And when an organization operates globally, in the twenty-four-hour cycle of outsourced software development, for example, the dynamics of knowledge organization and production acquire a geopolitical tinge. From this heteroclite point of view, when the organization of knowledge comes into focus, management theory not only needs to become a kind of media studies but needs to develop a much finer sense of the microtextures of everyday life.

Theories of distributed cognition do draw our attention to the role of mediation in propagating, amplifying, and embedding intelligent behavior in collective processes, pointing toward the crucial importance of media operations more generally in the genesis of thinking and knowing. But the role of media in propagating, amplifying, embedding, and redistributing stupidity is not one that has been studied in any great detail. This is not about dumbing down—a complaint that retains the neat separation of producer and consumer—and generally only concerns the specific contents of media rather than the concatenation of effects of media forms as such (as well as assuming that stupidity is a psychological characterization of the other). So the question must become one of how to grasp the distribution of stupidity throughout particular kinds of assemblage as such. Or to put it a slightly different way, how is knowledge at work reorganized so as to render thought inhibitory?

Knowledge management, which has been loosely defined as the concern for and organization of "knowing what we know,"[48] brings epistemological speculations of various sorts, economics, and information technology into a heady and problematic conjunction. Within knowledge management practices, the question of knowing what you know has a direct *material* shape, depending on the way in which knowledge assets are organized and put into communication. While knowledge management is often understood conceptually as a matter of making explicit what rests at a tacit level, more prosaically it is a matter of identifying, configuring, and leveraging the concrete knowledge resources (artifacts, databases, communications technologies, wikis, books and other forms of document, personal and organizational memories) on which an organization depends. And as recent projects concerned with "communities of practice" demonstrate, this gives knowledge management a scope that extends well beyond the confines of the organization and into the problematic differentiation between work and life.[49]

For the knowledge manager, the task is to find a way of articulating what an organization knows so as to make it smarter, more flexible, better able to rise to the challenges posed by the milieu in which it finds itself, better able to monetize its knowledge assets and realize their value. At its most crude, this will consist in creating more channels of communication—from the suggestions box to rebadging managers as "listeners" and "facilitators." On a more sophisticated level, it might consist in replacing one technology with another: databases instead of filing cabinets; wikis instead of e-mails; content management systems and virtual private networks (VPNs) instead of offices, colleagues, and a physically structured working environment. On a global level, this might extend into a full-fledged strategy for knowledge transfer and outsourcing practices.

However, becoming more fully connected, in the sense of materially linking more and more knowledge resources, within and without an organization, does not of itself suffice to make anyone or anything any smarter, even if the broader availability of information within an organization is an important prerequisite to making informed decisions.

We might compare the tireless work of the knowledge manager, assembling resources, writing documents, compiling flowcharts, speccing software, configuring databases, strategizing knowledge transfer processes, to the industrious laborings of Flaubert's inimitable double act Bouvard and Pécuchet. Their assiduous adventures in the acquisition of knowledge, their questing for the compilation of a comprehensively encyclopedic set of statements about what is known, betrays the active, even ardent, nature with which stupidity insists, and for which no knowledge is ever a sufficient antidote. For all their encyclopedic adventures, Bouvard and Pécuchet just don't get it.[50] This fictional example carries over, though, because as a recent philosophical review of theories of knowledge management has asked (and it was not a rhetorical question): what *is* the problem to which knowledge management is the answer?[51] A good question, although *solutions without problems* might actually be the very definition of a stupid knowledge: a solution without the problem that gave rise to it is a solution that has dispensed with the need for any thought and really only poses the problem of its application. If that judgment sounds harsh, let us admit that in the broader interests of efficiency and clarity, it is at least important to ask what kind of tacit knowledge the knowledge manager draws on.

Processes of knowledge management—and the consequent attempts to engineer systems or processes or policies that best facilitate its production—often rest on the presumption of a dialectic between the tacit and the explicit. Ingenious means are proposed for accomplishing the process that translates knowledge from its inchoate, scarcely articulated, tacit state to an explicit, codifiable, transmissible, and reproducible state. But what is less easily translated in this process is the way in which tacit knowledge itself translates inventive responses to problematic situations, and these are not always a matter of the irenic pursuit of knowledge—as references to the sociologist Pierre Bourdieu's conception of the *habitus* in the work of knowledge extraction suggests.

A knowledge-managed solution will be explicit, generic, and codifiable. In any set of circumstances, for any particular organization, it will define what is currently held to count as accountable knowledge. This will, in turn, produce a new domain of ideas, skills, and practices that do not count and can be safely forgotten while promoting others to the realm of signifying intelligence.

Leveraging the unknowns of technology is a useful possibility here: the machine whose dumbly insistent intransigence—it won't do what you want it to do—leaves the user making allowances for its stupidity, figuring out work-arounds or patches. In fact the machine *requires* that allowances be made for it, because unlike its human user, the machine won't get sacked if it fails to do its job properly, and the user has a vested interest in at least pretending to know what she is doing. Make allowances for the dumb terminal or risk looking terminally dumb.

But the tacit assumption so far has been that stupidity is a bad thing: for an image of thought that links thought to knowledge and knowledge to the good, this is an assumption that goes without saying. From a stratagematic point of view, of course, this may not be the case. Indeed, the great virtue of stupidity, at least if we do a stratagematic reading of Flaubert and those after him who have attempted to finger stupidity's irreducibility to other negative figures (error, ignorance, illusion, etc.), is precisely the way in which it gets confused with intelligence. Stupidity is difficult to locate in a clearly circumscribed domain—hence the need to attribute it to others, psychologically. However, the possibility that stupidity might be not a psychological state but something that, as we have emphasized, has an organizational form and a mediational configuration (and perhaps even a professional ethos) does not mean it does not have psychological effects. The feeling that positive psychologists call "flow" is endemic in stupidity: flow is the automation of habits, the blissful reinforcing of preexisting synaptic connections, a comforting transfer of feelings of cognitive security onto well-established territories. Perhaps the compulsive search for flow lies behind the way in which stupidity hijacks intelligence, seizing hold of agents who then acquire a missionary zeal, the glinting eyes of the convert, an algorithmic certainty.[52] In any case, the ease with which stupidity clothes itself in all the other virtues—hard work, eloquence, clarity—facilitates its insinuating propagation. Seeking to motivate his team to think about the next project, clicking his fingers impatiently, the project manager calls on them to brainstorm, to come up with ideas fast. Recalcitrance, a justifiable inability to process the latest blue-skies initiative, is at this point the sign of certain idiocy, and dissent a threat to team morale.

In truth, the propagation of stupidity, its zealous, even assiduous promotion, carefully fabricated through the creation of structures that do not tolerate the divergent possibilities of alternatives (not that way! don't be daft! chaos awaits you!), is easily accomplished: it suffices to confer the responsibility for thinking about what you are doing on others, to delegate authority. That stupidity hides out in intelligence and so easily translates into error or ignorance makes it difficult to pin down. While your enemies are still trying to figure out the thinking behind your next stupid move— making themselves look a bit slow-witted in the process—you can move on. Next project. Next target. Next goal. Click, click, click. And, of course, when confronted with stupidity's consequences, you can always point to an error, one you can acknowledge with more or less sincere, more or less real, humility—one would not want to be seen as being evil, after all.

Notes

Introduction

1. Or mantra, as it is invoked as part of Google's mission statement. See http://investor.google .com/corporate/code-of-conduct.html.

2. See, e.g., Peter Galison, "The Ontology of the Enemy: Norbert Wiener and the Cybernetic Vision," *Critical Inquiry* 21, no. 1 (Autumn 1994): 228–266.

3. Roger Silverstone, "The Rhetoric of Evil," chap. 3 of *Media and Morality* (London: Polity, 2007).

4. A sort of functionalist reversal of the dictum that information is the difference that "makes a difference."

5. See, e.g., David Nye, *The American Technological Sublime* (Cambridge, MA: MIT Press, 1994). For Nye, the technological sublime is associated with the spectacular quality of large-scale engineering projects in particular. Perhaps something similar can be said for the recent mass participation in the products of software engineering.

6. Indeed, the distinction consecrated by aesthetics—the difference between the spectator and the artist—may be one of the ethical stakes for contemporary media forms. As Giorgio Agamben has put it, the split between art such as it is lived by the spectator and art such as it is lived by the artist is, "precisely, Terror." Giorgio Agamben, *The Man without Content*, trans. Georgia Albert (Stanford: Stanford University Press, 1999).

7. Steven Shaviro has suggested a connection between thinking about affect and Raymond Williams's conception of "structures of feeling" that offers one way into exploring the broader configurations of affect in society. Steven Shaviro, *Post-Cinematic Affect* (Winchester: Zero Books, 2010). Sianne Ngai explores this reference in more detail in her research on "ugly" feeling. Ngai's work is largely restricted to the study of literary texts, but it does have a purchase on broader practices of mediation. Sianne Ngai, *Ugly Feelings* (Cambridge, MA: Harvard University Press, 2005). Ethnographic research has been equally suggestive of ways to get past the abstract generality of much of the work on affect. See, e.g., Kathleen Stewart, *Ordinary Affects* (Durham, NC: Duke University Press, 2007).

8. For Whitehead, the world itself is a medium. Given two entities A and D, for example, he says, "The medium between A and D consists of all those actual entities which lie in the actual world of A and not in the actual world of D." Alfred North Whitehead, *Process and Reality*, 2nd ed. (London: Macmillan–Free Press, 1978), 226; see pt. 3, chap. 1, more generally on objects as mediators or bearers of feeling.

9. For Jean Baudrillard, the abstract social relations constituted by the media—and hence the abolition of symbolic reciprocity they produce—are something of a given, a macroscopic social fact. It is more practical, though, to explore the constitution of these relations (which are no less real for it) as molar effects. Failure to do so in the case of media technologies usually results in some kind of deterministic argument. Baudrillard's argument is developed in his "Requiem for the Media," in *For a Critique of the Political Economy of the Sign*, trans. Charles Levin (St. Louis: Telos Press, 1981).

10. Eyal Weizman, *The Least of All Possible Evils: Humanitarian Violence from Arendt to Gaza* (London: Verso, 2012).

11. The distinction between transparent intermediaries and active mediators is important for the understanding proposed by science and technology studies of various sorts. See the discussion in Bruno Latour, *Re-assembling the Social* (Oxford: Oxford University Press, 2005), 39.

12. Graham Harman, *Tool-Being* (Peru, IL: Open Court, 2002).

13. Sophistry, says Nietzsche, begins where the "boundary between good and evil is erased." Quoted in Barbara Cassin, *L'Effet sophistique* (Paris: Gallimard, 1995), 7.

14. According to François Flahault, the monotheistic roots that have been so crucial for dualistic thinking about good and evil develop from Parmenides' poem *On Nature* and the Book of Job. As Flahault puts it, "Both of them mark the disappearance of Chaos and the coming of Being as simultaneously One and above alteration," a thinking that, developed in the culture of hellenized Jews, feeds into Christianity. François Flahault, *Malice*, trans. Liz Heron (London: Verso, 2003), 23.

15. To seduce, one must be able to be seduced in turn—a point that one might argue originates with the sophists. The point is an important one, because it suggests the need to cultivate a certain kind of sensibility, an ethic that is at the same time an aesthetic.

16. Or what Machiavelli would call *virtù*.

17. Niccolò Machiavelli, *The Prince*, trans. George Bull (London: Penguin, 1964), 131.

18. See, e.g., Jack Goody, *Domestication of the Savage Mind* (Cambridge: Cambridge University Press, 1977).

19. Susan Leigh Star and James L. Griesemer, "Institutional Ecology, 'Translations,' and Boundary Objects: Amateurs and Professionals in Berkeley's Museum of Vertebrate Zoology, 1907–39," *Social Studies of Science* 19 (1989); and Susan Leigh Star, "This Is Not a Boundary Object: Reflections on the Origin of a Concept," *Science, Technology, and Human Values* 35, no. 5 (2010).

20. See Carlo Ginzburg's essay on Menocchio, the miller of Friuli, whose aberrant learnings at the end of the sixteenth century earned him a trial and subsequent burning for heresy: *The Cheese and the Worms: The Cosmos of a Sixteenth-Century Miller*, trans. John Tedeschi and Anne C. Tedeschi (Baltimore, MD: Johns Hopkins University Press, 1992). Menocchio's cosmology seems to us an excellent example of the "ill-formed use" of the Bible (and of Ovid) as a boundary object.

21. Benedict Anderson, *Imagined Communities: Reflections on the Origin and Spread of Nationalism* (London: Verso, 1991).

22. Cf. Cassin, *L'Effet sophistique*. "Homologia," not "homonoia," implying not a meeting of minds, but rather only the sympathetic resonance of the sound of words. We do not actually agree with or understand each other; it just sounds as if we do.

23. Menocchio, in Ginzburg, *The Cheese and the Worms*, 53.

24. But not just Schopenhauer. We are thinking also of the writings of the Jesuit Balthasar Gracián (of whom Schopenhauer was a fan), as well as of Machiavelli. See below. A pertinent exponent of the work of both these figures is Guy Debord, e.g., in *The Society of the Spectacle* (Detroit: Black and Red, 1970).

25. As a more contemporary source of guidance and advice would have it: see the stratagem entitled "Structure Data."

26. See, e.g., the work of Chomsky.

27. E.g., Jerome Nriagu et al., "Saturnine Gout among Roman Aristocrats: Did Lead Poisoning Contribute to the Fall of the Empire?" *New England Journal of Medicine* 308, no.11 (March 1983): 660–663.

28. Alfred Crosby Jr., *Ecological Imperialism*, 2nd ed. (Cambridge: Cambridge University Press, 2004).

29. WikiLeaks may be one explicit case in point, but perhaps more telling are the complaints about the occlusive power of presentation software that the military uses for its internal communications. See Elizabeth Bumiller, "We Have Met the Enemy and He Is PowerPoint," *New York Times*, April 26, 2010, for a discussion of the various positions taken within the U.S. military on the use of presentation software.

30. Roland Barthes, *The Neutral*, trans. Rosalind E. Krauss and Denis Hollier (New York: Columbia University Press, 2005). We should note that Barthes himself did not associate the neutral and grayness.

31. See Primo Levi, *The Drowned and the Saved*, trans. Raymond Rosenthal (London: Abacus, 1989), chap. 2, esp. p. 27. See also Alan Blum's efforts to develop the notion of the gray zone in *The Grey Zone in Health and Illness* (London: Intellect, 2010). Gilles Deleuze and Félix Guattari refer to the notion with reference to Martin Heidegger, wondering whether "all concepts include this grey zone and indiscernibility where for a moment the combatants on the ground are confused and the thinker's tired eyes mistake one for the other." Gilles Deleuze and Félix Guattari, *What is Philosophy?* trans. Graham Burchell and Hugh Tomlinson (London: Verso, 1994), 109.

32. In Whitehead's pan-experiential—rather than pan-psychic—philosophy, everything in the universe is experience; everything is feeling, complex and interconnected. In its precision, his metaphysics offers a way of conceptualizing the immanence of affective and perceptual dispositions to technical and material apparatus. See Alfred North Whitehead, *Process and Reality*.

33. Ibid., 18.

34. The ongoing research of Mark Andrejevic in his *iSpy: Surveillance and Power in the Interactive Era* (Lawrence: University Press of Kansas, 2009) develops arguments that are pertinent here, as is Armand Mattelart's *The Globalization of Surveillance* (London: Polity, 2010). Not drawing too much attention to oneself is characteristic of the operations by which "infernal alternatives" are produced. See Isabelle Stengers and Philippe Pignarre, *Capitalist Sorcery: Breaking the Spell*, trans. Andrew Goffey (London: Palgrave, 2011).

35. Cf. Susan Leigh Star, "The Ethnography of Infrastructure," *American Behavioral Scientist* 43 (1999): 377.

36. See the work of Donald MacKenzie in particular; and Philip Mirowski, *Machine Dreams: Economics Becomes a Cyborg Science* (Cambridge: Cambridge University Press, 2002).

37. Andrew Barry, *Political Machines* (London: Athlone, 2001), and Michel Callon et al., *Acting in an Uncertain World* (Cambridge, MA: MIT Press, 2009), offer detailed analyses of these socio-technical conditions of contemporary politics. It seems to us that grayness is the aesthetic sensibility that best corresponds to these developments.

38. Jean-Luc Marion, *Sur l'ontologie grise de Descartes* (Paris: J. Vrin, 1975), 190.

39. For an analysis and discussion of Klee, see Gilles Deleuze and Félix Guattari, *A Thousand Plateaus* (Minneapolis: University of Minnesota Press, 1987), 344–345.

40. Félix Guattari, *Chaosmosis*, trans. Paul Bains and Julian Pefanis (Sydney: Power Institute, 1995).

41. Alberto Moravia, *Boredom*, trans. Angus Davidson (New York: NYRB, 1999), 8.

42. Cf. Richard Coyne, *The Tuning of Place* (Cambridge, MA: MIT Press, 2010).

43. Cf. "Micropolitics and Segmentarity" and the discussion of Gabriel Tarde and the "cycle" of assemblages in Deleuze and Guattari, *A Thousand Plateaus*.

44. Christian Marazzi, *Capital and Language* (New York: Semiotext[e], 2008); Paolo Virno, *The Grammar of the Multitude*, trans. Isabella Bertoletti, James Cascaito, and Andreas Casson (New York: Semiotext[e], 2004). But see also work on economics as performative such as that collected in Donald MacKenzie, Fabian Muniesa, and Lucia Siu, *Do Economists Make Markets? On the Performativity of Economics* (Princeton, NJ: Princeton University Press, 2007).

45. The key text for all this discussion is Cassin, *L'Effet sophistique*.

46. In addition to Paolo Virno and Jürgen Habermas, the work of the German philosopher Karl-Otto Apel is also an important contemporary reference.

47. Right down to the ambiguities of the vindication of elitism, the potential for demagoguery, and the pragmatic attitude toward truth. Edward Bernays's book *Propaganda* (New York: Horace Liveright, 1928) exemplifies this. The argument is made directly, albeit from a position somewhat different to the one taken here, in Romain Laufer and Catherine Paradeise, *Marketing Democracy: Public Opinion and Media Formation in Democratic Societies*, trans. Noel Castelino (New Brunswick, NJ: Transaction, 1990).

48. See the commentary on Odysseus in Theodor Adorno and Max Horkheimer, "The Concept of Enlightenment," chap. 1 of *The Dialectic of Enlightenment* (London: Verso, 1997).

49. Balthasar Gracián, *The Art of Worldly Wisdom*, trans. Joseph Jacobs (London: Shambhala, 1993).

50. "Radical evil" is how Cassin characterizes it in her discussion of Aristotle. See also her *L'Effet sophistique*, 234, for a connection with Bataille's notion of the accursed share.

51. The reference to sophistry proposed here equally reframes efforts to theorize "persuasive technology" or "persuasive games." An understanding of technology in terms of rhetoric gets us only as far as the forms of codification by which such devices capture and modulate attention.

52. In an essay called "Truth and Proof," Tarski offers a discussion of the well-known antinomy of the liar paradox—the statement "I am lying" attributed to Eubulides—arguing that in natural language, it appears "as a kind of evil force with a great destructive power," which further compels us "to abandon all attempts at clarifying the notion of truth for natural languages." Alfred Tarski, "Truth and Proof," *Scientific American*, June 1969; reprinted in R. I. G. Hughes, *A Philosophical Companion to First-Order Logic* (Cambridge, MA: Hackett, 1993). In her discussion of the paradox, Claude Imbert wryly characterizes the Cretan liar as a kind of "double agent" and points more generally to the occulting of the underhanded reliance that formal logic has on natural language. Claude Imbert, *Phénoménologies et langues formulaires* (Paris: PUF, 1992), 357.

53. In a slightly different context, it is worth noting that Kevin Mitnick devotes a great deal of his work on the security of computational systems to a discussion of social engineering (see below), or what the FBI described, in a 1956 monograph, as "pretexts and cover techniques." See http://mitnicksecurity.com/FBI_Pretexts_and_Cover_Techniques_May-1956.pdf.

54. Bruno Latour, *The Pasteurization of France*, trans. Alan Sheridan and John Law (Cambridge, MA: Harvard University Press, 1988), 158. Latour's interest in sophistry should also be noted here. See, e.g., his commentary on the debate between Socrates and Callicles in the final chapter of *Pandora's Hope: Essays on the Reality of Science Studies* (Cambridge, MA: Harvard University Press, 1999), 216–236. His essay "On Technical Mediation" invokes the ruseful spirit of Daedalus and the cunning of *metis* in its discussion of the operations of technique. Making the connection with sophistry seems an obvious extension for exploring the power and politics involved.

55. The commentary by Graham Harman in the first half of his book on Latour is useful in this regard. Graham Harman, *Prince of Networks* (Melbourne: re.press, 2009).

56. Bruno Latour, *Science in Action* (Cambridge, MA: Harvard University Press, 1987), 128.

57. The process of "delegation" is crucial in the conception of technical mediation proposed by Latour. It might be considered here in a manner more akin to the operations of delegation explored critically by Deleuze and Guattari in *Anti-Oedipus* (Minneapolis: University of Minnesota Press, 1983).

58. See, e.g., the work of W. Brian Arthur.

59. Stratagems seek to "do" things. In this sense they may be linked to ideas about the performative utterance. It is all the more tempting to make this link for the connections that have been established (a) between sophistry and Austinian performatives in the work of Cassin and (b) between the performative and contemporary knowledge practices, especially in the field of economics. If we avoid the notion of the performative here, we do so because in (b) it seems too readily to elide the distinction between knowledge and technique and in (a) retains a focus on the centrality of language. See MacKenzie et al., *Do Economists Make Markets?*

60. As the writings of Luc Boltanski and Giorgio Agamben underline respectively. Luc Boltanski, *Different Suffering* (Cambridge: Cambridge University Press, 1999); Agamben, *The Man without Content*. See also Alain Badiou, *Ethics: An Essay on the Understanding of Evil*, trans. Peter Hallward (London: Verso, 2001).

61. Isabelle Stengers has proposed the notion of the operative construct in an essay on Félix Guattari, "Relaying the War Machine," in *The Guattari Effect*, ed. Eric Alliez and Andrew Goffey (London: Continuum, 2011).

62. Michel Foucault, "Nietzsche, Genealogy, History," in *Language, Counter-memory, Practice*, ed. Donald F. Bouchard (Ithaca, NY: Cornell University Press, 1977), 139–164. As the editor of this collection points out, Foucault deploys the notion of disparity more fully in his *The Archaeology of Knowledge*. The spin that we give here to disparity is not, of course, one to be located in Foucault's work.

63. Max Atkinson, *Our Masters' Voices: The Language and Body-Language of Politics* (London: Routledge, 1984).

64. The scope that Foucault accords to strategies seems strictly circumscribed by the specific focus of his historical research. As a consequence, it is difficult to see how such work can be effective when taken up and treated in terms of unstated but much broader generalizations.

65. Schopenhauer, *The Art of Always Being Right*.

66. E.g., 50 Cent and Robert Greene, *The 50th Law* (New York: Harper, 2009).

67. Benner suggests a strong degree of continuity between Machiavelli and ancient Greek and Roman writers and glosses the difference between deception and dissimulation thus: "Deception involves the attempt to persuade others that one's intentions are altogether different from what they truly are. By contrast, dissimulation conceals some intentions or qualities while revealing others in indirect ways." Erica Benner, *Machiavelli's Ethics* (Princeton, NJ: Princeton University Press, 2009), 65.

68. Ibid., 101.

Intelligence

1. Giving the lie to the well-known hypodermic-syringe model of media effects, in its interest in "influence," Paul Lazarfeld's two-step flow model, outlined in his *Personal Influence*, arguably develops the insights of Gabriel Tarde in a manner consonant with ideas about brainwashing. Paul Lazarfeld, *Personal Influence: The Part Played by People in the Flow of Mass Communications* (Piscataway, NJ: Transaction, 2006). Tarde famously argued that "the social state, like the hypnotic state, is a dream of control and a dream in action." Gabriel Tarde, *The Laws of Imitation*, trans. Elsie Parsons (New York: Henry Holt, 1903), 77.

2. Arthur Schopenhauer, *The Art of Always Being Right* (London: Gibson, 2005), 28.

3. In ancient Greece, the sophists had a neologism for this: "to citizen." Its analogy with Kantian practical reason is underlined by Barbara Cassin in *L'Effet sophistique*.

4. Dominic Streatfield, *Brainwashing: The Secret History of Mind Control* (London: Hodder, 2006), 23; Philippe Pignarre, *Les malheurs des psys* (Paris: Découverte, 2006), 143–162.

5. Jean-François Lyotard, *The Differend* (Minneapolis: University of Minnesota Press, 1988), 84.

6. See Georges Didi-Huberman on Charcot, hypocrisy as a method, and the "hypnotic theater" through which Charcot staged hysteria. Georges Didi-Huberman, *Invention of Hysteria* (Cambridge, MA: MIT Press, 2003). The complex play of suggestion, the epistemic hall of mirrors at the birth of psychoanalysis, is discussed directly by Borch-Jacobsen in *Remembering Anna O.: A Century of Mystification* (New York: Routledge, 1996).

7. Edward Hunter, *Brain-washing in Red China: The Calculated Destruction of Men's Minds* (New York: Vanguard Press, 1951).

8. John von Neumann and Oskar Morgenstern, *Theory of Games and Economic Behavior* (Princeton, NJ: Princeton University Press, 1944). In "The Ontology of the Enemy," Galison characterizes game theory as one of three of the "Manichaean sciences" predicated on a characterization of the enemy, who is strangely similar to his opponent, as evil.

9. As in the work of Jacques Lacan, whose own interest in formalisms is well known. See, e.g., Lacan, *Ecrits: A Selection*, trans. Alan Sheridan (London: Routledge, 1977).

10. Isabelle Stengers, *The Invention of Modern Science*, trans. Daniel W. Smith (Minneapolis: University of Minnesota Press, 2000).

11. A point that seems to be lost on Kathleen Taylor in her updating of brainwashing via neuroscience, *Brainwashing: The Science of Thought Control* (Oxford: Oxford University Press, 2004). On the links between brainwashing and torture, see Streatfield, *Brainwashing*, esp. 29–59, 102–140, 338–402.

12. Attributed to James Jesus Angleton by the journalist Edward Jay Epstein. See the discussion in Michael Holzman, *James Jesus Angleton: The CIA and the Craft of Counterintelligence* (Amherst: University of Massachusetts Press, 2008), 40–41.

13. See Holzman, *James Jesus Angleton*; and the review by Terence Hawkes, "William Empson's Influence on the CIA," *Times Literary Supplement*, June 10, 2009.

14. William Empson, *The Seven Types of Ambiguity*, 2nd ed. (London: Chatto & Windus, 1949), 2.

15. See the discussion in Empson's preface to the second edition (ibid., xv).

16. Ibid., 3.

17. Ibid., 237.

18. Terence Hawkes makes the crucial point that while Empson may have thought ambiguity would never be resolvable, this appears not to have been the case for Angleton. See Hawkes, "William Empson's Influence."

19. Gilles Deleuze, *The Logic of Sense*, trans. Mark Lester (London: Athlone, 1990), 114.

20. A specific characteristic of the systemic ambiguity whose *mise en stratageme* we are mapping here is that it is the expression of an objective indeterminacy. Ambiguity is not the merely subjective form of mental conflict, as it is in Empson. See Deleuze, *The Logic of Sense*, and equally *The Fold: Leibniz and the Baroque,* trans. Tom Conley (London: Athlone, 1993), where the ambiguous sign is linked to Henry James as much as to Leibniz.

21. Cf. Marvin Minsky, "Jokes and Their Relation to the Cognitive Unconscious" (1981), http://web.media.mit.edu/~minsky/papers/jokes.cognitive.txt.

22. See the discussion of Tarski in the introduction.

23. Agre refers to this as a "grammar of action," a characterization that is helpful provided one recalls also that judgments of grammaticality can serve as markers of power. Philip Agre, "Surveillance and Capture: Two Models of Privacy," in *The New Media Reader*, ed. Noah Wardrip-Fruin and Nick Montfort (Cambridge, MA: MIT Press, 2003). On the links between grammar and power, see Gilles Deleuze and Félix Guattari, *A Thousand Plateaus* plateau 4, "The Postulates of Linguistics."

24. The debates about artificial intelligence are a useful indicator of the terms of reference of corporate power structures. If machines do all the work, the human command structure provides a convenient mechanism for apportioning responsibility. Harry Collins and Trevor Pinch, *The Shape of Actions* (Cambridge, MA: MIT Press, 1998); Hubert Dreyfus, *What Computers Still Can't Do* (Cambridge, MA: MIT Press, 1979).

25. Management theory typically focuses on "symbolic action." E. M. Eisenberg, "Ambiguity as Strategy in Organizational Communication," *Communication Monographs* 51 (1984): 227–242.

26. The concept of "repair" comes from ethnomethodology. Collins and Pinch use it in their work; our use of the concept is slightly different. Collins and Pinch, *The Shape of Actions*.

27. That power relations are inherently reversible is a point that Foucault, often considered intolerably pessimistic, makes with humor. Maurizio Lazzarato has extended this insight in his

work on "les intermittents du spectacle." However, Lazzarato prefers to see ambiguity as something separate from the techniques, technologies, and practices that are used to codify and regulate behavior. On the contrary, if power relations are formed and (literally) formatted through technologies, holding to and exploiting their reversibility entails exploring the ambiguities created by those regularizing technologies themselves. Maurizio Lazzarato, *Expérimentations politiques*, translation forthcoming from MIT Press.

28. On trials of strength and the problems of generalized translation failure, see Bruno Latour, "Irreductions," in *The Pasteurization of France*, trans. John Law and Alan Sheridan (Cambridge, MA: Harvard University Press, 1993); and *Science in Action* (Cambridge, MA: Harvard University Press, 1987). See also the first half of Harman, *Prince of Networks*.

29. Quoted in Slavoj Žižek, *Living in the End Times* (London: Verso, 2010).

30. We are not trying here to make a point about science in general but simply observing that the psy disciplines are a fascinating resource and topic for explorations of the interests of power. See, e.g., Isabelle Stengers, *Cosmopolitiques*, vol. 7, *Pour en finir avec la tolérance* (Paris: Découverte, 1997).

31. Marcel Gauchet, *L'inconscient cérébral* (Paris: Seuil, 1992).

32. Stengers, *Pour en finir avec la tolérance.*

33. Deleuze and Guattari, *Anti-Oedipus*, 46.

34. See, e.g., the comments in Sigmund Freud, *Beyond the Pleasure Principle*, Standard Edition, vol. 18 (1955), chap. 2.

35. Francoise Sironi, *Bourreaux et victimes* (Paris: Odile Jacob, 1992).

36. Jacques Lacan, cited in Avital Ronell, *Crack Wars* (Lincoln: University of Nebraska Press, 1992), 53.

37. Mikkel Borch-Jacobsen, "L'inconscient simulé," in *La guerre des psys*, ed. Tobie Nathan (Paris: Les Empêcheurs de Penser en Rond, 2006).

38. Jean Baudrillard, *In the Shadow of the Silent Majorities* (New York: Semiotext[e], 1983); Homi Bhabha, "Sly Civility," *October* 34 (1985): 71–80.

39. Freud, *Beyond the Pleasure Principle.*

40. Cf. Anna Munster, "Nerves of Data: The Neurological Turn in/against Networked Media," *Computational Culture* 1 (December 2011), http://computationalculture.net/.

41. Vinciane Despret, "Le secret est une dimension politique de la thérapie," in Nathan, *La guerre des psys.*

42. In the words of Walter Freeman, the intent was to turn "taxeaters" into "taxpayers." Jack Pressman, *The Last Resort: Psychosurgery and the Limits of Medicine* (Cambridge: Cambridge University Press, 1998).

43. Marshall McLuhan, *Understanding Media: The Extensions of Man* (Cambridge, MA: MIT Press, 1994).

44. The ARTICHOKE program, for example. See Alan Scheflin and Edward Opton, *The Mind Manipulators* (London: Paddington Press, 1978); and Streatfield, *Brainwashing*.

45. Cf. Retort, *Afflicted Powers: Capital and Spectacle in a New Age of War* (London: Verso, 2005), 20.

46. Cf. Thomas Pynchon, *Gravity's Rainbow* (London: Penguin, 1995).

47. As in the scenario imagined by Hitchcock and relayed by Slavoj Žižek in *The Puppet and the Dwarf: The Perverse Core of Christianity* (Cambridge, MA: MIT Press, 2003). See the brief discussion of this in Pignarre, *Les malheurs des psys*, 44–45. On specificity, see Jean-Jacques Kupiec and Pierre Sonigo, *Ni Dieu ni gène* (Paris: Seuil, 2000), 17–60.

48. Streatfield, *Brainwashing*, 44–49.

49. The ventilation system of a theater holding several hundred hostages taken by Chechen militants was flooded with an unspecified gas, killing or injuring both hostages and combatants.

50. Reid Kirby, "Paradise Lost: The Psycho Agents," *Quarterly Journal of the Harvard Sussex Program on CBW Armament and Arms Limitation* 71 (May 2006): 1.

51. Ibid., 4.

52. Cf. Chalmers Johnson, *Blowback* (New York: Holt Paperbacks, 2004).

53. Félix Guattari, "Machinic Junkies," in *Soft Subversions* (New York: Semiotext[e], 1996). See also Marazzi, *Capital and Language*, on the short-term movements of credulity inherent in the financial markets.

54. Ian Sample, "Leo Sternbach: Chemist Who Invented Librium and Valium, Drugs Whose Uses Are Still Being Explored," *Guardian*, March 10, 2005, http://www.guardian.co.uk/society/2005/oct/03/health.guardianobituaries.

55. Pignarre develops the full argument in *Les malheurs des psys*. His *Comment la dépression est devenue une épidémie* (Paris: Découverte, 2001) is a crucial text for following the logic of recruitment in the pharmaceutical industry.

56. See Sylvie le Poulichet, *Toxicomanies et psychanalyse: Les narcoses du désir* (Paris: PUF, 1987), on the fate of the transference in addiction; Pignarre, *Les malheurs des psys*, and Tobie Nathan, *A qui j'appartiens* (Paris: Seuil, 2007), on new complexes of attachments in psychology; and Carole Rivière, "Le lien de dépendance addictive à Internet: Une nouvelle forme d'addiction?" http://www.omnsh.org/article.php3?id_article=94 (accessed February 9, 2009), for an analytic approach to new media.

57. Emilie Gomart, "Surprised by Methadone: In Praise of Drug Substitution Treatment in a French Clinic," *Body and Society* 10, nos. 2–3 (2004): 85–110.

58. "Freedom Fighter's Manual," http://www.ballistichelmet.org/school/free.html.

59. Elizabeth Gurley Flynn, *Sabotage: The Conscious Withdrawal of Workers' Industrial Efficiency* (Cleveland: Industrial Workers of the World, 1916).

60. "Psychological Operations in Guerrilla Warfare" is available online in numerous locations.

61. Bertrand Gille, *The Renaissance Engineers* (London: Lund Humphries, 1966), 58.

62. Guy Debord, "Report on the Construction of Situations and on the International Situationist Tendency's Conditions of Organization and Action" (June 1957), in *Situationist International Anthology*, ed. Ken Knabb (Berkeley: Bureau of Public Secrets, 1981), 25.

63. Situationist International, "Preliminary Problems in Constructing a Situation" (1958), in *Situationist International Anthology*, ed. Ken Knabb (Berkeley: Bureau of Public Secrets, 1981), 44.

64. Asger Jorn, "The Situationists and Automation," in *Situationist International Anthology*, ed. Ken Knabb (Berkeley: Bureau of Public Secrets, 1981), 47.

65. Situationist International, "Preliminary Problems," 43.

66. Ibid.

Togetherness

1. StankDawg, "Hacking Google AdWords," in *The Best of 2600: A Hacker Odyssey*, ed. Emmanuel Goldstein (Indianapolis: Wiley, 2008), 800.

2. Herbert A. Simon, *Administrative Behavior: A Study of Decision-Making Processes in Administrative Organizations*, 4th ed. (New York: Free Press, 1997), 252.

3. Mark Bishop, "Dancing with Pixies: Strong Artificial Intelligence and Panpsychism," in *Views into the Chinese Room: New Essays on Searle and Artificial Intelligence*, ed. John Preston and Mark Bishop (Oxford: Oxford University Press, 2002), 360–378.

4. Stanley Milgram, *Obedience to Authority: An Experimental View* (London: Harper Collins, 1974).

5. Leo Szilard, "On the Decrease of Entropy in Thermodynamic Systems by the Intervention of Intelligent Beings," in *Maxwell's Demon 2: Entropy, Classical and Quantum Information, Computing*, ed. Harvey S. Leff and Andrew F. Rex (Bristol: Institute of Physics Publications, 2003), 110–119. Szilard's attempts to mediate the entry into history of the atomic weapons stemming from his involvement in the Manhattan Project, by requesting that they should be demonstrated before "actual" use, can perhaps be seen in this light.

6. On general intellect, see Karl Marx's *Grundrisse*, where the term originates in the "fragment on machines" and its development in the work of a number of theorists such as Negri, Berardi, and Virno. For the early stages of the idea of the noösphere, see Vladimir Vernadsky, *The Biosphere*, trans. David B. Langmuir (New York: Copernicus, 1998); and for its later development, various texts by Teilhard de Chardin.

7. Jeff Howe, "The Rise of Crowdsourcing," *Wired* 14.06 (June 2006).

8. James R. Beniger, *The Control Revolution: Technological and Economic Origins of the Information Society* (Cambridge, MA: Harvard University Press, 1986), 391.

9. Christopher Kelty, *Two Bits: The Cultural Significance of Free Software* (Durham: Duke University Press, 2008).

10. Howe, "The Rise of Crowdsourcing."

11. Howard Rheingold, *Smart Mobs: The Next Social Revolution* (New York: Basic Books, 2002), 117.

12. Knuth Dohse, Ulrich Jurgens, and Thomas Malsch, "From 'Fordism' to 'Toyotism'? The Social Organization of the Labor Process in the Japanese Automobile Industry," International Institute for Labour Policy, Working Paper, Berlin, April 1984.

13. Victor Shklovsky, *Zoo, or Letters Not about Love: A Novel*, trans. Richard Sheldon (Normal, IL: Dalkey Archive Press, 2001).

14. Nicholas Lobachevski, "The Theory of Parallels," trans. George Bruce Halsted, appendix to *Non-Euclidean Geometry: A Critical and Historical Study of Its Development*, by Roberto Bonola, trans. H. S. Carslaw (New York: Dover Books, 1955).

15. Kenneth Dean and Brian Massumi, *First and Last Emperors: The Absolute State and the Body of the Despot* (New York: Autonomedia, 1992).

16. Henri Bergson, *Creative Evolution* (New York: Dover Books, 1998), 100.

17. Frank Ball, Denis Mollison, and Gianpaolo Scalia-Tomba, "Epidemics with Two Levels of Mixing," *Annals of Applied Probability* 7, no. 1 (1997): 46–89, 61.

18. Chris Anderson, *The Long Tail: How Endless Choice Is Creating Unlimited Demand* (London: Random House, 2006); Erik Brynjolfsson, Yu Jeffrey Hu, and Duncan Simester, "Goodbye Pareto Principle, Hello Long Tail: The Effect of Search Costs on the Concentration of Product Sales," November 2007, http://ssrn.com/abstract=953587.

19. Mirowski, *Machine Dreams*.

20. See, e.g., Marazzi, *Capital and Language*.

21. In a manner somewhat analogous to that suggested by Donald MacKenzie in *An Engine, Not a Camera: How Financial Models Shape Markets* (Cambridge, MA: MIT Press, 2006).

22. Theories that extend economic logic beyond the normal bounds of markets predate behavioral economics, as in the work of Gary Becker, for example.

23. Such a connection might have taken Akerloff and Shiller, in their discussion of Keynes's "animal spirits," in a rather different direction. George Akerloff and Robert Shiller, *Animal Spirits: How Human Psychology Drives the Economy, and Why It Matters* (Princeton, NJ: Princeton University Press, 2009).

24. Ibid., 4.

25. On alpha-male behavior, see Vinciane Despret, *Quand le loup habitera avec l'agneau* (Paris: Les Empêcheurs de Penser en Rond, 2002); on simulated symptoms, see Borch-Jacobsen, *Anna O.*

26. See Baudrillard's infamous essay *In the Shadow of the Silent Majorities*.

27. Deleuze and Guattari make the point amply in *Anti-Oedipus*.

28. In this respect, behavioral economics occupies a position analogous to that of Leibniz in relation to God. Where Leibniz proposes a sort of psychotic effort to save theological reason, behavioral economics operates the delirious reconstruction of economic reason, saving it by finding it everywhere. Not all economic behavior is rational, but all behavior is economic. Regarding Leibniz, see Deleuze, *The Fold*.

29. Such as, presently, the Wii or Xbox with Kinect.

30. If you are reading this book on certain e-readers, for instance, your scrolling, noting, and searching will be recorded and sent back to the great river of servers for analysis and for the derivation of future product.

31. Cf. Dan Ariely, *Predictably Irrational*, rev. ed. (London: HarperCollins, 2009), 173–194.

32. Robert Rogers, *Rogers' Rangers Rules* (Rogers Island, 1757); Robert Taber, *The War of the Flea* (New York: Brassey's, 2002).

33. Vladimir Tasić, "Politics of Chaos," manuscript, n.d.; Richard K. Guy, "The Strong Law of Small Numbers," *American Mathematical Monthly* 95, no. 8 (October 1988): 697–712.

34. Casey Alt, "Viral Load: The Fantastic Rhetorical Power of the Computer Virus in the Contemporary U.S. Technoscape," in "Fremdkörper," ed. Philipp Sarasin, special issue, *Österreichische Zeitschrift für Geschichtswissenschaft* 16, no. 3 (2005): 133–149; Jussi Parikka, *Digital Contagions* (New York: Peter Lang, 2007).

35. Malcolm Gladwell, *The Tipping Point* (London: Abacus, 2001).

36. Niccolò Machiavelli, *The Prince*, XXV, 130–133.

37. Leo Strauss, *The City and Man* (Chicago: Rand McNally, 1964). For Strauss, the noble lie is the untruth required to engender the most moral, brave, or noble behavior.

38. Michael Power, *Organized Uncertainty: Designing a World of Risk Management* (Oxford: Oxford University Press, 2007).

39. See Tony Sampson, "How Networks Become Viral: Three Questions concerning Universal Contagion," in *The Spam Book: On Viruses, Porn, and Other Anomalies from the Dark Side of Digital Culture*, ed. Jussi Parikka and Tony D. Sampson (Cresskill, NJ: Hampton Press, 2009).

40. Alluquére Roseanne Stone, *The War of Desire and Technology at the Close of the Machine Age* (Cambridge, MA: MIT Press, 1996).

41. Rhodri Hayward, "The Tortoise and the Love-Machine: Grey Walter and the Politics of Electroencephalography," *Science in Context* 14, no. 4 (2001): 615–641. For a critical analysis of Internet dating sites, see Eva Illouz, *Cold Intimacies: The Making of Emotional Capitalism* (Cambridge: Polity, 2007).

42. Schopenhauer, *The Art of Being Right*, §38.

43. For instructors in "the art of the pickup," see various online training courses and forums.

44. See, e.g., Catherine Hakim, "Erotic Capital," *European Sociological Review* 26, no. 5 (2010): 1–20.

45. Matt Ridley, *The Red Queen: Sex and the Evolution of Human Nature* (London: Viking, 1993).

46. Franco "Bifo" Berardi, *The Soul at Work: From Alienation to Autonomy*, trans. Francesca Cadel and Giuseppina Mecchia (New York: Semiotext[e], 2009).

47. Olga Goriunova, *Art Platforms and Cultural Production on the Internet* (London: Routledge, 2011).

48. Gilles Deleuze, "The Exhausted," in *Essays Critical and Clinical*, trans. Daniel W. Smith and Michael A. Greco (London: Verso, 1998), 152–174.

Algorithms

1. Vladimir Sorokin, "Afterword," in *The Queue*, trans. Sally Laird (New York: NYRB Classics, 2008), 256.

2. See, for an evaluation of such claims, Matthias Scheutz, ed., *Computationalism: New Directions* (Cambridge, MA: MIT Press, 2002).

3. Harvey M. Wagner, *Principles of Operations Research with Applications to Managerial Decisions*, 2nd ed. (Englewood Cliffs, NJ: Prentice Hall, 1975).

4. Beniger, *The Control Revolution*, 333–336.

5. Max Horkheimer, *Critique of Instrumental Reason* (London: Continuum, 1983).

6. See, e.g., David Lyon, ed., *Surveillance and Social Sorting* (London: Routledge, 2002).

7. Lizette Alvarez, "Meet Mikey, 8: U.S. Has Him on Watch List," *New York Times*, January 13, 2010.

8. Algorithms exemplifying such an approach include heapsort, quicksort, insertion sort, merge sort, cocktail sort, and others.

9. A classic problem in computer science, in which the shortest path between several different points (cities to be visited by a salesman) is to be calculated.

10. Roy Mayall, *Dear Granny Smith* (London: Short Books, 2009).

11. Gilles Deleuze, *Difference and Repetition*, trans. Paul Patton (London: Athlone, 1994).

12. Ulas Vural and Yusuf Akgul, "Eye-Gaze Based Real-Time Surveillance Video Synopsis," *Pattern Recognition Letters* 30, no. 12 (September 2009): 1151–1159.

13. Mark Fisher, *Capitalist Realism: Is There No Alternative?* (Winchester: Zero Books, 2009), 17.

14. See Stephen Toulmin's account of various versions of the founding of modernity as the establishment of a rational society de novo in *Cosmopolis: The Hidden Agenda of Modernity* (Chicago: University of Chicago Press, 1990).

15. Isaac Newton, preface to *Philosopiae Naturalis Principia Mathematica* (London: S. Pepys, 1687).

16. See Toscano's efforts to rethink the notion of "real abstraction" in Marx. Alberto Toscano, "The Open Secret of Real Abstraction," *Rethinking Marxism* 7, no. 2 (April 2008): 273–287.

17. For further discussion of the regular expression, see the stratagem "Express Regularly, But Not Too Regularly" in the essay titled "Technicalities."

18. See, e.g., Gary Klein, *Sources of Power: How People Make Decisions* (Cambridge, MA: MIT Press, 1999).

19. The invention of the finite-state machine is attributed to McCulloch and Pitts. Papers by Huffman and by Moore in the 1950s are crucial references; paradoxically, the Turing machine generalizes its logic before the invention of the finite-state machine per se.

20. We encounter here the notion of simulation that Manuel De Landa deploys in *Simulation and Philosophy* (London: Continuum, 2011).

21. See, e.g., George C. Caffentzis, "Crystals and Analytic Engines: Historical and Conceptual Preliminaries to a New Theory of Machines," *Ephemera* 7, no. 1 (2007): 24–45, http://www .ephemeraweb.org/journal/7-1/7-1caffentzis.pdf.

22. Yuri Gurevich, *Logic and the Challenge of Computer Science* (New York: Computer Science Press, 1988), 4.

23. E. Börger, "High Level System Design and Analysis Using Abstract State Machines," in *Proceedings of the International Workshop on Current Trends in Applied Formal Method: Applied Formal Methods*, October 7–9, 1998, Lecture Notes in Computer Science, vol. 1641, ed. D. Hutter, W. Stephan, P. Traverso, and M. Ullmann (London: Springer, 1999), 1.

24. Enthusiasm for economic globalization would be somewhat attenuated if the digital connections that delocalized working practices requires were not seen to work seamlessly. See the stratagem on workflow in the "Technicalities" chapter.

Structures

1. Addressing machine memory might be considered an elementary process of semioticization. See P. B. Andersen, *A Theory of Computer Semiotics* (New York: Cambridge University Press, 1991); and P. B. Andersen, B. Holmqvist, and J. F. Jensen, *The Computer as Medium* (New York: Cambridge University Press, 1993).

2. Bjarne Stroustrup, the inventor of the enormously successful programming language C++, quotes Machiavelli in the epigraph to the section titled "Abstraction Mechanisms," in *The C++ Programming Language*, 3rd ed. (Reading: Addison-Wesley, 1997): "There is nothing more difficult to carry out, nor more doubtful of success, nor more dangerous to handle, than to initiate a new order of things. For the reformer makes enemies of all those who profit by the old order, and only lukewarm defenders in all those who would profit by the new order" (222).

3. See also the stratagem titled "Abstract Captures" in the previous essay.

4. David Allen, *Getting Things Done: The Art of Stress-Free Productivity* (London: Penguin, 2001).

5. A Petri net is a system for graphing the structure of events caused by interacting elements in mutual reaction and dependency, originally deriving from analysis of chemical reactions.

6. The significance of the "life hacks" trend can be attributed to this sense of a need to adapt to the imperatives of information.

7. Cf. Berardi, *The Soul at Work*; Fisher, *Capitalist Realism*.

8. D. T. Ross and K. E. Schoman, "Structured Analysis for Requirements Definitions," in *Classics in Software Engineering*, ed. Edward Nash Yourdon (New York: Yourdon Press, 1979), 365–388.

9. Michel Foucault, *The Birth of Biopolitics: Lectures at the Collège de France, 1978–1979*, trans. Graham Burchell (London: Palgrave Macmillan, 2008).

10. John Seely Brown and Paul Duguid, *The Social Life of Information* (Cambridge: Harvard Business School Press, 2000).

11. Herman Melville, *Bartleby the Scrivener* (London: Hesperus, 2007).

12. Geoffrey C. Bowker and Susan Leigh Star, *Sorting Things Out: Classification and Its Consequences* (Cambridge, MA: MIT Press, 1999), 298.

13. Geert Lovink and Nathaniel Tkacz, eds., *Critical Point of View: A Wikipedia Reader* (Amsterdam: Institute of Network Cultures, 2011).

14. Brown and Duguid, *The Social Life of Information*, 47.

15. Eric Raymond, *The Cathedral and the Bazaar* (Sebastopol, CA: O'Reilly Media, 2001).

16. It would be interesting to see the results of the application of peer production to utilities to maintain limits on this way of working and to reemphasize the market as the primary mechanism for self-organization and the realization of desires. From a technical perspective, it is useful to maintain and cultivate forms of cunning that can operate in multiple conditions.

17. As exemplified in initial versions of Windows Vista or KDE 4, among others.

18. Edgar F. Codd, "A Relational Model of Data for Large Shared Data Banks," *Communications of the ACM* 13, no. 6 (June 1970): 377–387.

19. Machiavelli, *The Prince*, 131.

20. A usage initiated in OS/360.

21. Ian Hacking, "How Should We Do the History of Statistics?" in *The Foucault Effect: Studies in Governmentality*, ed. Graham Burchell, Colin Gordon, and Peter Miller (Hemel Hempstead: Harvester Wheatsheaf, 1991).

22. Friedrich Kittler's development of Foucault's archaeology turns precisely on the fulcrum produced by this shift.

23. Chris Thornton, *Truth from Trash: How Learning Makes Sense* (Cambridge, MA: MIT Press, 2000).

24. This expression may sound a little odd. However, it is not unprecedented. See the discussion of "plug-ins" and "psychomorphs" in Latour, *Re-assembling the Social*, 207–218; and more generally Guattari, *Chaosmosis*. The recent research of Armand Mattelart in *The Globalization of Surveillance* and, in a different way, that of Mark Andrejevic have started to develop a more detailed analysis of the links between gathering data and marketing processes.

25. See Marazzi, *Capital and Language*.

26. The argument that the consumption of advertisements represents a form of labor is an old one and can be attributed to, for example, Dallas Smythe; see his *Dependency Road: Communications, Capitalism, Consciousness* (Toronto: Ablex, 1981). For a more recent update of the argument, see, e.g., Mark Andrejevic, "The Work of Being Watched: Interactive Media and the Exploitation of Self-Disclosure," *Critical Studies in Media Communication* 19, no. 2 (June 2002).

27. In *Anti-Oedipus*, Deleuze and Guattari insist on the distinction between the singularity of desiring machines and the statistical aggregates of social production. The distinction is relevant here for what it suggests about the antagonism between singularity and probability.

28. See, e.g., Felix Salmon, "Recipe for Disaster: The Formula That Killed Wall Street," *Wired* 17.03 (February 2009).

Technicalities

1. Workflow Management Coalition, "The Workflow Management Coalition Terminology and Glossary," document no. WFMC-TC-1011, p. 8, http://www.wfmc.org/standards/docs/TC-1011_term_glossary_v3.pdf.

2. Thomas L. Friedman, *The World Is Flat: The Globalized World in the Twenty-first Century* (London: Penguin, 2006), 78.

3. For further discussion, see http://www.oasis-open.org/committees/tc_home.php?wg_abbrev =wsbpel.

4. Friedman, *The World Is Flat*, 79.

5. Pointing in turn to the difficulty of saying with any precision what activities actually count as work in some cases.

6. Toscano, "Open Secret of Real Abstraction."

7. Wil van der Aalst and Kees van Hee, *Workflow Management: Models, Methods, and Systems* (Cambridge, MA: MIT Press, 2002), 2.

8. A helpful cataloging of standard patterns may be found at the YAWL Web site: http://www .yawlfoundation.org.

9. Harry Braverman, *Labor and Monopoly Capital* (New York: Monthly Review Press, 1974).

10. Friedman, *The World Is Flat.*

11. Perhaps an adept of neurolinguistic programming, Friedman favors the term "seamless" in his account of workflow.

12. Mark Klein and Chrysanthos Dellarocas, "A Knowledge-Based Approach to Exception Handling," *Computer Supported Collaborative Work* 9, nos. 3–4 (2000): 399–412.

13. The creation of a regular expression is the creation of a specific set of instructions or rules about what counts or can be "recognized" as an acceptable string. A regular-expression engine, such as that incorporated into the Perl scripting language, provides a series of "metacharacters" that allow an expression for matching to be constructed. ^(Mary|Mungo|Midge)$ will match lines of text solely comprising either "Mary," "Mungo," or "Midge," for example (the ^ metacharacter specifies the start of a line, the | specifies "or," and the $ specifies the end of a line). The regular expression. * will match anything at all, because the . metacharacter matches any character and the * says "any number of times." Regular-expression engines also feature a number of functions that extend the capacity of what can be done to process text, such as replacing strings, storing expressions, and so on.

14. The concept of the regular expression can be traced back to S. C. Kleene's 1951 Rand Corporation memorandum demonstrating the formal equivalence of the logic of the finite automaton and McCulloch and Pitts's "logical calculus" of nervous activity. Stephen C. Kleene, "Representation of Events in Nerve Nets and Finite Automata," in *Automata Studies*, ed. C. Shannon and J. McCarthy (Princeton, NJ: Princeton University Press, 1956).

15. The Internet Engineering Taskforce's Request for Comments Repository is maintained at http://www.ietf.org/rfc.html/.

16. Niklaus Wirth, *Algorithm + Data Structure = Program* (London: Prentice Hall, 1976).

17. Cf. Barbara Cassin and Philippe Büttgen, "The Performative without Condition: A University sans Appel," *Radical Philosophy* 162 (July–August 2010): 31–37.

18. One might also consider the filing and documentation structures of an organization in terms of this process of regularization.

19. See the discussion of formalism and discipline in chap. 3 of Marc Berg, *Rationalizing Medical Work* (Cambridge, MA: MIT Press, 1997).

20. See the discussion of the "recognition-primed decision model" and its relation to intuition in Klein, *Sources of Power*, 15–45.

21. In the informational sense that pattern is redundancy.

22. For a discussion, see Kleene, "Representation of Events."

23. A minor reworking of Jacques Lacan's "that one speaks remains hidden behind what is heard of what is said." Cf. Barbara Cassin, "Performance before the Performative" (forthcoming). The interest of speech act theory for a consideration of computing technology is a feature of the work of Winograd and Flores. One critique has been developed by Lucy Suchman in "Do Categories Have Politics?" *Computer-Supported Co-operative Work* 2 (1994): 177–190. The view we propose here is slightly different: computers translate speech acts into signals.

24. Weibe Bijker and John Law have developed the notion of obduracy in the afterword to *Shaping Technology*; Madeleine Akrich and Bruno Latour examine the prescriptive aspect of technology in their essays in the same collection. Weibe Bijker and John Law, eds., *Shaping Technology* (Cambridge, MA: MIT Press, 1992).

25. Which is not without analogy to the numbering systems used to organize nomadic warriors. See the discussion of "numbering number" in Deleuze and Guattari's exploration of the war machine and countersignifying semiotics in *A Thousand Plateaus*.

26. An advantage mined by the field of usability in, for instance, Steve Krug, *Don't Make Me Think! A Common Sense Approach to Web Usability*, 2nd ed. (Berkeley: New Riders, 2005).

27. The idea of "implicatures" in language use is associated with the work of H. P. Grice on the pragmatic maxims of conversation. See "Logic and Conversation," in *Studies in the Way of Words*, ed. H.P. Grice (Cambridge, MA: Harvard University Press, 1989).

28. Cf. chap. 5 of Harry Collins, *Artificial Experts: Social Knowledge and Intelligent Machines* (Cambridge, MA: MIT Press, 1990), 62–71.

29. Cf. the tension between, and gradual merging of, information systems and communication systems described by Enrico Coiera in his "Informality," HP Laboratories technical document HPL-97-37.

30. Edgar Codd, "A Relational Model for Large Shared Data Banks." See also Edgar Codd, *The Relational Model for Database Management: Version 2* (Reading: Addison-Wesley, 1990).

31. Yochai Benkler, *The Wealth of Networks: How Social Production Transforms Markets and Freedom* (New Haven: Yale University Press, 2006).

32. Herbert A. Simon, *Sciences of the Artificial*, 3rd ed. (Cambridge, MA: MIT Press, 1996).

33. J. L. Kuhns, *Answering Questions by Computer: A Logical Study* (Santa Monica, CA: Rand Corporation, 1967).

34. See, e.g., the United Kingdom's Regulation of Investigatory Powers Act 2000 (RIPA).

35. Alain Badiou and Giorgio Agamben exemplify this trend. See Alain Badiou, *Theory of the Subject*, trans. Bruno Bosteels (London: Continuum, 2009); and Giorgio Agamben, *The State of Exception* Chicago: University of Chicago Press, 2005).

36. Carl Schmitt, *Political Theology: Four Chapters on the Concept of Sovereignty* (Cambridge, MA: MIT Press, 1985), 15. In the same text, Schmitt says, more infamously, that the "sovereign decides on the exception." We examine this claim in more detail when we address decision support systems. Schmitt is thought to be glossing Kierkergaard's discussion of the exception in his *Repetition*.

37. From a different point of view, the sociologist Harry Collins has argued in his *Artificial Experts* that debates about computing (he is thinking in particular of AI) are inseparable from metaphysical questions.

38. Alfred Jarry, *The Exploits and Opinions of Dr. Faustroll, Pataphysician*, trans. Simon Watson Taylor (Cambridge, MA: Exact Change, 1997).

39. This, at least, is how it appears to Badiou in his *Theory of the Subject*, and more generally in his magnum opus *Being and Event* (London: Continuum, 2007). Agamben comments on related concerns in *The Coming Community*, trans. Michael Hardt (Minneapolis: University of Minnesota Press, 1993), among other places.

40. Lawrence Lessig's optimistic social engineering maxim "code is law" can usefully be viewed in the light of this imminence to collapse. Lawrence Lessig, *Code, Version 2.0* (New York: Basic Books, 2006).

41. Michael Howard and David LeBlanc, *Writing Secure Code*, 2nd ed. (Seattle: Microsoft Press, 2002).

42. Grady Booch, *Object-Oriented Analysis and Design with Applications* (Reading: Addison-Wesley, 2007), 51–52.

43. In the Java programming language, the exception belongs to the java.lang.Throwable class. This class contains one basic type of exception, and then further extensions. The java.lang. NullPointerException extends java.lang.RuntimeException, which itself extends java.lang. Exception.

44. Bertrand Russell, "Letter to Frege" (1902), in *From Frege to Gödel: A Sourcebook in Mathematical Logic, 1879–1931*, ed. Jean van Heijenoort (Cambridge, MA: Harvard University Press, 1967), 124–125.

45. Friedrich Nietzsche, *Untimely Meditations*, trans. R. J. Hollingdale (Cambridge: Cambridge University Press, 1997), 123.

46. Bryan Cantrill, "A Spoonful of Sewage," in *Beautiful Code: Leading Programmers Explain How They Think*, ed. Andy Oram and Greg Wilson (Sebastopol, CA: O'Reilly Media, 2007), 353–369.

47. A summary of this work can be found in John Johnson, *The Allure of Machinic Life: Cybernetics, Artificial Life, and the New AI* (Cambridge, MA: MIT Press, 2008).

48. Rodney A. Brooks and Lynn Andrea Stein, "Building Brains for Bodies," in *Autonomous Robots*, vol. 1 (Boston: Kluwer Academic, 1994), 7–25.

49. Rodney A. Brooks, "Elephants Don't Play Chess," *Robotics and Autonomous Systems* 6 (1990): 3–15.

50. Friedrich Nietzsche, *Beyond Good and Evil: Prelude to a Philosophy of the Future*, ed. Rolf-Peter Horstmann and Judith Norman, trans. Judith Norman (Cambridge: Cambridge University Press, 2002), 78.

Productivity

1. It might seem idiosyncratic to treat a concept as a mediator in the sense we propose here for this term; concepts are more usually thought of as more or less adequate representations of some aspect of states of affairs. But from a pragmatic view, building on the formulations in the stratagem "Multiply Interfaces" (in the essay titled "Structures"), concepts operate to capture some aspect or another of a situation, an operation that occurs more or less successfully according to the transverse sets of connections they make.

2. Harry Collins, *Tacit and Explicit Knowledge* (Chicago: University of Chicago Press, 2010), provides a helpful account of the semantic drift to which Polanyi's concept has been subjected. Collins's argument that the explicit, rather than the tacit, is the variety of knowledge that requires more understanding provides a cautionary reminder that in matters of knowledge management, issues are considerably more complex than they might seem. What we are interested in here, though, is the way that the drift to which the concept of the tacit has been subjected itself offers scope for the mischief of abuse and misappropriation.

3. See, e.g., Antonio Damasio, *Descartes' Error* (London: Penguin, 2005). Let us not forget in passing the way that Polanyi's work makes itself available to an evolutionistic reading.

4. J. C. Spender and Andreas Georg Scherer, "The Philosophical Foundations of Knowledge Management: Editors' Introduction," *Organization* 14, no. 1 (2007): 5–28, http://ssrn.com/abstract=958768.

5. In science, the history of the development of the Royal Society and the allocation of roles in the development of experiments and instruments arranged between artisan and gentleman scientist exemplifies this differentiation.

6. See the stratagem "Work Abstraction Layers" in the essay titled "Structures."

7. Pierre Bourdieu, *Outline of a Theory of Practice* (Cambridge: Cambridge University Press, 1977), 83.

8. Nietzsche, *On the Genealogy of Morality*, 2nd essay, §1.

9. Friedrich Nietzsche, *Writings from the Late Notebooks*, ed. Rüdiger Bittner, trans. Kate Sturge (Cambridge: Cambridge University Press, 2003), §10 (165).

10. James Burnham, *The Managerial Revolution* (Harmondsworth: Pelican, 1945).

11. Marilyn Strathern, *Audit Cultures: Anthropological Studies in Accountability, Ethics, and the Academy* (London: Routledge, 2000), 4.

12. For a discussion of the neutral, see the stratagem "Grayness" in the introduction.

13. As Peter F. Drucker so handsomely reminds us, "Indeed, one of the major contributions of management by objectives is that it enables us to substitute management by self-control for management by domination." Drucker, *The Practice of Management* (1955; Oxford: Butterworth Heinemann, 1995), 129.

14. Niccolò Machiavelli, *The Prince*, trans. George Bull (London: Penguin, 1964), 101.

15. Louis Althusser, *Machiavelli and Us* (London: Verso, 2001).

16. See, e.g., Friedrich Kittler, "Code," in *Software Studies: A Lexicon*, ed. Matthew Fuller (Cambridge, MA: MIT Press, 2008).

17. Michel Foucault, *Security, Territory, Population: Lectures at the Collège de France, 1977–78*, ed. Michel Senellart, trans. Graham Burchell (London: Palgrave Macmillan, 2007).

18. See Adrian Johns's mammoth reconstruction, *The Nature of the Book: Print and Knowledge in the Making* (Chicago: University of Chicago Press, 2000).

19. An amusing fiction, and one that is less evident than it might seem—Hollywood, for example, routinely displays a clear anxiety that the Other might be more intelligent than "us."

20. E.g., the gender performance involved in the Turing test.

21. Pedagogical literature often restricts the "decision support system" even further, sandwiching it somewhere between transaction systems, executive information, and expert systems. For a general background, see D. J. Power, "A Brief History of Decision Support Systems," http://dssresources.com/history/dsshistory.html. For the place of Herbert Simon, see also Jean-Charles Pomerol and Frédéric Adam, "On the Legacy of Herbert Simon and His Contribution to Decision Making Support Systems and Artificial Intelligence," in *Intelligent Decision-Making Support Systems (i-DMSS): Foundations, Applications, and Challenges*, ed. J. Gupta, G. Forgionnne, and M. Mora (Frankfurt: Springer, 2005), 25–44.

22. OLAP stands for online analytic processing, a way of extracting information from a database and presenting in a multidimensional format. It is common to a number of large database management systems.

23. Herbert Simon, *Administrative Behavior: A Study of Decision-Making Processes in Administrative Organizations* (New York: Free Press, 1997). This text lists the first three stages; the fourth stage appears to have been added later. See Herbert Simon, *The New Science of Management Decision*, 3rd rev. ed. (Englewood Cliffs, NJ: Prentice-Hall, 1977) (the first edition was published in 1960).

24. Whether the model is a cause or an effect of decision support systems implemented in software does not matter here: Simon was no more able to think outside the assemblages in which he found himself than is anyone else. The development of the sciences of the artificial, as he

liked to call them, during the Cold War was patently a closed-world phenomenon. See Paul N. Edwards, *The Closed World* (Cambridge, MA: MIT Press, 1996).

25. A pertinent conception of the perpetuation of evil might be the one proposed by Alain Badiou in his *Ethics*, wherein an evil is what emerges in the simulation of truth.

26. Edward Yourdon, *Death March*, 2nd ed. (Hemel Hempstead: Prentice Hall, 2003). Yourdon specifies that such assessment "includes an assessment of technical risks, personnel risks, legal risks, political risks, etc." (3).

27. The death march is, of course, a military term, but one derived from administration and its imaginary rather than from combat action. One can see this in the victory for abstraction and the sumptuary expenditure of Cold War vanity projects, and in a more dispersed way in the asymmetric projections of force of the present. In the world of software engineering, Jerry Manas's *Napoleon on Project Management: Timeless Lessons in Planning, Execution, and Leadership* (Nashville, TN: Thomas Nelson, 2006) is not untypical. Alan Axelrod's *Patton on Leadership: Strategic Lessons for Corporate Warfare* (Hemel Hempstead: Prentice Hall, 2001) offers a good example of the figurative resonances on which such thinking depends more generally.

28. While not a study per se of project management, Gillian Tett's study of the invention of credit default swaps by a team of bankers at J. P. Morgan, *Fool's Gold*, is highly suggestive with regard to the possibilities for mobilization when a group finds itself working in a subjectively demarcated space-time. Gillian Tett, *Fool's Gold: How Unrestrained Greed Corrupted a Dream, Shattered Global Markets, and Unleashed a Catastrophe* (New York: Little, Brown, 2009).

29. The 'Project Initiation Document' is a key element of the PRINCE2 methodology and is widely adopted as a key element of project management. Little work has been done on initiation processes. However, see Stengers and Pignarre, "Minions," chap. 4 of *Capitalist Sorcery*.

30. Burkard Sievers, "Psychotic Organization as a Metaphoric Frame for the Socioanalysis of Organizational and Interorganizational Dynamics," *Administration and Society* 31, no. 5 (1999): 588–615. The field of research known as "socio-analysis" tends to ignore the role of techniques, technologies, and tools in shaping the organizational unconscious.

31. Paul O. Gaddis, "The Project Manager," *Harvard Business Review* 37 (1959): 89–97.

32. It is noteworthy that Morris does not consider the mental environment at all in the list of externalities (roughly, side effects or indirect consequences) that he produces in his discussion of project management. Peter W. G. Morris, *The Management of Projects* (London: Thomas Telford, 1997).

33. Cf. R. Thomsett, "Double Dummy Spit and Other Estimating Games," *American Programmer* 9, no. 6 (1996): 16–22.

34. In this sense, we might say that the project is to work what utopias are to politics. For more on utopias and semantic neutralization, see Louis Marin, *Utopics: The Semiotics of Spatial Play*, trans. Robert Vollrath (Amherst, NY: Humanity Books, 1984).

35. The Gantt chart was developed in 1917 by Henry Gantt as a way of organizing the production of armaments at the Frankford Arsenal in Pennsylvania.

36. To borrow the title of Edward Tufte's well-known book. See *The Visual Display of Quantitative Information*, 2nd ed. (Cheshire, CT: Graphic Press, 2001). The discussion forum on Tufte's Web site contains a number of threads on project plans. See, e.g., http://www.edwardtufte.com/bboard/q-and-a-fetch-msg?msg_id=000076.

37. A notion owed to Deleuze and Guattari's *Anti-Oedipus*.

38. For the early proponents of project management, it was a matter of "making" the work of scientists fit in with strategic and economic goals of the U.S. military-industrial complex. See Gaddis, "The Project Manager."

39. "Delegation" is a role that STS theorists often attribute to technological devices. See Madeline Akrich, "The De-scription of Technical Objects," in Bijker and Law, *Shaping Technology*. It is also a role that psychoanalysts attribute to representations. In the psychoanalytic sense, delegation is equally a form of displacement of energy, a redirection.

40. Project management handbooks insist that communication is the key skill of the project manager.

41. Michel Callon, "Some Elements of a Sociology of Translation: Domestication of the Scallops and the Fishermen of Saint Brieuc Bay," in *Power, Action, and Belief: A New Sociology of Knowledge?* Sociological Review Monograph 32, ed. John Law (London: Routledge and Kegan Paul, 1986).

42. Herbert A. Simon, *Administrative Behavior* (New York: Macmillan, 1947), 47.

43. Alfred Sohn-Rethel, *Intellectual and Manual Labour: A Critique of Epistemology* (London: Macmillan, 1978).

44. Franco "Bifo" Berardi, *The Soul at Work: From Alienation to Autonomy*, trans. Cadel F. and G. Mecchia (New York: Semiotext[e], 2009).

45. The terms used by I. Nonaka and H. Takeuchi, *The Knowledge-Creating Company* (Oxford: Oxford University Press. 1995).

46. Rationalizing the organization as a quasi-computational input-output system is one of the features of Simon's work.

47. Nonaka and Takeuchi, *The Knowledge-Creating Company*, 156.

48. On the growing importance of oxymoron in contemporary discourse, see Bertrand Meheust, *La politique de l'oxymore* (Paris: Découverte, 2009).

49. Thierry Melchior, *Créer le reel* (Paris: Seuil, 1998), 247–392.

50. K. C. Laudon and J. P. Laudon, *Management Information Systems: New Approaches to Organization and Technology*, 5th ed. (New York: Macmillan, 1998); cited in Marc Berg, "Patient Care Information Systems and Health Care Work: A Sociotechnical Approach," *International Journal of Medical Informatics* 55 (1999): 88.

51. Warren G. Bennis, *The Unconscious Conspiracy: Why Leaders Can't Lead* (New York: AMACOM, 1976).

52. Edgar Schein, *Organizational Culture and Leadership* (Hoboken, NJ: John Wiley, 2004).

53. R. L. Daft and R. H. Lengel, "Information Richness: A New Approach to Managerial Behavior and Organizational Design," in *Research in Organizational Behavior*, vol. 6, ed. L. L. Cummings and B. M. Staw (Homewood, IL: JAI Press, 1984).

Excellence

1. It is, in a sense, what Agre is pointing toward in his article "Surveillance and Capture: Two Models of Privacy."

2. Romilla Ready and Kate Burton, *NLP for Dummies* (Chichester: John Wiley and Sons, 2004), 9. The key text is Richard Bandler and John Grinder, *The Structure of Magic I: A Book about Language and Therapy* (Palo Alto: Science & Behavior Books, 1975).

3. This is a highly simplified account of mathematical modeling as used in more or less scientific research: a model of sorts itself, then. Our account differs somewhat from model theory as it is understood in mathematics and computing science. On the model theory, see Alain Badiou, *The Concept of Model*, trans. Zachary Fraser and Tzuchien Tho (Melbourne: re.press, 2007). The history of the use of models in science is explored in, e.g., Daniela Bailer-Jones, "Tracing the Development of Models in the Philosophy of Science," in *Model-Based Reasoning in Scientific Discovery*, ed. Lorenzo Magnani, Nancy J. Nersessian, and Paul Thagard (Berlin: Springer, 1999).

4. Some confusion arises between modeling and models, particularly in cognitive science. For techniques of influence, such confusions are both felicitous and propitious.

5. Compare this with Virno, who adopts an Aristotelian principle of virtuosity in his exploration of the role of language in production, or with Cassin's reading of the performative nature of sophist eloquence. Virno, *The Grammar of the Multitude*; Cassin, *L'Effet sophistique*.

6. See the detailed discussion of these in Bandler and Grinder, *Structures of Magic*.

7. The notion of the "well-formed" is everywhere present in NLP. It comes from formal logic.

8. This may be one way to distinguish between the metamodeling of neurolinguistic programming and the metamodeling of schizoanalysis. Regrettably, the take-up of schizoanalysis in business circles has been somewhat limited. See Félix Guattari, *Les cartographies schizoanalytiques* (Paris: Galilée, 1989).

9. Mary S. Morgan and Margaret Morrison, eds., *Models as Mediators: Perspectives on Natural and Social Science* (Cambridge: Cambridge University Press, 1999), esp. chaps. 2 and 3.

10. NLP theorists sometimes bemoan resistance to the unconscious assimilation of patterns of excellence (perhaps a residual or vestigial resistance to the authority, the glory of the guru). Self-modeling is encouraged under such circumstances.

11. NLP arguably improves on SMART thinking by complementing Specific, Measurable, Attainable, and Relevant outcomes with sensory experience. On SMART see George T. Doran, "There's a S.M.A.R.T. Way to Write Management's Goals and Objectives," *Management Review* 70, no. 11 (1981).

12. Giorgio Agamben explores the possibility that money and mysticism share a somewhat more involved relationship in *La regne et la gloire* (Paris: Seuil, 2008).

13. That pragmatic, and more exactly stratagematic, considerations are operative in computation is made evident in textbooks on a regular basis. See, e.g., Stephane Faroult, *The Art of SQL* (Sebastopol, CA: O'Reilly Media, 2006).

14. Jean-Pierre Dupuy, *On the Origins of Cognitive Science: The Mechanization of the Mind* (Cambridge, MA: MIT Press, 2009).

15. Edwards, *The Closed World*.

16. Robert Putnam, *Bowling Alone: The Collapse and Revival of American Community* (New York: Simon & Schuster, 2000).

17. For the detail, see Teuvo Kohonen, *Self-Organizing Maps* (Berlin: Springer, 2001).

18. Saul D. Alinsky, *Rules for Radicals: A Pragmatic Primer for Realistic Radicals* (New York: Vintage, 1989).

19. See, e.g., Tom Peters, *Thriving on Chaos: Handbook for a Management Revolution* (New York: Harper Perennial, 1987).

20. Varlam Shalamov, *Kolyma Tales*, trans. John Glad (London: Penguin, 1994), 127.

21. Sergey Brin and Lawrence Page, "The Anatomy of a Large-Scale Hypertextual Web Search Engine," *Computer Networks and ISDN Systems* 30, nos. 1–7 (April 1998): 107–117, §1.3.2.

22. Stephen Baker, *The Numerati* (New York: Houghton Mifflin Harcourt, 2008).

23. Philip Agre, "The Practical Logic of Computer Work," in *Computationalism: New Directions*, ed. Matthias Scheutz (Cambridge, MA: MIT Press, 2002).

24. On the "parliament of things," see Bruno Latour, *We Have Never Been Modern*, trans. Catherine Porter (Cambridge, MA: Harvard University Press, 1993).

25. Jean-Paul Sartre, *Being and Nothingness* (London: Methuen, 1958), 59–61.

26. Erving Goffman, *The Presentation of Self in Everyday Life* (London: Penguin, 1990); R. C. Schank and R. Abelson, *Scripts, Plans, Goals, and Understanding* (Hillsdale, NJ: Erlbaum, 1977).

27. A minor point, perhaps, but the increasing penetration of information technology into everyday life would not have happened if every software upgrade required the direct intervention of a computer engineer.

28. Ronald Loui, "In Praise of Scripting: Real Programming Pragmatism," *IEEE Computer* 41, no. 7 (2008).

29. Félix Guattari explores the concept of the "universe of reference" in his *Cartographies schizoanalytiques*.

30. Bhabha, "Sly Civility."

31. Performative utterances, like scripts, can be used to configure roles: "I thee wed."

32. "Rapport" is an important element of neurolinguistic programming and allegedly derives from observations of the excellence of the hypnosis strategies of Milton Erickson. See Jay Haley, *Uncommon Therapy: Psychiatric Techniques of Milton H. Erickson, M.D.* (New York: W. W. Norton, 1993).

33. The "Collateral Murder" video published on the WikiLeaks Web site displays the confusion of scaling and universes of reference particularly clearly.

34. Quoted in Bill Moggridge, *Designing Interactions* (Cambridge, MA: MIT Press, 2006), 466.

35. Jean Baudrillard, *The System of Objects*, trans. James Benedict (London: Verso, 1996).

36. Victor Tausk, "The Influencing Machine," in *Zone 6: Incorporations*, ed. Jonathan Crary and Sanford Kwinter (New York: Zone Books, 1992), 542–569.

37. Melanie Klein, "A Contribution to the Psychogenesis of Manic-Depressive States," in *Contributions to Psychoanalysis, 1921–1945* (London: Hogarth, 1948).

38. D. W. Winnicott, "Transitional Objects and Transitional Phenomena: A Study of the First Not-Me Possession," *International Journal of Psychoanalysis* 34 (1953).

39. Andy Clark and David Chalmers, "The Extended Mind," *Analysis* 58, no. 1 (1982): 7–19.

40. Michael Wheeler, "Minds, Things, and Materiality," in *The Cognitive Life of Things: Recasting Boundaries of the Mind*, ed. Lambros Malafouris and Colin Renfrew (Cambridge: McDonald Institute for Archaeological Research, 2010).

41. Ben Schneiderman, "Direct Manipulation: A Step beyond Programming Languages," *IEEE Computer* 16, no. 8 (August 1983): 57–69.

42. Scott Forstall, iPad promotional video, http://www.apple.com/ipad (accessed May 12, 2010).

43. Gustave Flaubert, quoted in "Stan and Ollie in the Lab," Mark Polizotti, introduction to *Bouvard and Pécuchet*, by Gustave Flaubert, trans. Mark Polizotti (Normal, IL: Dalkey Archive Press, 2005), xv.

44. Linsey McGoey, "On the Will to Ignorance in Bureaucracy," *Economy and Society* 36, no. 2 (2007): 212–235.

45. Avital Ronell, *Stupidity* (Chicago: University of Illinois Press, 2003), 10. On the "image of thought," see Deleuze, *Difference and Repetition*, chap. 3.

46. Ed Hutchins, *Cognition in the Wild* (Cambridge, MA: MIT Press, 1996).

47. Anselm Strauss, "The Articulation of Project Work: An Organizational Process," *Sociological Quarterly* 29, no. 2 (1988): 63–178; Lucy Suchman, "Supporting Articulation Work," in *Computerization and Controversy: Value Conflicts and Social Choices*, ed. Rob Kling (London: Academic Press, 1991), 407–423.

48. Ann Macintosh, "Position Paper on Knowledge Asset Management," http://www.aiai.ed.ac .uk/~alm/kam.html. More explicitly, Macintosh defines knowledge management as "the identification and analysis of available and required knowledge, and the subsequent planning and control of actions to develop knowledge assets so as to fulfill organizational objectives."

49. See, e.g., Etienne C. Wenger, *Communities of Practice: Learning, Meaning, and Identity* (Cambridge: Cambridge University Press, 1998).

50. Flaubert, *Bouvard and Pécuchet*.

51. See J.-C. Spender and Andreas Georg Scherer, "The Philosophical Foundations of Knowledge Management: Editors' Introduction," *Organization* 14, no. 1 (2007): 5–28.

52. As the work of Alain Badiou suggests, thinking is affirmed in the interruption of the algorithms of subjectivity. Badiou, *Theory of the Subject*, esp. sec. 4.

Bibliography

Aalst, Wil van der, and Kees van Hee. *Workflow Management: Models, Methods, and Systems*. Cambridge, MA: MIT Press, 2002.

Adorno, Theodor, and Max Horkheimer. *The Dialectic of Enlightenment*. London: Verso, 1997.

Agamben, Giorgio. *The Coming Community*. Trans. Michael Hardt. Minneapolis: University of Minnesota Press, 1993.

Agamben, Giorgio. *La regne et la gloire*. Paris: Seuil, 2008.

Agamben, Giorgio. *The Man without Content*. Trans. Georgia Albert. Stanford: Stanford University Press, 1999.

Agamben, Giorgio. *The State of Exception*. Chicago: University of Chicago Press, 2005.

Agre, Philip. The practical logic of computer work. In *Computationalism: New Directions*, ed. Matthias Scheutz. Cambridge, MA: MIT Press, 2002.

Agre, Philip. Surveillance and capture: Two models of privacy. In *The New Media Reader*, ed. Noah Wardrip-Fruin and Nick Montfort. Cambridge, MA: MIT Press, 2003.

Akerloff, George, and Robert Shiller. *Animal Spirits: How Human Psychology Drives the Economy, and Why It Matters*. Princeton, NJ: Princeton University Press, 2009.

Akrich, Madeline. The de-scription of technical objects. In *Shaping Technology*, ed. Weibe Bijker and John Law. Cambridge, MA: MIT Press, 1992.

Alinsky, Saul D. *Rules for Radicals: A Pragmatic Primer for Realistic Radicals*. New York: Vintage, 1989.

Allen, David. *Getting Things Done: The Art of Stress-Free Productivity*. London: Penguin, 2001.

Alt, Casey. Viral load: The fantastic rhetorical power of the computer virus in the contemporary U.S. technoscape. In *Fremdkörper*, ed. Philipp Sarasin, special issue, *Österreichische Zeitschrift für Geschichtswissenschaft* 16 (3) (2005): 133–149.

Althusser, Louis. *Machiavelli and Us*. London: Verso, 2001.

Alvarez, Lizette. Meet Mikey, 8: U.S. has him on watch list. *New York Times*, January 13, 2010.

Andersen, P. B. *A Theory of Computer Semiotics*. New York: Cambridge University Press, 1991.

Andersen, P. B., B. Holmqvist, and J. F. Jensen. *The Computer as Medium*. New York: Cambridge University Press, 1993.

Anderson, Benedict. *Imagined Communities: Reflections on the Origin and Spread of Nationalism*. London: Verso, 1991.

Anderson, Chris. *The Long Tail: How Endless Choice Is Creating Unlimited Demand*. London: Random House, 2006.

Andrejevic, Mark. *iSpy: Surveillance and Power in the Interactive Era*. Lawrence: University Press of Kansas, 2009.

Andrejevic, Mark. The work of being watched: Interactive media and the exploitation of self-disclosure. *Critical Studies in Media Communication* 19 (2) (June 2002): 230–248.

Anonymous. Psychological operations in guerrilla warfare. New York: Vintage Books, 1985.

Ariely, Dan. *Predictably Irrational*. Rev. ed. London: HarperCollins, 2009.

Arthur, Brian W. *The Nature of Technology: What It Is and How It Evolves*. London: Penguin, 2010.

Atkinson, Max. *Our Masters' Voices: The Language and Body-Language of Politics*. London: Routledge, 1984.

Axelrod, Alan. *Patton on Leadership: Strategic Lessons for Corporate Warfare*. Hemel Hempstead: Prentice Hall, 2001.

Badiou, Alain. *Being and Event*. London: Continuum, 2007.

Badiou, Alain. *The Concept of Model*. Trans. Zachary Fraser and Tzuchien Tho. Melbourne: re.press, 2007.

Badiou, Alain. *Ethics: An Essay on the Understanding of Evil*. Trans. Peter Hallward. London: Verso, 2001.

Badiou, Alain. *Theory of the Subject*. Trans. Bruno Bosteels. London: Continuum, 2009.

Bailer-Jones, Daniela. Tracing the development of models in the philosophy of science. In *Model-Based Reasoning in Scientific Discovery*, ed. Lorenzo Magnani, Nancy J. Nersessian, and Paul Thagard. Berlin: Springer, 1999.

Ball, Frank, Denis Mollison, and Gianpaolo Scalia-Tomba. Epidemics with two levels of mixing. *Annals of Applied Probability* 7 (1) (1997): 46–89.

Baker, Stephen. *The Numerati*. New York: Houghton Mifflin Harcourt, 2008.

Bandler, Richard, and John Grinder. *The Structure of Magic I: A Book about Language and Therapy*. Palo Alto: Science & Behavior Books, 1975.

Barry, Andrew. *Political Machines*. London: Athlone, 2001.

Barthes, Roland. *The Neutral*. Trans. Rosalind E. Krauss and Denis Hollier. New York: Columbia University Press, 2005.

Baudrillard, Jean. *For a Critique of the Political Economy of the Sign*. Trans. Charles Levin. St. Louis, MO: Telos Press, 1981.

Baudrillard, Jean. *In the Shadow of the Silent Majorities*. New York: Semiotext(e), 1983.

Baudrillard, Jean. *The System of Objects*. Trans. James Benedict. London: Verso, 1996.

Beniger, James R. *The Control Revolution: Technological and Economic Origins of the Information Society*. Cambridge, MA: Harvard University Press, 1986.

Benkler, Yochai. *The Wealth of Networks: How Social Production Transforms Markets and Freedom*. New Haven: Yale University Press, 2006.

Benner, Erica. *Machiavelli's Ethics*. Princeton, NJ: Princeton University Press, 2009.

Bennis, Warren G. *The Unconscious Conspiracy: Why Leaders Can't Lead*. New York: AMACOM, 1976.

Berardi, Franco "Bifo." *The Soul at Work: From Alienation to Autonomy*. Trans. Francesca Cadel and Giuseppina Mecchia. New York: Semiotext(e), 2009.

Berg, Marc. Patient care information systems and health care work: A sociotechnical approach. *International Journal of Medical Informatics* 55 (1999): 87–101.

Berg, Marc. *Rationalizing Medical Work: Decision Support Techniques and Medical Practices*. Cambridge, MA: MIT Press, 1997.

Bergson, Henri. *Creative Evolution*. New York: Dover Books, 1998.

Bernays, Edward. *Propaganda*. New York: Horace Liveright, 1928.

Bhabha, Homi. Sly civility. *October* 34 (1985): 71–80.

Bijker, Weibe, and John Law, eds. *Shaping Technology*. Cambridge, MA: MIT Press, 1992.

Bishop, Mark. Dancing with pixies: Strong artificial intelligence and panpsychism. In *Views into the Chinese Room: New Essays on Searle and Artificial Intelligence*, ed. John Preston and Mark Bishop, 360–378. Oxford: Oxford University Press, 2002.

Blum, Alan. *The Grey Zone in Health and Illness*. London: Intellect, 2010.

Boltanski, Luc. *Different Suffering*. Cambridge: Cambridge University Press, 1999.

Booch, Grady. *Object-Oriented Analysis and Design with Applications*. Reading: Addison-Wesley, 2007.

Borch-Jacobsen, Mikkel. L'inconscient simulé. In *La guerre des psys*, ed. Tobie Nathan. Paris: Les Empêcheurs de Penser en Rond, 2006.

Borch-Jacobsen, Mikkel. *Remembering Anna O.: A Century of Mystification*. New York: Routledge, 1996.

Börger, E. High level system design and analysis using abstract state machines. In *Proceedings of the International Workshop on Current Trends in Applied Formal Method: Applied Formal Methods*, ed. D. Hutter, W. Stephan, P. Traverso, and M. Ullmann. Lecture Notes in Computer Science, vol. 1641. London: Springer, 1999.

Bourdieu, Pierre. *Outline of a Theory of Practice*. Cambridge: Cambridge University Press, 1977.

Bowker, Geoffrey C., and Susan Leigh Star. *Sorting Things Out: Classification and Its Consequences*. Cambridge, MA: MIT Press, 1999.

Braverman, Harry. *Labor and Monopoly Capital*. New York: Monthly Review Press, 1974.

Brin, Sergey, and Lawrence Page. The anatomy of a large-scale hypertextual web search engine. *Computer Networks and ISDN Systems* 30 (1–7) (April 1998): 107–117.

Brooks, Rodney A. Elephants don't play chess. *Robotics and Autonomous Systems* 6 (1990): 3–15.

Brooks, Rodney A., and Lynn Andrea Stein. Building brains for bodies. In *Autonomous Robots*, vol. 1, 7–25. Boston: Kluwer Academic, 1994.

Brown, John Seely, and Paul Duguid. *The Social Life of Information*. Cambridge: Harvard Business School Press, 2000.

Brynjolfsson, Erik, Yu Jeffrey Hu, and Duncan Simester. Goodbye Pareto principle, hello long tail: The effect of search costs on the concentration of product sales. November 2007. http://ssrn.com/abstract=953587.

Bumiller, Elizabeth. We have met the enemy and he is PowerPoint. *New York Times*, April 26, 2010.

Burnham, James. *The Managerial Revolution*. Harmondsworth: Pelican Books, 1945.

Caffentzis, George C. Crystals and analytic engines: Historical and conceptual preliminaries to a new theory of machines. *Ephemera* 7 (1) (2007): 24–45. http://www.ephemeraweb.org/journal/7-1/7-1caffentzis.pdf.

Callon, Michel. Some elements of a sociology of translation: Domestication of the scallops and the fishermen of Saint Brieuc Bay. In *Power, Action, and Belief: A New Sociology of Knowledge?* ed. John Law. Sociological Review Monograph 32. London: Routledge & Kegan Paul, 1986.

Callon, Michel, Pierre Lascoumes, and Yannick Barthe. *Acting in an Uncertain World*. Trans. Graham Burchell. Cambridge, MA: MIT Press, 2009.

Cantrill, Bryan. A spoonful of sewage. In *Beautiful Code: Leading Programmers Explain How They Think*, ed. Andy Oram and Greg Wilson, 353–369. Sebastopol, CA: O'Reilly Media, 2007.

Cassin, Barbara. *L'Effet sophistique*. Paris: Gallimard, 1995.

Cassin, Barbara. Performance before the performative. Forthcoming.

Cassin, Barbara, and Philippe Büttgen. The performative without condition: A university sans appel. *Radical Philosophy* 162 (July–August 2010): 31–37.

Clark, Andy, and David Chalmers. The extended mind. *Analysis* 58 (1) (1982): 7–19.

Codd, Edgar. *The Relational Model for Database Management: Version 2*. Reading: Addison-Wesley, 1990.

Codd, Edgar F. A relational model of data for large shared data banks. *Communications of the ACM* 13 (6) (June 1970): 377–387.

Coiera, Enrico. Informality. HP Laboratories technical document HPL-97-37.

Collins, Harry. *Artificial Experts: Social Knowledge and Intelligent Machines*. Cambridge, MA: MIT Press, 1990.

Collins, Harry. *Tacit and Explicit Knowledge*. Chicago: University of Chicago Press, 2010.

Collins, Harry, and Trevor Pinch. *The Shape of Actions*. Cambridge, MA: MIT Press, 1998.

Coyne, Richard. *The Tuning of Place*. Cambridge, MA: MIT Press, 2010.

Crosby, Alfred, Jr. *Ecological Imperialism*, 2nd ed. Cambridge: Cambridge University Press, 2004.

Daft, R. L., and R. H. Lengel. Information richness: A new approach to managerial behavior and organizational design. In *Research in Organizational Behavior*, vol. 6, ed. L. L. Cummings and B. M. Staw, 191–233. Homewood, IL: JAI Press, 1984.

Damasio, Antonio. *Descartes' Error*. London: Penguin, 2005.

Dean, Kenneth, and Brian Massumi. *First and Last Emperors: The Absolute State and the Body of the Despot*. New York: Autonomedia, 1992.

Debord, Guy. Report on the construction of situations and on the International Situationist tendency's conditions of organization and action (June 1957). In *Situationist International Anthology*, ed. Ken Knabb. Berkeley: Bureau of Public Secrets, 1981.

Debord, Guy. *The Society of the Spectacle*. Detroit: Black and Red, 1970.

De Landa, Manuel. *Simulation and Philosophy*. London: Continuum, 2011.

Deleuze, Gilles. *Difference and Repetition*. Trans. Paul Patton. London: Athlone, 1994.

Deleuze, Gilles. The exhausted. In *Essays Critical and Clinical*, trans. Daniel W. Smith and Michael A. Greco, 152–174. London: Verso, 1998.

Deleuze, Gilles. *The Fold: Leibniz and the Baroque*. Trans. Tom Conley. London: Athlone, 1993.

Deleuze, Gilles. *The Logic of Sense*. Trans. Mark Lester. London: Athlone, 1990.

Deleuze, Gilles, and Félix Guattari. *Anti-Oedipus*. Minneapolis: University of Minnesota Press, 1983.

Deleuze, Gilles, and Félix Guattari. *A Thousand Plateaus*. Trans. Brian Massumi. Minneapolis: University of Minnesota Press, 1987.

Deleuze, Gilles, and Félix Guattari. *What Is Philosophy?* Trans. Graham Burchell and Hugh Tomlinson. London: Verso, 1994.

Despret, Vinciane. Le secret est une dimension politique de la thérapie. In *La guerre des psys, manifeste pour une psychothérapie democratique*, ed. T. Nathan. Paris: Les Empêcheurs de Penser en Rond, 2006.

Despret, Vinciane. *Quand le loup habitera avec l'agneau*. Paris: Les Empêcheurs de Penser en Rond, 2002.

Didi-Huberman, Georges. *Invention of Hysteria: Charcot and the Photographic Iconography of the Salpêtrière*. Cambridge, MA: MIT Press, 2003.

Dohse, Knuth, Ulrich Jurgens, and Thomas Malsch. From "Fordism" to "Toyotism"? The social organization of the labor process in the Japanese automobile industry. International Institute for Labour Policy, Working Paper, Berlin, April 1984.

Doran, George T. There's a S.M.A.R.T. way to write management's goals and objectives. *Management Review* 70 (11) (1981): 35–36.

Dreyfus, Hubert. *What Computers Still Can't Do*. Cambridge, MA: MIT Press, 1979.

Drucker, Peter F. *The Practice of Management*. 1955; Oxford: Butterworth Heinemann, 1995.

Dupuy, Jean-Pierre. *On the Origins of Cognitive Science: The Mechanization of the Mind*. Cambridge, MA: MIT Press, 2009.

Edwards, Paul N. *The Closed World*. Cambridge, MA: MIT Press, 1996.

Eisenberg, E. M. Ambiguity as strategy in organizational communication. *Communication Monographs* 51 (1984): 227–242.

Empson, William. *The Seven Types of Ambiguity*, 2nd ed. London: Chatto and Windus, 1949.

Faroult, Stephane. *The Art of SQL*. Sebastopol, CA: O'Reilly Media, 2006.

50 Cent and Robert Greene. *The 50th Law*. New York: Harper, 2009.

Fisher, Mark. *Capitalist Realism: Is There No Alternative?* Winchester: Zero Books, 2009.

Flahault, Francois. *Malice*. Trans. Liz Heron. London: Verso, 2003.

Flaubert, Gustave. *Bouvard and Pécuchet*. Trans. Mark Polizotti. Normal, IL: Dalkey Archive Press, 2005.

Flynn, Elizabeth Gurley. *Sabotage: The Conscious Withdrawal of Workers' Industrial Efficiency*. Cleveland: Industrial Workers of the World, 1916.

Forstall, Scott. iPad promotional video. http://www.apple.com/ipad (accessed May 12, 2010).

Foucault, Michel. *The Birth of Biopolitics: Lectures at the Collège de France, 1978–1979*. Trans. Graham Burchell. London: Palgrave Macmillan, 2008.

Foucault, Michel. Nietzsche, genealogy, history. In *Language, Counter-memory, Practice*, ed. Donald F. Bouchard. Ithaca, NY: Cornell University Press, 1977.

Foucault, Michel. *Security, Territory, Population: Lectures at the Collège de France, 1977–78*. Ed. Michel Senellart, trans. Graham Burchell. London: Palgrave Macmillan, 2007.

Freedom Fighter's Manual. http://www.ballistichelmet.org/school/free.html.

Freud, Sigmund. *Beyond the Pleasure Principle*, Standard Edition, vol. 18. New York: W. W. Norton, 1955.

Friedman, Thomas L. *The World Is Flat: The Globalized World in the Twenty-first Century*. London: Penguin, 2006.

Gaddis, Paul O. The project manager. *Harvard Business Review*, no. 37 (1959): 89–97.

Galison, Peter. The ontology of the enemy: Norbert Wiener and the cybernetic vision. *Critical Inquiry* 21 (1) (autumn 1994): 228–266.

Gauchet, Marcel. *L'inconscient cérébral*. Paris: Seuil, 1992.

Gille, Bertrand. *The Renaissance Engineers*. London: Lund Humphries, 1966.

Ginzburg, Carlo. *The Cheese and the Worms: The Cosmos of a Sixteenth-Century Miller*. Trans. John Tedeschi and Anne C. Tedeschi. Baltimore, MD: Johns Hopkins University Press, 1992.

Gladwell, Malcolm. *The Tipping Point*. London: Abacus, 2001.

Goffman, Erving. *The Presentation of Self in Everyday Life*. London: Penguin, 1990.

Gomart, Emilie. Surprised by methadone: In praise of drug substitution treatment in a French clinic. *Body and Society* 10 (2–3) (June 2004): 85–110.

Goody, Jack. *Domestication of the Savage Mind*. Cambridge: Cambridge University Press, 1977.

Google. Code of Conduct. http://investor.google.com/corporate/code-of-conduct.html.

Goriunova, Olga. *Art Platforms and Cultural Production on the Internet*. London: Routledge, 2011.

Gracián, Balthasar. *The Art of Worldly Wisdom*. Trans. Joseph Jacobs. London: Shambhala, 1993.

Grice, H. P. Logic and conversation. In *Studies in the Way of Words*, ed. H. P. Grice. Cambridge, MA: Harvard University Press, 1989.

Guattari, Félix. *Chaosmosis*. Trans. Paul Bains and Julian Pefanis. Sydney: Power Institute, 1995.

Guattari, Félix. *Les cartographies schizoanalytiques*. Paris: Galilée, 1989.

Guattari, Félix. Machinic junkies. In *Soft Subversions*. New York: Semiotext(e), 1996.

Gurevich, Yuri. *Logic and the Challenge of Computer Science*. New York: Computer Science Press, 1988.

Guy, Richard K. The strong law of small numbers. *American Mathematical Monthly* 95 (8) (October 1988): 697–712.

Hakim, Catherine. Erotic capital. *European Sociological Review* 26 (5) (2010): 1–20.

Hacking, Ian. How should we do the history of statistics? In *The Foucault Effect: Studies in Governmentality*, ed. Graham Burchell, Colin Gordon, and Peter Miller. Hemel Hempstead: Harvester Wheatsheaf, 1991.

Haley, Jay. *Uncommon Therapy: Psychiatric Techniques of Milton H. Erickson, M.D.* New York: W. W. Norton, 1993.

Harman, Graham. *Prince of Networks: Bruno Latour and Metaphysics*. Melbourne: re.press, 2009.

Harman, Graham. *Tool-being*. Peru, IL: Open Court, 2002.

Hawkes, Terence. William Empson's influence on the CIA. *Times Literary Supplement* (June 2009): 10.

Hayward, Rhodri. The tortoise and the love-machine: Grey Walter and the politics of electroencephalography. *Science in Context* 14 (4) (2001): 615–641.

Holzman, Michael. *James Jesus Angleton: The CIA and the Craft of Counterintelligence*. Amherst: University of Massachusetts Press, 2008.

Horkheimer, Max. *Critique of Instrumental Reason*. London: Continuum, 1983.

Howard, Michael, and David LeBlanc. *Writing Secure Code*, 2nd ed. Seattle: Microsoft Press, 2002.

Howe, Jeff. The rise of crowdsourcing. *Wired* 14.06 (June 2006).

Hunter, Edward. *Brain-Washing in Red China: The Calculated Destruction of Men's Minds*. New York: Vanguard Press, 1951.

Hutchins, Ed. *Cognition in the Wild*. Cambridge, MA: MIT Press, 1996.

Illouz, Eva. *Cold Intimacies: The Making of Emotional Capitalism*. Cambridge: Polity, 2007.

Imbert, Claude. *Phénoménologies et langues formulaires*. Paris: PUF, 1992.

Internet Engineering Taskforce. Request for comments repository. http://www.ietf.org/rfc.html.

Jarry, Alfred. *The Exploits and Opinions of Dr. Faustroll, Pataphysician*. Trans. Simon Watson Taylor. Cambridge, MA: Exact Change, 1997.

Johns, Adrian. *The Nature of the Book: Print and Knowledge in the Making*. Chicago: University of Chicago Press, 2000.

Johnson, Chalmers. *Blowback*. New York: Holt Paperbacks, 2004.

Johnson, John. *The Allure of Machinic Life: Cybernetics, Artificial Life, and the New AI*. Cambridge, MA: MIT Press, 2008.

Jorn, Asger. The situationists and automation. In *Situationist International Anthology*, ed. Ken Knabb. Berkeley: Bureau of Public Secrets, 1981.

Kelty, Christopher. *Two Bits: The Cultural Significance of Free Software*. Durham: Duke University Press, 2008.

Kirby, Reid. Paradise lost: The psycho agents. *Quarterly Journal of the Harvard Sussex Program on CBW Armament and Arms Limitation*, no. 71 (May 2006): 1.

Kittler, Friedrich. Code. In *Software Studies: A Lexicon*, ed. Matthew Fuller. Cambridge, MA: MIT Press, 2008.

Kleene, Stephen C. Representation of events in nerve nets and finite automata. In *Automata Studies*, ed. C. Shannon and J. McCarthy. Princeton, NJ: Princeton University Press, 1956.

Klein, Gary. *Sources of Power: How People Make Decisions*. Cambridge, MA: MIT Press, 1999.

Klein, Mark, and Chrysanthos Dellarocas. A knowledge-based approach to handling exceptions in workflow systems. *Computer Supported Collaborative Work* 9 (3–4) (2000): 399–412.

Klein, Melanie. A contribution to the psychogenesis of manic-depressive states. In *Contributions to Psychoanalysis, 1921–1945*. London: Hogarth Press and the Institute of Psychoanalysis, 1948.

Kohonen, Teuvo. *Self-Organizing Maps*. Berlin: Springer, 2001.

Krug, Steve. *Don't Make Me Think! A Common Sense Approach to Web Usability*, 2nd ed. Berkeley: New Riders, 2005.

Kuhns, J. L. *Answering Questions by Computer: A Logical Study*. Santa Monica, CA: Rand Corporation, 1967.

Kupiec, Jean-Jacques, and Pierre Sonigo. *Ni Dieu ni gène: Pour une autre théorie de l'hérédité*. Paris: Seuil, 2000.

Lacan, Jacques. *Ecrits: A Selection*. Trans. Alan Sheridan. London: Routledge, 1977.

Latour, Bruno. Irreductions. In *The Pasteurization of France*, trans. Alan Sheridan and John Law. Cambridge, MA: Harvard University Press, 1993.

Latour, Bruno. *Pandora's Hope: Essays on the Reality of Science Studies*. Cambridge, MA: Harvard University Press, 1999.

Latour, Bruno. *The Pasteurization of France*. Trans Alan Sheridan and John Law. Cambridge, MA: Harvard University Press, 1988.

Latour, Bruno. *Re-assembling the Social*. Oxford: Oxford University Press, 2005.

Latour, Bruno. *Science in Action*. Cambridge, MA: Harvard University Press, 1987.

Latour, Bruno. *We Have Never Been Modern*. Trans. Catherine Porter. Cambridge: Harvard University Press, 1993.

Laudon, K. C., and J. P. Laudon. *Management Information Systems: New Approaches to Organization and Technology*, 5th ed. New York: Macmillan, 1998.

Laufer, Romain, and Catherine Paradeise. *Marketing Democracy: Public Opinion and Media Formation in Democratic Societies*. Trans. Noel Castelino. New Brunswick, NJ: Transaction, 1990.

Lazarfeld, Paul. *Personal Influence: The Part Played by People in the Flow of Mass Communications*. Piscataway, NJ: Transaction, 2006.

Lazzarato, Maurizio. *Expérimentations politiques*. Paris: Editions Amsterdam, 2009. Translation forthcoming from MIT Press.

Le Poulichet, Sylvie. *Toxicomanies et psychanalyse: Les narcoses du désir*. Paris: PUF, 1987.

Lessig, Lawrence. *Code, Version 2.0*. New York: Basic Books, 2006.

Levi, Primo. *The Drowned and the Saved*. Trans Raymond Rosenthal. London: Abacus, 1989.

Lobachevski, Nicholas. The theory of parallels, trans. George Bruce Halsted, appendix to *Non-Euclidean Geometry: A Critical and Historical Study of Its Development*, by Roberto Bonola, trans. H. S. Carslaw. New York: Dover Books, 1955.

Loui, Ronald. In praise of scripting: Real programming pragmatism. *IEEE Computer* 41 (7) (2008): 22–26.

Lovink, Geert, and Nathaniel Tkacz, eds. *Critical Point of View: A Wikipedia Reader*. Amsterdam: Institute of Network Cultures, 2011.

Lyon, David, ed. *Surveillance and Social Sorting*. London: Routledge, 2002.

Lyotard, Jean-François. *The Differend*. Minneapolis: University of Minnesota Press, 1988.

Machiavelli, Niccolò. *The Prince*. Trans. George Bull. London: Penguin, 1964.

Macintosh, Ann. Position paper on knowledge asset management. http://www.aiai.ed.ac.uk/~alm/kam.html.

MacKenzie, Donald. *An Engine, Not a Camera: How Financial Models Shape Markets*. Cambridge, MA: MIT Press, 2006.

MacKenzie, Donald, Fabian Muniesa, and Lucia Siu. *Do Economists Make Markets? On the Performativity of Economics*. Princeton, NJ: Princeton University Press, 2007.

Manas, Jerry. *Napoleon on Project Management: Timeless Lessons in Planning, Execution, and Leadership*. Nashville, TN: Thomas Nelson, 2006.

Marazzi, Christian. *Capital and Language*. New York: Semiotext(e), 2008.

Marin, Louis. *Utopics: The Semiotics of Spatial Play*. Trans. Robert Vollrath. Amherst, NY: Humanity Books, 1984.

Marion, Jean-Luc. *Sur l'ontologie grise de Descartes*. Paris: J. Vrin, 1975.

Mattelart, Armand. *The Globalization of Surveillance*. London: Polity, 2010.

Mayall, Roy. *Dear Granny Smith*. London: Short Books, 2009.

McGoey, Linsey. On the will to ignorance in bureaucracy. *Economy and Society* 36 (2) (May 2007): 212–235.

McLuhan, Marshall. *Understanding Media: The Extensions of Man*. Cambridge, MA: MIT Press, 1994.

Meheust, Bertrand. *La politique de l'oxymore*. Paris: Découverte, 2009.

Melchior, Thierry. *Créer le reel*. Paris: Seuil, 1998.

Melville, Herman. *Bartleby the Scrivener*. London: Hesperus Press, 2007.

Milgram, Stanley. *Obedience to Authority: An Experimental View*. London: Harper Collins, 1974.

Minsky, Marvin. Jokes and their relation to the cognitive unconscious. 1981. http://web.media .mit.edu/~minsky/papers/jokes.cognitive.txt.

Mirowski, Philip. *Machine Dreams: Economics Becomes a Cyborg Science*. Cambridge: Cambridge University Press, 2002.

Moggridge, Bill. *Designing Interactions*. Cambridge, MA: MIT Press, 2006.

Moravia, Alberto. *Boredom*. Trans. Angus Davidson. New York: NYRB, 1999.

Morgan, Mary S., and Margaret Morrison, eds. *Models as Mediators: Perspectives on Natural and Social Science*. Cambridge: Cambridge University Press, 1999.

Morris, Peter W. G. *The Management of Projects*. London: Thomas Telford, 1997.

Munster, Anna. Nerves of data: The neurological turn in/against networked media. *Computational Culture* 1 (December 2011), http://www.computationalculture.net.

Nathan, Tobie. *A qui j'appartiens?* Paris: Seuil, 2007.

Newton, Isaac. *Philosopiae Naturalis Principia Mathematica (The Mathematical Principles of Natural Philosophy)*. London: S. Pepys, 1687.

Nietzsche, Friedrich. *Beyond Good and Evil: Prelude to a Philosophy of the Future*. Ed. Rolf-Peter Horstmann and Judith Norman, trans. Judith Norman. Cambridge: Cambridge University Press, 2002.

Nietzsche, Friedrich. *On the Genealogy of Morality*. Ed. Keith Ansell-Pearson, trans. Carol Diethe. Cambridge: Cambridge University Press, 1994.

Nietzsche, Friedrich. *Untimely Meditations*. Trans. R. J. Hollingdale. Cambridge: Cambridge University Press, 1997.

Nietzsche, Friedrich. *Writings from the Late Notebooks*. Ed. Rüdiger Bittner, trans. Kate Sturge. Cambridge: Cambridge University Press, 2003.

Ngai, Sianne. *Ugly Feelings*. Cambridge, MA: Harvard University Press, 2005.

Nonaka, I., and H. Takeuchi. *The Knowledge-Creating Company.* Oxford: Oxford University Press, 1995.

Nriagu, Jerome, et al. Saturnine gout among Roman aristocrats: Did lead poisoning contribute to the fall of the Empire? *New England Journal of Medicine* 308 (11) (March 1983): 660–663.

Nye, David. *The American Technological Sublime.* Cambridge, MA: MIT Press, 1994.

Office of Government Commerce. Project initiation documentation. http://www.ogc.gov.uk/documentation_and_templates_project_initiation_document_pid.asp (accessed February 28, 2010. Site now defunct).

Parikka, Jussi. *Digital Contagions.* New York: Peter Lang, 2007.

Peters, Tom. *Thriving on Chaos: Handbook for a Management Revolution.* New York: Harper Perennial, 1987.

Pignarre, Philippe. *Comment la dépression est devenue une épidémie.* Paris: Découverte, 2001.

Pignarre, Philippe. *Les malheurs des psys.* Paris: Découverte, 2006.

Pomerol, Jean-Charles, and Frédéric Adam. On the legacy of Herbert Simon and his contribution to decision making support systems and artificial intelligence. In *Intelligent Decision-Making Support Systems (i-DMSS): Foundations, Applications, and Challenges,* ed. J. Gupta, G. Forgionnne, and M. Mora, 25–44. Frankfurt: Springer, 2005.

Power, D. J. A brief history of decision support systems. http://dssresources.com/history/dsshistory.html.

Power, Michael. *Organized Uncertainty: Designing a World of Risk Management.* Oxford: Oxford University Press, 2007.

Pressman, Jack. *The Last Resort: Psychosurgery and the Limits of Medicine.* Cambridge: Cambridge University Press, 1998.

Putnam, Robert. *Bowling Alone: The Collapse and Revival of American Community.* New York: Simon & Schuster, 2000.

Pynchon, Thomas. *Gravity's Rainbow.* London: Penguin, 1995.

Raymond, Eric. *The Cathedral and the Bazaar: Musings on Linux and Open Source by an Accidental Revolutionary.* Sebastopol, CA: O'Reilly Media, 2001.

Ready, Romilla, and Kate Burton. *NLP for Dummies.* Chichester: John Wiley and Sons, 2004.

Retort. *Afflicted Powers: Capital and Spectacle in a New Age of War.* London: Verso, 2005.

Rheingold, Howard. *Smart Mobs: The Next Social Revolution.* New York: Basic Books, 2002.

Ridley, Matt. *The Red Queen: Sex and the Evolution of Human Nature.* London: Viking, 1993.

Rivière, Carole. Le lien de dépendance addictive à Internet: Une nouvelle forme d'addiction? Observatoire des Mondes Numériques en Sciences Humaines. http://www.omnsh.org/article .php3?id_article=94.

Rogers, Robert. *Rogers' Rangers Rules*, 1757. http://www.military-info.com/freebies/roger.htm.

Ronell, Avital. *Crack Wars: Literature, Addiction, Mania*. Lincoln: University of Nebraska Press, 1992.

Ronell, Avital. *Stupidity*. Chicago: University of Illinois Press, 2003.

Ross, D. T., and K. E. Schoman. Structured analysis for requirements definitions. In *Classics in Software Engineering*, ed. Edward Nash Yourdon, 365–388. New York: Yourdon Press, 1979.

Russell, Bertrand. Letter to Frege (1902). In *From Frege to Gödel: A Sourcebook in Mathematical Logic, 1879–1931*, ed. Jean van Heijenoort, 124–125. Cambridge, MA: Harvard University Press, 1967.

Sampson, Tony. How networks become viral: Three questions concerning universal contagion. In *The Spam Book: On Viruses, Porn, and Other Anomalies from the Dark Side of Digital Culture*, ed. Jussi Parikka and Tony D. Sampson. Cresskill, NJ: Hampton Press, 2009.

Sartre, Jean-Paul. *Being and Nothingness*. London: Methuen, 1958.

Schank, R. C., and R. Abelson. *Scripts, Plans, Goals, and Understanding*. Hillsdale, NJ: Erlbaum, 1977.

Scheflin, Alan, and Edward Opton. *The Mind Manipulators*. London: Paddington Press, 1978.

Schein, Edgar. *Organizational Culture and Leadership*. Hoboken, NJ: John Wiley, 2004.

Scheutz, Matthias, ed. *Computationalism: New Directions*. Cambridge, MA: MIT Press, 2002.

Schmitt, Carl. *Political Theology: Four Chapters on the Concept of Sovereignty*. Cambridge, MA: MIT Press, 1985.

Schneiderman, Ben. Direct manipulation: A step beyond programming languages. *IEEE Computer* 16 (8) (August 1983): 57–69.

Schopenhauer, Arthur. *The Art of Always Being Right*. London: Gibson, 2005.

Shalamov, Varlam. *Kolyma Tales*. Trans. John Glad. London: Penguin, 1994.

Shaviro, Steven. *Post-Cinematic Affect*. Winchester: Zero Books, 2010.

Shklovsky, Victor. *Zoo, or Letters Not about Love: A Novel*. Trans. Richard Sheldon. Normal, IL: Dalkey Archive Press, 2001.

Sievers, Burkard. Psychotic organization as a metaphoric frame for the socioanalysis of organizational and interorganizational dynamics. *Administration and Society* 31 (5) (1999): 588–615.

Silverstone, Roger. *Media and Morality*. London: Polity, 2007.

Simon, Herbert A. *Administrative Behavior: A Study of Decision-Making Processes in Administrative Organizations*. 4th ed. New York: Free Press, 1997.

Simon, Herbert A. *The New Science of Management Decision*, 3rd rev. ed. Englewood Cliffs, NJ: Prentice Hall, 1977.

Simon, Herbert A. *Sciences of the Artificial*, 3rd ed. Cambridge, MA: MIT Press, 1996.

Sironi, Francoise. *Bourreaux et victimes*. Paris: Odile Jacob, 1992.

Situationist International. Preliminary problems in constructing a situation (1958). In *Situationist International Anthology*, ed. Ken Knabb. Berkeley: Bureau of Public Secrets, 1981.

Sohn-Rethel, Alfred. *Intellectual and Manual Labour: A Critique of Epistemology*. London: Macmillan, 1978.

Smythe, Dallas. *Dependency Road: Communications, Capitalism, Consciousness*. Toronto: Ablex, 1981.

Sorokin, Vladimir. *The Queue*. Trans. Sally Laird. New York: NYRB Classics, 2008.

Spender, J. C., and Andreas Georg Scherer. The philosophical foundations of knowledge management: Editors' introduction. *Organization* 14 (1) (2007): 5–28.

StankDawg. Hacking Google AdWords. In *The Best of 2600: A Hacker Odyssey*, ed. Emmanuel Goldstein. Indianapolis: Wiley, 2008.

Star, Susan Leigh. The ethnography of infrastructure. *American Behavioral Scientist* 43 (1999): 377–391.

Star, Susan Leigh. This is not a boundary object: Reflections on the origin of a concept. *Science, Technology, and Human Values* 35 (5) (2010): 601–617.

Star, Susan Leigh, and James L. Griesemer. Institutional ecology, "translations," and boundary objects: Amateurs and professionals in Berkeley's Museum of Vertebrate Zoology, 1907–39. *Social Studies of Science* 19 (3) (August 1989): 387–420.

Stengers, Isabelle. *Cosmopolitiques*, vol. 7: *Pour en finir avec la tolerance*. Paris: Découverte, 1997.

Stengers, Isabelle. *The Invention of Modern Science*. Trans. Daniel W. Smith. Minneapolis: University of Minnesota Press, 2000.

Stengers, Isabelle. Relaying the war machine. In *The Guattari Effect*, ed. Eric Alliez and Andrew Goffey. London: Continuum, 2011.

Stengers, Isabelle, and Philippe Pignarre. *Capitalist Sorcery: Breaking the Spell*. Trans. Andrew Goffey. London: Palgrave, 2011.

Stewart, Kathleen. *Ordinary Affects*. Durham, NC: Duke University Press, 2007.

Stone, Alluquére Roseanne. *The War of Desire and Technology at the Close of the Machine Age*. Cambridge, MA: MIT Press, 1996.

Strathern, Marilyn, ed. *Audit Cultures: Anthropological Studies in Accountability, Ethics, and the Academy*. London: Routledge, 2000.

Strauss, Anselm. The articulation of project work: An organizational process. *Sociological Quarterly* 29 (2) (1988): 163–178.

Strauss, Leo. *The City and Man*. Chicago: Rand McNally, 1964.

Streatfield, Dominic. *Brainwashing. The Secret History of Mind Control*. London: Hodder, 2006.

Stroustrup, Bjarne. *The C++ Programming Language*, 3rd ed. Reading: Addison-Wesley, 1997.

Suchman, Lucy. Do categories have politics? *Computer Supported Cooperative Work* 2 (1994): 177–190.

Suchman, Lucy. Supporting articulation work. In *Computerization and Controversy: Value Conflicts and Social Choices*, ed. Rob Kling, 407–423. London: Academic Press, 1991.

Szilard, Leo. On the decrease of entropy in thermodynamic systems by the intervention of intelligent beings. In *Maxwell's Demon 2: Entropy, Classical and Quantum Information, Computing*, ed. Harvey S. Leff and Andrew F. Rex, 110–119. Bristol: Institute of Physics Publications, 2003.

Taber, Robert. *The War of the Flea*. New York: Brassey's, 2002.

Tarde, Gabriel. *The Laws of Imitation*. Trans. Elsie Parsons. New York: Henry Holt, 1903.

Tarski, Alfred. Truth and proof. In *A Philosophical Companion to First-Order Logic*, ed. R. I .G. Hughes. Cambridge, MA: Hackett, 1993. Originally published in Scientific American, June 1969.

Tasić, Vladimir. Politics of chaos. n.d.

Tausk, Victor. The influencing machine. In *Zone 6: Incorporations*, ed. Jonathan Crary and Sanford Kwinter, 542–569. New York: Zone Books, 1992.

Taylor, Kathleen. *Brainwashing: The Science of Thought Control*. Oxford: Oxford University Press, 2004.

Thomsett, R. Double dummy spit and other estimating games. *American Programmer* 9 (6) (1996): 16–22.

Thornton, Chris. *Truth from Trash: How Learning Makes Sense*. Cambridge, MA: MIT Press, 2000.

Tett, Gillian. *Fool's Gold: How Unrestrained Greed Corrupted a Dream, Shattered Global Markets, and Unleashed a Catastrophe*. Boston: Little, Brown, 2009.

Toscano, Alberto. The open secret of real abstraction. *Rethinking Marxism* 7 (2) (April 2008): 273–287.

Toulmin, Stephen. *Cosmopolis: The Hidden Agenda of Modernity*. Chicago: University of Chicago Press, 1990.

Tufte, Edward. *The Visual Display of Quantitative Information*, 2nd ed. Cheshire, CT: Graphic Press, 2001.

Virno, Paolo. *The Grammar of the Multitude*. Trans. Isabella Bertoletti, James Cascaito, and Andrea Casson. New York: Semiotext(e), 2004.

von Neumann, John, and Oskar Morgenstern. *Theory of Games and Economic Behavior*. Princeton, NJ: Princeton University Press, 1944.

Vural, Ulas, and Yusuf Akgul. Eye-gaze based real-time surveillance video synopsis. *Pattern Recognition Letters* 30 (12) (September 2009): 1151–1159.

Wagner, Harvey M. *Principles of Operations Research with Applications to Managerial Decisions*, 2nd ed. Englewood Cliffs, NJ: Prentice Hall, 1975.

Weizman, Eyal. *The Least of All Possible Evils: Humanitarian Violence from Arendt to Gaza*. London: Verso, 2012.

Wenger, Etienne C. *Communities of Practice: Learning, Meaning, and Identity*. Cambridge: Cambridge University Press, 1998.

Wheeler, Michael. Minds, things, and materiality. In *The Cognitive Life of Things: Recasting Boundaries of the Mind*, ed. Lambros Malafouris and Colin Renfrew. Cambridge: McDonald Institute for Archaeological Research, 2010.

Whitehead, Alfred North. *Process and Reality*, 2nd ed. London: Macmillan–Free Press, 1978.

WikiLeaks. Collateral murder. April 5, 2010. http://www.collateralmurder.com.

Winnicott, D. W. Transitional objects and transitional phenomena: A study of the first not-me possession. *International Journal of Psychoanalysis* 34 (1953): 89–97.

Wirth, Niklaus. *Algorithm + Data Structure = Program*. Upper Saddle River, NJ: Prentice Hall, 1976.

Workflow Management Coalition. The workflow management coalition terminology and glossary. Document no. WFMC-TC-1011, p. 8. http://www.wfmc.org/standards/docs/TC-1011_term_glossary_v3.pdf.

YAWL Foundation. YAWL: Yet another workflow language. http://www.yawl-system.com/resources/patterns.html.

Yourdon, Edward. *Death March*, 2nd ed. Upper Saddle River, NJ: Prentice Hall, 2003.

Žižek, Slavoj. *Living in the End Times*. London: Verso, 2010.

Žižek, Slavoj. *The Puppet and the Dwarf: The Perverse Core of Christianity*. Cambridge, MA: MIT Press, 2003.

Index

Index prepared by M. Beatrice Fazi.